WHEN ALL IS SAID
AND DONE

DOLLY BLOUNT LAMAR

WHEN ALL IS SAID AND DONE

BY
DOLLY BLOUNT LAMAR

THE UNIVERSITY OF GEORGIA PRESS
ATHENS
1952

Paperback edition, 2010
© 1952 by the University of Georgia Press
Athens, Georgia 30602
www.ugapress.org
All rights reserved
Printed digitally in the United States of America

The Library of Congress has cataloged the hardcover edition
of this book as follows:
Library of Congress Cataloging-in-Publication Data
LCCN Permalink: http://lccn.loc.gov/52010106

Lamar, Eugenia Dorothy Blount, 1867–1955.
    When all is said and done.
    286 p. illus. 22cm.
    Autobiographical.
    1. Lamar, Eugenia Dorothy Blount, 1867–1955. I. Title
CT275.L2528 A3
920.7   52-10106

Paperback ISBN-13: 978-0-8203-3541-4
ISBN-10: 0-8203-3541-X

Affectionately dedicated to my parents
EUGENIA WILEY BLOUNT
and
JAMES HENDERSON BLOUNT

CONTENTS

	FOREWORD	XI
I	YOUNG JIM BLOUNT	1
II	A LITTLE LADY—CIRCA 1870	21
III	CAMPAIGNS AND CHINQUAPINS	39
IV	WASHINGTON CITY	53
V	REBEL AT WELLESLEY	74
VI	DEBUT IN THE EIGHTIES	82
VII	PARAMOUNT BLOUNT	92
VIII	COURTSHIP AND MARRIAGE	101
IX	A DAUGHTER OF THE CONFEDERACY	110
X	MACON'S REUNION OF CONFEDERATE VETERANS	144
XI	LOST CAUSE OF THE TWENTIES	151
XII	SIDNEY LANIER ADVANCEMENT	170
XIII	MIRACLE OF THE DEPRESSION	199
XIV	RELUCTANT POLITICIAN	208
XV	NOTABLES: LITERARY AND OTHERWISE	221
XVI	TRAVEL MEMORIES	234
XVII	AND THEN SOME	256
	CONCLUSION	273
	INDEX	277

ILLUSTRATIONS

DOLLY BLOUNT LAMAR .... Frontispiece

facing page

BIRTHPLACE OF MRS. LAMAR 20
MRS. LAMAR AT THE AGE OF TWO 21
JAMES H. BLOUNT 100
MR. AND MRS. JAMES H. BLOUNT 101
MRS. C. HELEN PLANE 116
MRS. JOHN B. GORDON 116
MRS. JAMES H. BLOUNT 116
JUDITH GAMBRELL WILEY 117
GROUP OF CONFEDERATE VETERANS AT THE REUNION IN MACON 148
EXECUTIVE COMMITTEE, REUNION OF CONFEDERATE VETERANS IN MACON 149
UNVEILING BUST OF SIDNEY LANIER IN THE HALL OF FAME 164
UNVEILING BUST OF SIDNEY LANIER IN THE MACON LIBRARY 165
BIRTHPLACE OF SIDNEY LANIER 196
MRS. LAMAR WITH 1934 GRADUATING CLASS AT THE TALLULAH FALLS SCHOOL 272

FOREWORD

IN SETTING DOWN THIS STORY, I HAVE GIVEN A PICTURE OF life in the South from the mid-sixties (as told to me) and on through my own childhood and later experiences at home and abroad. I have described social events and outstanding personalities during colorful times in Washington; I have told of historical happenings in my work with the United Daughters of the Confederacy, of the Stone Mountain Memorial difficulties, of my work to advance Sidney Lanier to his rightful place in the Hall of Fame, of my anti-suffrage work and subsequent political activities. These and other subjects denote some of the many activities that mark my ambitious urge, "driven by an onward ache," to be of service as a private soldier in the ranks of humanity.

This is the story of a heritage and of one woman's effort to live by it. It is a heritage of gentle manners, of ethics and morals rooted in orthodox religion, of spiritual values too real to be bought, sold, or compromised for material things.

This heritage which is mine has been described in song and story, glorified in history, pictured on canvas and in films until it has become a romantic part of our country's culture. In fact, in latter days, it seems to me, it has become too much a matter of romance, poetry, and sighing over a civilization long dead. Even the phrase "Old South" is said with nostalgia and regret for a lost way of life.

For those born in the twilight of the Old South—of that time, that place, that way of life—this heritage still works and lives and has value. It has meaning and value too, we hope, for later generations to whom the heritage is dimmed, lost, and forgotten in the hurry, cynicism, and venality of today.

It is my hope that in this book the young people of this day and time may see their heritage and its vitality and be moved

FOREWORD

to return to it and employ its ideals and standards to cope with the social, moral, and political problems of today.

The heritage of which I write brought an earlier generation of Southerners through bitterer defeat, greater hardships, and more dreadful political threats than any of us face today. And the standards they believed in and lived by led the best of them through stronger temptations toward compromise and even corruption than most of us know today.

I was born in the late sixties of young parents stripped of wealth and prospects—and even table silver—by Sherman's march through Georgia. They faced a bleak and bitter future as disfranchised subjects of a devastated "conquered territory," and I have inevitably felt the impress of those times.

Some of the hardships and humiliations I remember. Others I know from stories of happenings before my birth, stories so oft-told and so vivid that I seem to have been there. Indeed, the whole story of my beginnings, from the time my father first came to Macon, is so clear to me that I can scarcely separate the events of the early sixties, as they were told to me, from my own family memories of the seventies.

Now, from the history of that period, from memories of my family and their friends, I begin the story by recalling the stirring days when my father, a fledgling lawyer from Jones County, loved, courted, and married a dark-haired belle of old Macon, an excited little firebrand who listened with shining eyes as the oldsters talked gravely of Georgia's secession.

I

YOUNG JIM BLOUNT

YOUNG JIM BLOUNT DESCENDED THE STAIRS FROM THE second floor offices of Anderson and Simmons, attorneys-at-law, and stepped with excitement into the spongy red dirt of Mulberry Street, the main street of Macon, Georgia, on a late March day of 1861.

His face was sallow and bone-sharpened and his normally well-muscled frame was wasted from recent typhoid, but he looked almost husky again today.

There was a bright heat from the sky and a tempering breeze on the town. The day brought a foretaste of the opulent green and gold blaze of Georgia May—a happy caprice the Southern weather is apt to serve up any time from November to April, an unexpected treat of spring to rouse young blood and warm old bones. Thus blessed, young Blount felt warmed, expanded, and renewed. And he looked it.

Also, he was exhilarated by two other tonic factors: love and war. The two stimuli were scarcely distinguishable right now in his agreeably disturbed heart. These incentives swelled vaguely and delightfully as he reached the street and met and fused with the smiling weather to bring him a surging conviction of health, heroism, and love already won.

The late afternoon sun filtered through the yellow-green lace of new buds on the mulberry trees lining the street, and struck a glint of red in his thick, fair hair. He paused, and his keen gray eyes took in the two downtown blocks of the street which was so highly charged these days.

WHEN ALL IS SAID AND DONE

Loungers around the big stable at the corner of Third and Mulberry talked wildly and constantly of next month's departure of the Macon Volunteers and the Floyd Rifles for Virginia. Barefoot black boys listened, mumbling and laughing with each other as the young gentlemen, hot-eyed and fervent, boasted of what the Macon boys would do to the Yankees.

Jim Blount's lower lip, out-thrust like an accent to his strong chin, curved quickly in a smile as he looked at the high facade of the Floyd Rifles Armory over the Floyd Hotel. There waved the spanking new "Stars and Bars," more stirringly beautiful than ever this fine day. His heart saluted this first Confederate flag for Macon. It had been raised March 5, the day after its design was adopted by the new Confederate Congress at Montgomery. Mrs. Tom Hardeman, wife of the Floyd Rifles' captain, had sewed all night of the fourth to complete the banner and present it to Captain Tom. Next day at drill, the company paraded downtown to cheers and applause, bearing the new flag. Then they raised it over the Armory and fired the first salute to the Confederate colors in Georgia.

Young Mr. Blount's heart took a thumping bump as he saw Dr. Jack Wiley's buggy across the street in front of the Lanier house. Rumpled and fagged as usual, the doctor leaned out of his buggy, dropped the reins, and used both hands—one forefinger striking the other palm for emphasis—as he talked to Judge Iverson Harris about the Georgia Secession Act passed two months before in Milledgeville.

Then Dr. Wiley sat back, relaxed, and added: "Eugenia, you know, is the most rabid little secessionist in my family." Whereat Jim's heart swelled and skipped. With his head turned the other way, he listened eagerly.

"Yes," the doctor was saying, "Ann and I—and my son, Charlie, too, for a while—had our doubts about the rupture, like the rest of you. But not Eugenia. John B. Lamar and Eugenius Nisbet had supper with us just before the convention at the capital, and our youngsters almost took the table talk away from us. Charlie was as eager as Eugenia. She implored Judge Nisbet to pass the act on her birthday, January 19. And, sure enough, in all the commotion, that's just the way it happened."

"Well," said Judge Harris, shaking his head, "it's all settled now, and I'm right behind it. I doubt if there is a Union man in Macon since Sumter—not one worth his salt, anyway. But I tell you, Jack, we're in for more than the youngsters figure on."

They nodded their graying heads in worried agreement as Dr. Wiley clucked to his horse and drove off.

As the ruddy dust subsided, Jim watched the buggy rumble up Mulberry and out of sight. Love-struck, he pictured its course up the hill, past the W. B. Johnstons' villa on the left and Cowles' Hill on the right, along Georgia Avenue to Orange Street and the white columns of the Thaddeus Holt house, and to the high terraced home of Parthenia and Cadwallader Raines, built in a modified Maltese cross at the corner of College Street and Georgia Avenue. Jim's heart followed the doctor's turn left and his progress along College, past Wesleyan Female College for two blocks to the home of that magic maiden, Eugenia.

Young Jim Blount was usually pretty sure of himself. He had enjoyed a happy childhood on the Blount Estate near Clinton in Jones County in the household of his older half-brother, David. Although his parents had died in his childhood (his father, Thomas Blount, came to Georgia from Virginia, by way of North Carolina, and married Mary Ricketts), the boy had grown up feeling secure in the affection of his foster family and the motherly devotion of his big sister, Mary. A bright, strong, extrovert child, he had easily distinguished himself at private school and was graduated from the University of Georgia with honors in 1858.

In 1860, he moved from the Blount plantation (chiefly cotton, of course) to seek his fortune with the law firm of Anderson and Simmons in nearby Macon. Well-connected, attractive, and happily aware of the force of his talkative, friendly magnetism, the boy from Jones easily assumed his place in the agreeable circle of well-born, well-to-do Macon. And he was, by grace of the same endowments, making his mark at reading the law.

So, he was usually a thoroughly self-confident young man.

This evening, however, making his careful toilet in his high-ceilinged room, he was beset by suspense and unaccustomed doubts. If Genie wouldn't accept him—well, it was an intolerable prospect. He must persuade her to marry him before the Rifles and Volunteers moved to Virginia at the call of President Davis and General Beauregard. Virginia Lamar was already Mrs. A. O. Bacon, he reflected, going over the roster of their contemporaries. Clifford Anderson and his wife, the former Anna LeConte, were going to Virginia together, as were also other couples.

Reviewing his romance as he dressed, Jim pondered something about Genie he couldn't quite fathom. He thought her spirited, entertaining, and beautiful, despite the frailty which so concerned Dr. Wiley. In fact, he was entranced to remember an ethereal aura about the dark grey eyes, the fine white skin, and the classic symmetry of her young face. She was flawlessly lovely and endlessly interesting to him, certainly.

But sometimes, just when he thought her most yielding and charming, and was quite sure he could persuade her, she would meet his eagerness with quick laughter, and something like derision—to deflate his hopes. It was provocative—and nerve-wracking.

She was a formidable girl, with her tall slim figure, and she had uncommon dignity for 18 years. This dignity and grace, with her provocative spirit, intrigued him even as they discouraged and intimidated him.

Buttoning his brocade waistcoat, Jim succumbed to his chronically recurrent distress over the way the Macon boys were forever hanging around the Wiley mansion since Eugenia came home from Miss Spangler's School in New York. It was her first season, really, and they had managed almost to monopolize her. He himself had lost a good six weeks by being sick with fever, leaving them a clear field.

That girl-faced, flute-playing Sidney Lanier, home for the holidays, had serenaded her with his ever ready flute, Jim heard. This 19-year-old versifying darling of Macon belles was a close friend of Genie's brother, Charlie, which made it worse. Thank God he was back at Oglethorpe University, tutoring. How the young ladies idolized him, laughing at his jokes, languishing over his music, and sighing into his great gray eyes! Genie had been riding often with Captain Robert A. Smith, who commanded the Volunteers. She was dazzled no doubt by his performance at Macon's independence meeting last election day. He was chairman of the committee which drew up resolutions calling on the governor to arm all the men in the state. Genie seemed to think him personally responsible for every Minute Man in Georgia. It was ridiculous how a young girl's head could be turned by an old man of nigh thirty.

And Phil Tracy. Jim remembered with anxiety and misery the great night of January 19, when Macon was celebrating Georgia's Secession. He remembered the laughing, shouting young men in the torchlight parade downtown, and the girls leaning over the iron balconies along Mulberry Street cheering them on.

It had been beautiful and thrilling as they neared the balcony next to his office and he saw Genie, her head high and her eyes shining. But then when Phil passed by, just ahead of Jim in the procession, and looked up at the girls, Genie waved her handkerchief at him! Why, Jim wondered now, re-living his jealousy, had she singled out Phil for this sign of public favor?

Dressed and ready, Jim paused at his door to reassure himself by recalling a meeting which gave him the right to hope. He had felt splendidly sure of himself for a while at the big party at the Wiley home last week. He had thought her exquisite in her white ruffled gown edged with cerise satin, moving taller, sweeter, and more stately than the other girls in the huge, candle-lit parlors. She had been like a première danseuse in a ballet of swaying hoop skirts among the gold-framed mirrors, scarlet draperies, and rich mahogany.

He waltzed her boldly into the dining room, around the great table and into a quiet corner between the china cabinet and a jardinière filled with magnolias. He had vowed to himself to ask her then, but his heart failed him. He had taken her hand, faltered, failed, and waltzed her right back into the great hall in a turmoil of happiness and disappointment.

Now, leaving his room and remembering, Jim cursed himself for being a dolt. At the same time he saw again how Genie's cool self-possession and quick laughter had deserted her in the dining room, and how a vulnerable quietude had come over her. And he felt quite a fellow again. He ran down the steps and into the street, and briskly walked to the Wileys.

Three hours later young Jim Blount walked home again, some of the bounce gone out of his stride. He was engaged and duly enraptured, but there was a proviso that worried him.

Eugenia had accepted him and they had planned with excited happiness to go with their friends to Virginia. How she had sparkled and how he had thrilled as they talked of the journey and the valiant distinction of forming the first troops from another Southern state to go to Virginia's aid!

But there was difficulty with Dr. Wiley during the formal visit to the library to ask for Genie's hand. The doctor did not want his daughter to become a war bride, to make a solemn decision under the influence of wartime excitements. She had enjoyed less than a year of young ladyhood; she was swept away by the fever of the times. And she was none too strong. Even dancing tired her. The doctor was never free of anxiety about her, and there was the dreaded possibility that she might go into a decline.

The doctor also cast a sharp professional eye on the boy's gaunt face, his unfleshed frame. And Jim's sense of health and well-being shrivelled under the appraisal. Dr. Wiley observed kindly that Mr. Blount himself didn't look any too robust as yet. With precarious health on both sides. . . .

However, 23-year-old Mr. Blount rallied and exerted all his powers of persuasion, which he usually found to be considerable. He won a conditional consent. Dr. and Mrs. Wiley would bestow their daughter's hand if Mr. Blount would take time after the wedding for them to visit the Blounts in Jones County.

That was the rub. It galled him to ask Captain Hardeman for a stay while his friends were marching off to war. His company might be called up any day and depart for Virginia, while he dallied in Jones County, acquainting his wife with Blounts.

Already, several score boys had gone to the defense of the Georgia coast, and Captain L. M. Lamar's Macon Guards would be off to Savannah in April. To wait now, a laggard, was a condition hard to accept.

At the thought of the radiant Genie, however, his sense of happiness and triumph returned. Now, he smiled over the easy disposition of his rivals. Why, everyone in Macon knew that Sid Lanier serenaded all the girls. He had, in fact, played under Eugenia's window at the behest of Phil Tracy. Delightful fellow, young Sid. Talented, full of fun and high spirits. As for Phil, well, Eugenia had been quite taken with him, but "that was before you came to call, Mr. Blount," she had explained. Phil was a prince of a chap, after all. As for Captain Smith, Dr. Wiley thought him a bit old for Genie, and Genie did too, it seems. John Baxter, being her cousin, was out of the running.

It all seemed feasible now. Jim would write Sister Mary, now Mrs. Thomas Bowen, at Belmont Farm, the Big House at Haddock, and tell her that Mr. and Mrs. James Henderson Blount were coming for a short visit to the beautiful, Pratt-built home. Then they would go to Virginia by train to prepare for battle, whip the Union forces, and return to Georgia. Just like that.

Already, Jim was dreaming of the household they would soon establish in Macon, Georgia, Confederate States of America.

The wedding plans worked out happily. The Wileys quickly mustered a lavish troùsseau. Since there wasn't time for a bridal outfit from New York or Paris, Genie wore a white silk wedding gown lent her by her dear friend Emma Townes Gaines. Seamstresses and friends with talented fingers worked with Mrs. Wiley to assemble the requisite piles of fine cambric and linen lingerie with minute and elaborate embroideries, puffs, tucks, laces, and ruffles.

There was a second-day dress, almost as important as the wedding dress in the sixties, when brides received at home on the second day instead of going off honeymooning. This gown was of dainty ashes-of-roses silk figured in small rosebuds with angel sleeves flaring wide below the elbow, a skirt many yards full, and narrow pleated pink ribbons outlining neck, sleeves, and diamond-shaped cutouts in the front of the skirt. Genie's royal blue silk had a cape for church and afternoon calls, to go over the off-shoulder décolletage for evening. The low-necked evening bodice was trimmed with white lace rosettes and the daytime basque jacket, with black lace. On her wedding day, Genie wore the décolleté basque to sit for her portrait in pastel, a gold-framed family treasure which now hangs in her daughter's home.

Two of her finest gowns were heavy silk lined with stiff cambric, full-skirted like the others to accommodate hoops. One of the handsomest was an apple green moiré stripe alternating with a cross-stripe of black and white centered with blurred pink chenét roses. This off-shoulder basque, too, could be covered with a short cape with angel sleeves for afternoon.

After the wedding, Mr. and Mrs. Blount departed for Haddock, where Genie and Sister Mary took to each other with a quick affection which delighted the bridegroom. When the

YOUNG JIM BLOUNT

David Blounts came from Clinton for a family party, Genie was as happy with her husband's family as the Wileys had hoped she would be.

Late in April, the young Blounts went to Virginia, following the Rifles and Volunteers, who had been called up April 19 and had left Macon the next day. With two other Georgia companies—Captain P. H. Colquitt's Columbus Light Guards and Captain L. T. Doyal's Spalding Grays of Griffin—the Macon men formed the Second Georgia Battalion. The Rifles' Captain Tom Hardeman was elected major to command the Battalion.

Never had such high-born, conventionally-reared Georgia girls such a honeymoon as the eight Macon war brides enjoyed at Portsmouth. They were installed in a hotel under chaperonage of Mrs. William Henry Ross, wife of a Second Battalion officer from Macon, who walked with them each afternoon to visit the Norfolk shipyards at Portsmouth. Here Confederate workmen had raised the sunken *Merrimac* from the harbor and were rebuilding the Yankee vessel for Southern service as the *Virginia*.

The boys—Jim, his married contemporaries, with Granville Connor, Genie's brother Charlie, Charles Campbell, and other bachelors—were stationed at the Norfolk fairgrounds at Sewell's Point opposite Fort Monroe. The Second Battalion drilled, trained, and picketed the beach in an atmosphere of valor and jubilation like plumed champions before a tournament. Almost every young soldier of the Second Battalion was attended by his black body servant; Private Jim Blount had Booz, who accompanied him first from Jones County to Macon, then from Macon to the war.

The single boys made socializing forays into society at Norfolk, Richmond, and surrounding Tidewater plantations. The gallant Georgians were heroic darlings of the countryside, as the first Southerners to come to aid the Virginians early in the war. Sometimes the bachelor soldiers surrendered their leaves of absence to the bridegrooms so that the young husbands might visit Portsmouth oftener.

This exciting state of affairs lasted nearly a year. The boys at Norfolk fretted through the rousing news of the victory at Manassas, Johnston's clashes with McClellan, and other demonstrations of Southern fighting quality in which they had, as yet, no part.

This festival prelude to war was interrupted for Genie by bitterly sad news from home. Her father was gravely ill and she was summoned back to Macon. He died in June of 1861, and there followed a period of intimate grief (she was the doctor's favorite child) and conventional mourning. It was the beginning of a series of personal sorrows which underscored for the young Blounts the tremendous tragedy of the war years.

Doubtless it seemed unbecoming to Mrs. Wiley and her friends that Eugenia should, in deep mourning, leave Macon and undertake alone the trip back to her husband in Virginia. But return she did, to cherish the little time remaining with her "Mr. Blount."

By fall she was in Portsmouth, saddened and black-gowned, taking her place with the other brides on afternoon expeditions to the *Merrimac* rebuilding, watching the Yankee vessel acquire its iron armor for Confederate fighting, forgetting her grief as best she could in her visits with "Mr. Blount" and in her interest in the conversion of the warship.

In March of 1862, however, Genie was obliged to return home to stay. She was expecting her first child and her condition made it both improper and foolhardy for her to remain away from home any longer.

Within a few days after Genie had come back and settled into the routine of war-bereft young brides in Macon, the Battle of the *Virginia* and the *Monitor* broke at Portsmouth. And Genie, who often said she felt as if she were the construction chief of the *Virginia*, never recovered from missing the battle itself.

YOUNG JIM BLOUNT

When April of 1862 rolled around the members of the Second Battalion, having enlisted for a year, were due to return to Georgia. But en route home, they were ordered to report to Goldsboro, North Carolina, by April 30. The war looked more serious than Southerners had anticipated.

The news reached Macon early in April and the town prepared a rousing welcome for its heroes. Wives, sweethearts, sisters, and mothers planned an intensive and happy time during the weeks the boys were to have at home.

Flags flew, bands played, and bunting draped the town when the Second Battalion arrived. Speechmaking, parades, and a warriors' welcome were scheduled for the afternoon arrival, but the Battalion came in on an early morning train. However, a crowd soon gathered as the gray-clad men of Macon with their friends from Griffin and Columbus reached the streets. They were escorted in fine, if informal, style to the Floyd Rifles' Hall at Mulberry and Third and the Volunteers' Armory at Mulberry and Second streets.

Ladies of Macon had worked arduously and lovingly to prepare a barbecue dinner for 1,000. Half were served at the Floyd Rifles' Hall and half at the Volunteers' Armory.

After their reunion with the homefolks, the Second Battalion boys entrained and reported to Goldsboro the last day of April. They were sent again to Virginia. There they got their first taste of gunpowder when the *Monitor* moved up the James River and fired on the small fort they were defending at Drury's Bluff. Their gala advance into war was over, and the reality had come.

In July, Private Jim Blount and his companions-at-arms went to Chickahominy for the Seven Days' fighting around Richmond. This was more than a taste of war. Private Blount was seriously wounded.

Young Blount came home to a long convalescence, and a house of private grief and war sorrow. He had gone to fight depleted in strength from typhoid, and recovery was long and hard. And, late that year, Genie bore and buried their first child, a girl.

For Mrs. Blount, however, there was little time for tears. Her "Mr. Blount," as she called him all their life together, was ill, and he fretted over his inactivity when all Macon's young men seemed to be at war. He had to be nursed, eased, and heartened. She could not, moreover, weep for a stillborn baby in the company of girls who went smiling about their war work with husbands dead, imprisoned, or missing in action.

By 1863, all of Macon was too busy for show of grief. Though Genie was expecting another baby, she decided that she would continue her service with the Ladies Soldiers' Relief Society. Indeed Mrs. Washington Poe, the president, Miss Julia Wrigley, and Miss Bass expected her to. She could sew, knit, and make lint bandages for the soldiers as fast as ever-scarcer materials came to hand. The young wives, all agreed, should overcome their natural modesty and the proprieties of normal times in the interests of high service. Genie would be excused later on from ministrations at the Soldiers' Wayside Home.

The town and the times had changed so much that it seemed easy to dispense with the old niceties that encumbered war work. The population of 8,000 seemed doubled since removal of the Savannah Arsenal to Macon, with a horde of artisans making cannon, shot, shells, and the 12-pound Napoleon guns which were the pride of commandeered Findlay's Foundry and of the whole Confederacy. The town was swelled with war refugees and wounded and convalescent soldiers going to and from battlefields and stopping for rest at the Wayside Home the ladies had established for their relief and comfort.

There were no more parties, new frocks, dancing, barbecues, picnics, or leisurely gatherings on the green lawns or in the mahogany-furnished, damask-hung drawing rooms and parlors of the big houses—except meetings of ladies who gathered to sew or knit. There was hardly any going out, except for expeditions to the Wayside Home, or calls on families stricken by news of the death of a loved one—a son, brother, or father.

But even these sad and Spartan times were not without their smiles and laughter. From the distress and suffering of the Wayside Home came a story the young ladies laughed over many times. One morning Genie, on her rounds of the rows of cots bearing wounded and convalescent soldiers, approached one patient and asked, "May I bathe your face, sir?"

"Why, yes, ma'am," replied the soldier with a sigh, and a smile. "I reckon so. It ain't been washed but six times this morning."

The number of ladies in black, with heavy crêpe veils on their bonnets was increasing. Genie, sometimes fingering the bright silks and rich brocades of her trousseau, wondered if she would ever use them again. Several of her loveliest gowns, like the green plaid with chenét roses, she had never worn at all. As the war years rolled relentlessly on, the beautiful dresses she didn't wear came to symbolize the family grief and war agonies they knew. After the summer of '62, throughout the young years for which her trousseau was designed, she was always in deep black or "expecting."

Before the birth of their second child, the Blounts left Macon for Jones County. They established themselves at Pitts Place, a family plantation of Thomas Blount's first wife, the mother of half-brother David. Here was a big house with enough acreage to appease the land hunger of the Blount men, a hunger which was growing in Genie's husband.

Edie, a devoted slave of the David Blount ménage, was detailed to help at Pitts Place. She was overjoyed to welcome Marse Jim and his wife, and to marshal the other slaves to the service of the new household. Booz, Marse Jim's body servant who had followed him to war, of course joined the household.

Here the new baby girl arrived and dispelled for a while the grief and anxiety of her parents. She grew fat and rosy, and Genie bloomed with her.

But there was trouble a-plenty on the outside. Middle Georgia was terrorized in 1864 by random raiders from the Sherman forces in North Georgia. Still disabled for active service, Mr. Blount served the cause by recruiting for the Confederate Army. He had organized several cavalry companies and now held a colonel's commission.

One day when the Colonel was away, a Negro rider came to Pitts Place with news that a detachment of Yankees was in Jones County, burning barns, stealing supplies, and killing or taking off livestock. They had even invaded some of the big houses and destroyed furniture and borne off silver and household treasures.

"Ain' no use to lock up, Miss Genie," the Negro said. "Dey jes' break down de do' and come trampin' in. Better take dat chile and git yo' foot in de road fer Macon. Leave Edie and de niggers heah. Dey 'low dey come to free us and dey ain' gwine hurt no niggers. Let Edie hide de silver and de money and save what she kin."

Genie took his advice and with the baby in one arm and the buggy reins in the other hand, she started on the rough country road for Macon.

As she approached East Macon, she noticed with alarm a whole battery of troops stationed on the Clinton Road. There were more soldiers at the bridge and they stopped the young woman to warn her of rising waters that had weakened the Fifth Street bridge.

She learned from them that Captain Dunlap's party of Scouts had sighted Yankee cavalry approaching Macon on the Clinton Road. Governor Brown was in the city, and had called young boys, old men, and convalescent soldiers to the defense of the town. In fact, Colonel Charlie Wiley, Genie's brother, was commanding a company of wounded soldiers on the Vineville road to protect Macon from the north approach. Also, Captain J. R. Armstrong and his Silver Grays, a company of aged gentlemen, were stationed in Vineville.

Frightened but resolute, Genie maneuvered the wavering

bridge, trembling as she felt it wave with the current when her buggy rattled across. It was still standing when she slowed the horses to look back. She hurried them up then along Walnut Street to Orange, and turned at Georgia Avenue to drive to College Street and thence along the last familiar blocks home. The bridge washed away later that day.

Next day the troops were engaged at East Macon. General Stoneman, ordered to Macon from Atlanta by Sherman to destroy the railroads, was met by a force of Major John W. Nisbet's Tennesseans. The Tennesseans, veterans en route to help defend Atlanta, arrived in Macon just in time to meet the Yankee cavalry attack. A column of Stoneman's Raiders, which was to join him in Macon, had been intercepted on the Atlanta road by some of Hood's forces. So, at Macon, Stoneman was repelled, and later captured in retreat near Clinton by General Iverson commanding a portion of "Little Joe" Wheeler's cavalry.

The Stoneman battery at Dunlap's Farm outside Macon had shelled the town, without any damage except on Mulberry Street, where one shot tore away a column from the front of the Asa Holt home. There were casualties, of course. One was sixteen-year-old Mike Barfield, wounded on the outskirts of East Macon and rescued by Negroes to die in their cabin a few hours later.

After a few days, when Middle Georgia seemed free of fighting, Genie returned to Clinton to see what the Raiders had done to the plantation. Edie met her, groaning and shaking her head. "Dey got de silver, de best weddin' china. Dey mess up de house, broke de furniture, and when dey couldn't do no mo' devilment, dey open up de trunks and scatter roun' de dead baby's clothes, and den light into dat weddin' trunk and trample on de veil til hit ain't nothin' but a tore up rag."

Genie sadly toured the house, and found one teaspoon left of her bridal treasures and household riches.

'Sixty-four and 'sixty-five were nightmare years at home for the Blounts and abroad throughout the Confederacy. Their baby girl, the second, died before the third child was born.

Before Atlanta fell, Governor Brown called out the State Militia and reserves of young boys, old men, and disabled veterans to help Johnston, and later Hood, defend the city. Blount's Cavalry with their convalescent colonel in command joined the fighting.

After Atlanta surrendered, Brown's troops and home-recruited companies like Blount's trudged or rode sniping after the edges of the Sherman army, fighting to abate the destruction in the terrible swath—thirty to fifty and eighty miles wide—which Sherman carved in the state. They attacked foraging parties and marching sections and took a toll of columns that proceeded to Milledgeville. After sacking the capital and plundering homes and estates at random in and around Clinton, Sherman made his annihilating way to Savannah, and thence back along the coast to burn Columbia, South Carolina.

More than two weeks after Lee's surrender on April 9, 1865, at Appomattox, Joseph E. Johnston surrendered to Sherman in North Carolina. Next month President Jefferson Davis was captured at Irwinville, Georgia.

In April of 1865, halted on the Atlanta road by a flag of truce, Colonel Blount turned and rode home to Clinton. The family then had moved from Pitts Place to Lowther Hall at Clinton, where Colonel Blount, returning, greeted his first son, Joseph, born in December. Colonel Blount's Confederate commission as brigadier general had been signed and was en route to him when the war ended. For the rest of his days, he remained "Colonel Blount" to friends, acquaintances, and clients.

Hard times gripped the community. The Blounts moved again, from Lowther Hall to a small, federal type, two-gallery house down the street—"Not fine," as Mrs. Blount described it, "but adequate." Colonel Blount settled down to law practice in the Jones County seat of Clinton, saddened by the changes around him and angered by the first revolutionary upheavals of Reconstruction in the South. He was excited and challenged, too, by the struggle for Southern survival through Yankee oppressions that were beginning.

Here, the Blounts' fourth child was born. She was named Eugenia Dorothy, the "Dorothy" for Genie's girlhood friend, Dorothy Lamar Chappell. They had promised to name their first girls for each other. However, Dorothy Chappell Toomer weakened or forgot, and named her daughter Loretta Lamar for her mother.

This was a very little girl, so tiny, in fact, that her parents were anxious about her. Genie was especially worried when the restless, excited, confused Negroes milled around the place and their shouting and mumbling wakened the baby.

She was even more uneasy in the early days of trouble, when Mr. Blount went out to quiet the freed slaves. She didn't know what he said, or how he calmed the menacing freedmen; but a combination of authority and friendly power in his ringing voice would always dispel the trouble. She was proud of him, too, when he strode into the ordinary's office at Clinton and forcibly ejected a mulatto who had come, with federal papers to back him up, to claim the office he was appointed to. She was not afraid of the marching, shouting, or grumbling of the Negroes when he was there. "Mr. Blount's presence," she reflected then, and many times later, "is always compelling."

Before 1870, when Georgia was still staggering under military rule, its gentry impoverished, its blacks seduced to power by carpetbaggers, and most Georgians floundering in the bitter chaos of the new order, the Blounts left Clinton. Though loath to leave the lands of his fathers, Colonel Blount took his family to Macon because the prostrate county seat offered no security in farming or in the law.

Clinton was not razed and ruined like towns in the direct path of Sherman's March, though raiders and foragers had, to be sure, burned, despoiled, and stripped a few plantations. Still, the quiet little town was suffering from the general prostration of the state—outlandish taxes, surrounding devastation and disruption, and the excited holiday for Negroes which deprived the farms and plantations of field hands.

Living, even table fare, came hard in Jones County now. Mrs. Blount recalled sadly but with affectionate pride the dinner that Sister Mary had served when the Blounts visited the Bowens at Haddock on a recent Sunday. Sister Mary's fine home—built by Daniel Pratt with exquisite use of gold on fluted woodwork, artful paint to transform Georgia pine to exotically patterned wood grains, and French and Greek motifs in small designs on mantels, windows, and mouldings—was undamaged by the detachment from Sherman's army which took over the lower floors in '65. Officers had pledged to restrain their troops in exchange for quarters in the house. So, Sister Mary and her children exiled themselves upstairs away from the Yankee officers. This arrangement saved the house, silver, furniture, and domestic finery. Troops were content with burning servant quarters and removing food and livestock.

At dinner this Sunday of 1867, Sister Mary presided with her usual regal grace over the long table in the huge, high-ceilinged dining room. The old cook served dinner on French china and heavy silver, with fine linen and flowers, so that even the children enjoyed an illusion of a pre-war feast as they ate their small servings of turnip greens, a sliver of fatback, and one thin white hoecake without butter. As a dessert treat the white and gold china plates bore a second hoecake with a teaspoon of cane syrup—a lavish company fling of the long-hoarded sweet.

Seeing little Joseph's delight at the taste of syrup, and the wild gleam, so politely subdued in repressed smiles, on the thin faces of Mary's children, and remembering the meager fare which graced her own table, Mrs. Blount was willing to concede that Jones County didn't offer an abundant living, and that the Macon move was economically wise.

She smiled at Mr. Blount's glowing eyes and vivid persuasions as he talked of the move to Macon, knowing that he was drawn by the tumultuous currents of change, struggle, and danger that surged through the town, waves of trouble and opportunity on which a bold man could ride to financial security and political power.

In Macon, former slaves and a handful of literate free Negroes held public offices, and Negroes sat with whites on Macon's city council. In Atlanta, Yankee scalawags and illiterate Negroes comprised the General Assembly and roistered over the charred, rebuilding capital, levying heavier taxes and more outrageous strictures on responsible Georgians as fast as they could think them up.

Old Macon friends of the Wileys and Blounts were losing their property. Many Macon ladies were working like scullery maids and washer-women in their own homes. The children, Mrs. Wiley wrote to her daughter, were eating meals such as the slaves had cooked in their cabins behind the Big Houses before the war. Still, that was pretty good fare. The cornbread, fatback, garden greens, and milk that nourished strong, working Negroes in the old days were better food than most gentle people were getting in the Georgia of the late sixties.

Macon was a good place to go, she decided. Macon, the Blounts estimated, was rich and undisturbed, compared to the rest of Georgia.

Young Mrs. Blount was happy to return to her mother, Brother Charlie, and her sister, Mary Wiley Harris, and the old friends who were left. And, too, she was feeling Mr. Blount's excitement over the times. All the hopes, troubles, and passions of Georgia in the late sixties seemed intensified in larger, growing Macon, right in the heart of the state.

They took Edie and Booz to Macon. Booz was still loyal in these curious days of "freedom" when the Negroes roamed up and down the roads, ran for the legislature, marched off to seek their fortunes, and as often as not straggled back, hungry and bewildered.

Mr. Blount secured a simple house and here Eugenia settled

down to make a home for him, Joseph, and Baby Dolly, just a short walk from the old Wiley place on College Street.

It was not without pangs that she left the two-story white house in Clinton. In later years the family made many a sentimental journey back to the "not fine, but adequate" early home where Eugenia Dorothy was born.

BIRTHPLACE OF MRS. LAMAR

MRS. LAMAR AT THE AGE OF TWO

A LITTLE LADY--
CIRCA 1870

RADICAL SECRETARY OF WAR STANTON WAS IN THE SADDLE, riding the South with Charles Sumner and Thad Stevens, and flooding the "conquered territory" with a vulture crew of adventurers when my family moved to Macon. Freedmen, native turncoats, known as Scalawags, and imported lower class whites sat in seats of power, bleeding the region with taxes, foreclosures, and oppressions of disfranchisement.

My parents' unpretentious two-story house on Bond Street was a few steps from Cowles' Hill, Macon's highest point. Here was a panoramic view of the green little town, crossed by the red Ocmulgee River, laced with red and brown dirt streets and dotted with small homes, white-columned mansions, and a few grand residences in high-styled Victorian.

On the south edge of town Schofield's Iron Works, another foundry or two, and the Massee Gin Works sent occasional plumes of smoke toward the sky, harbingers of economic recovery and growth that accompanied the political distress of the times. Across the Ocmulgee on the east bank the Macon Cotton Factory, soon to consolidate with another textile plant to become the Bibb Manufacturing Company, was drawing war-impoverished country folk to town. The Central Railroad, the Southwestern, the Macon and Brunswick, and the Macon and Augusta lines met at the terminal on Broadway and were again beginning to move cotton, as well as passengers.

WHEN ALL IS SAID AND DONE

Downtown, around Mulberry, Cherry, and the cross streets of Cotton Avenue, and Second, Third, and Fourth streets, new shops opened up near old ones. Many a son of a planter or town professional man was in trade now, selling groceries, clothing, shoes, hardware, to support his family and the Negroes who stayed on after freedom. The old folks sometimes sighed and suffered over the disgrace of turning to "trade," but gratefully shared in the profits from selling to Yankee officials, Negro officeholders, and despised Northern adventurers, as well as to their own friends.

We could not see the village of Vineville from Cowles' Hill, but it was growing apace to the north, a brisk walk or a short leisurely ride from the best residential part of town proper, the College-Bond-Orange-High Street section and the streets edging the business district. Smaller houses were being built or were already occupied in Vineville around the Clisbys' huge brick home, the Lamar place, the Troutman Greek revival house, the columned Corbin mansion, and other great homes.

Wesleyan Female College, more than 30 years old, was polishing Macon girls into cultivated young ladies. Mercer University, not so long removed from its small beginnings at Penfield, was educating the boys. In an advertisement in the back of *Butler's Historical Record of Macon,* Mount de Sales Academy on the hill at the west end of Orange Street was "acknowledged to be the Cheapest First Class Boarding School in the States." There was also on the edge of Vineville the Jesuit Pio Nono College, where "Discipline is Mild, but Firm," and where was offered a "complete Scientific, Classical and Commercial Course." Mr. Polhill, instructing boys, and Miss Clifford Cotton, instructing girls, gave elementary education to younger Maconites at their respective private schools.

Many young men like my father took to the law. That paid, too, as life during Reconstruction seemed at times one tangled maze of suits, counter-suits, and altercations in the courts over taxes, confiscated property, carpetbaggers' claims, and Geor-

A LITTLE LADY—CIRCA 1870

gians' protests. It was no way to get rich, for fees were slim or not forthcoming at all in some cases, but it paid a living.

The more ambitious young attorneys watched politics, biding their time until Georgians could rid themselves of President Grant's radical exploiters.

At this time there seems to have been a quiet, passionate re-dedication to the old virtues and manners of the defeated gentlepeople. There was an equal devotion to the ante-bellum concept of state sovereignty for which they had fought and which was now submerged in oppressions and violations from Washington.

Upper class Southerners, shabby, outraged, and dispossessed, moved proudly through the black time of injustice, thieving, and opportunism which possessed the town. The hardiest and best of them bent to the requirements of survival with little compromise of old, exalted standards. They ran their shops, practiced law, even sat with blacks and carpetbaggers in city council when they could get elected without turning Radical Republican. Mayor O'Bear and later Mayor Huff handled as best they could their councils of mixed aldermen.

Contact with the rascals who usurped the town strengthened the old attachment to the Lost Cause.

I was a curly-haired toddler in the early eighteen seventies. If Mama economized, I didn't know it. I had never seen the heavy silks, braided velvets, plumes, and imported laces of her trousseau. Much later, I was to revel in the sight of these rich relics when a favorite gown was taken from the closet to be re-fashioned into a frock for me.

If the table fare was plain, it was sufficient and rather ceremoniously served. I remember Booz's batter cakes were a treat; my parents had brought him to Macon partly because of his magic with a bowl of batter.

While the interlopers talked of prices, and riches gained from their prostrate, disfranchised betters, the ladies and gentlemen did not. They behaved with the old, outward disdain for money, as if wealth were still a basic certainty which relieved gentlepeople from concern with it. Such matters were beneath the notice of well-born, well-educated best families. Nice little girls didn't know whether they were rich or poor.

On Bond Street we children were too young to attend talk of politics. But even then I must have been aware of the sacredness surrounding phrases like "States' Rights," "the Confederate Cause," "the Bill of Rights" denying to Washington any powers not granted in the Constitution. I absorbed the Southern reverence for these subjects which so concerned my parents and their friends, as a baby learns the meaning of words and phrases from grownup tones and emphasis.

In March of 1869, Baby Jim was born. Around 1871, when dark-eyed Joseph was seven and I was not quite five, my father bought a big house at the far end of College Street, across from Tattnall Square.

It was a square frame house with an observatory on top, a center hall and four big rooms to each of the two stories. Papa bought it with seventeen acres of ground around the house, bordering one side of Tattnall Square Park across the street. Mercer University faced the park on the west side of the square and stood at the end of College Street, and across the park were our new neighbors, the William Hazlehursts.

Here, we played under the chinaberry trees in the back yard —at climbing, building playhouses, making up and enacting stories. Ours was a pleasant, quiet childhood shielded from the stinging anger and hardships behind the authoritative, loving certainty with which our parents faced us.

When the Klan rode in and around Macon, frightening Negroes and the more credulous and tyrannical carpetbaggers with ghostly robes, macabre makeup, and demon tricks, we didn't know it. If Papa was gone and Mama had a long evening with us, it was occasion for story-reading, play-acting, and recitations. When the housebreaking and violence of Reconstruc-

A LITTLE LADY—CIRCA 1870

tion Days abated, and the federal authorities couldn't seem to unmask the Klan, we were none the wiser; for we hadn't known about the molested ladies, the robbed homes, or the dangers of a lonely walk or ride in Bibb County.

During the hard times and accompanying great need of some of the Confederate veterans, most of Macon's social life seems to have centered around benefit entertainments for former soldiers. The old families were preoccupied, outside of the struggle for survival, with easing these needs, memoralizing the Lost Cause and doing honor to the soldier martyrs who died for it. The ladies especially dedicated their spare time and effort to the new demands on their old loyalties. One of the postwar projects carried out in this spirit was establishment of the Appleton Church Home for orphans of Confederate heroes, an Episcopalian institution where later many little girls in town were sent for music lessons.

One of my most charmed memories of Mama is the evening she dressed for a benefit masquerade given by the Ladies Memorial Association.

This dedicated band was headed by Mrs. Isaac Winship, a heroine in the annals of Georgia during the war. Her service to the wounded during the siege of Atlanta, when she turned her house into a hospital, was prodigious. She was the Virginia Dare of local history, the first white child born at Fort Hawkins where Macon began. She moved to Atlanta after her marriage and returned to Macon when her home was burned and the Winship fortunes were leveled for a time. Back home, she became president of the Ladies Memorial Association, which was the converted Soldiers' Relief Society, and led the ladies in removal of the battle-slain from hasty burial places to marked graves at Rose Hill Cemetery. Soon thereafter the ladies bent their efforts to raising funds for a monument to war dead.

In this cause Mama was beautifully costumed on the night she dazzled her little daughter. She was always beautiful, with naturally wavy hair and drooping eyelids that gave her a look of melancholy. Acquaintances sometimes judged her haughty, perhaps from her dignity of demeanor and the hauteur that is suggested by high carriage of the head. This ball night she wore one of her trousseau dresses retrimmed to represent Night. Its cloudy black tulle skirt was sprinkled with silver stars, and she wore stars in her black hair. She was idyllic.

Another hit of the masquerade was Judge L. N. Whittle, who went dancing in frayed and rusty black. Like many a sartorially seedy gentleman of that period in Macon, he wore his old dress suit and gaily called himself an S.F.V., or Second Family of Virginia.

At five or six I was dispatched to Miss Clifford Cotton's school on Washington Avenue, in a small house across the street from the Wesleyan campus. Little girls of all sizes, dressed in calico with white aprons, with hair curled or braided, sat in one room and learned their reading, writing, and arithmetic. Miss Clifford at the end of the day would kiss the little girls who had been good. I don't remember being kissed very often. I don't remember wanting to be, either.

I, neatly braided and pinafored, was infatuated with the Coleman girls. How glossy their pigtails, how beautiful their pinafores, rolled and whipped with lace inserts and ruffles, and how enticing their pretty lunchbaskets with two handles and hinged covers! The Sam Colemans were former neighbors of ours on Bond Street. Their home was the showplace commanding the top of Cowles' Hill, a majestically columned piece of perfection designed by Elam Alexander for Jere Cowles. The house is to this day a symbol of grace, spaciousness, and tradition as it stands atop the town, its columns gleaming behind giant magnolias, the home of a succession of first families in Macon's social life. Cowles' Hill became Coleman's Hill (as it has remained since) when the Sam Colemans and my friends, Birdie and Daisy, lived there. Today it is the home of another friend, Mrs. B. P. O'Neal.

Birdie and Daisy were so proper and pretty in every way that

A LITTLE LADY—CIRCA 1870

I thought them exquisite and was happy when invited to put my lunch with theirs.

I, too, had my days of splendor. Even now I recall with pleasure my picture at the age of two in my best dress. It was pale gray silk poplin piped with cherry, which I proudly wore with high button shoes betasseled at the top, and a white silk beaver hat "wif a feaver what blows"—my enraptured description of the play of the little plume on the hat.

For fine occasions there was a solemn and ceremonious curling of my auburn hair. Mother seemed very proud of my curls, and would stand me up for what seemed like hours, forming the long, round curls on a wooden stick. It was very tiring, but very compensating. Joseph would stand and watch, always proud and admiring. After a while, the ritual would be too much for Jimmy, and he would run up to us and pull the curls.

Sometimes I was very carefully dressed to go calling on family friends. Among them was Mrs. William B. Johnston in the big brick palace on Georgia Avenue. Copied from an old world villa, its parlors and great ballroom were furnished sumptuously to befit the imposing plans and decoration of the house. Mother would garb me in my most beautiful dress, a fine white thread cambric with a great many ruffles edged with lace and hemstitching from waist to hem. When I fared forth in the family carriage, resplendent in my finery, curled, ruffled, and ribbon-sashed, I doubtless deemed myself quite as fine and dainty as the ineffable Birdie and Daisy Coleman.

Such vanities, however, were highlights in the Blount ménage, rather than daily doings which set the tone of our home. My father was a serious and ambitious young man beneath the hearty charm of his manner. For all her wit, Mama was a serious woman, who valued good talk, good literature, and the problems of politics above fripperies of dress and society and the absorptions of housekeeping.

When all three children were old enough, and Papa was in Washington at short sessions of Congress, there were evenings of play acting. As a reward for diligence when we finished our lessons early, Mama would produce and participate in a Shakespearean play. She'd take the minor parts and assign the great, juicy mouthfuls of the big parts to Joseph, Jimmy, and me. There were no costumes, stage sets, or trappings—just Shakespeare, Mama, and us. And that was enough. In our parlor productions of Shakespeare I was both Ophelia and Gertrude, Lady Macbeth, Queen Catherine, Cordelia, Portia, or Rosalind, striving mightily to blend Mama's corrections in diction and inflection with my own pleasure in performing.

I remember our play acting more vividly than our Christmases. Here Joe shone. He played Hamlet, Macbeth, Lear, and Shylock, his innate aptitude for acting tempered and polished by Mama's direction.

Remembering his part in our home theatricals calls up a picture of talented, endearing Joseph and of how he brought to our life a long, sad note of pathos, a story of trouble and failure such as saddens nearly every family history.

He was Mama's favorite, although she would never admit it or indicate it by any act of favoritism. But we knew it, and we thought it quite right, for we loved him, too, and thought he deserved her special love.

Joseph early excelled at the Shakespearean evenings and charmed Mama with his love of the bard, his aptitude for expression, and his grace and spirit in acting. He sang sweetly and played the piano by ear, a Wiley inheritance which was of course not cultivated in a boy of that time. Unmusical though I was, as the young lady of the family I received lessons in such parlor graces, as did my little sister Fanny later on.

As Joe grew older and his taste and talent for the stage became more marked, the boy bloomed with all the endowments for a brilliant career. He was as handsome as a matinee idol, and he eagerly absorbed Mama's love of great drama and her training in diction and expression.

So, he determined to become an actor, an unthinkable ambi-

A LITTLE LADY—CIRCA 1870

tion for a gentleman. Papa ordered his son to read law. With rebellion of spirit, but dutiful application, Joe studied at Mercer and was graduated with a law degree.

Mama, moved by love and pride and the independence of outlook which distinguished her all her life, pleaded Joe's cause. She saw that he was a natural artist, devoted with all the ardor of his nature to the theater, and she thought he should do the work he loved and was fitted for. But Papa was adamant. He did not think the calling an honorable one, even though the stage was occasionally redeemed by a Booth, a Jefferson, or a Frederick Ward.

We other children were not privy to such conflicts. We knew only that Joe wanted to go on the stage, but that Papa, like the fathers of his day, had the final say-so.

The edict was too much for Joe at last, and he left home in the late eighties to tour with a stock company. His break may have been delayed too long, or badly planned. Certainly it proved expensive beyond his means away from home. I recall that his frequent frustration was purchase of rich costumes which he must provide for himself.

And he never reached his stride. For about 20 years he worked at a series of unremarkable positions, including a Western post with the federal land office and some Washington jobs, never happy and dogged by misfortune.

He was married in 1901 to Mrs. Bowie Dorsey Griffith of Maryland. The Joseph Blounts had three daughters. Dorothy, a beauty with Joe's dark eyes and lovely features, spent much of her girlhood with my husband and me. The second daughter, Maude, was gray-eyed and fair-haired like her mother, and was often in Macon with Grandmother Blount. Maude was married at an early age to Dr. L. K. Fargo, a Baltimore physician much older than she. The youngest, Eugenia, was also a frequent visitor to the family in Macon, and was married to Charles Roberts Anderson at my home on Georgia Avenue.

Joe came home in 1910 ill with pernicious anemia. Papa

had died seven years before, and Joe stayed with Mama at her Orange Street home with Fanny. As his weakness increased, he thought longingly of the country quiet and boyhood happiness he remembered at Hale Nui. So Mama took him home to the Big House, with only the servants and his male nurse.

There at Hale Nui my mother lost her most beautiful and best loved child. She was white-haired and almost seventy, and Joe was thin and graying. But reading, talking, reminiscing together, they felt the old love and pride and tenderness between them grow stronger than ever in those last weeks.

Mama had a lofty scorn for what was slovenly or silly in speech, reading, or thinking. She did not hesitate to counteract any outside influences which she thought worked for inferior performances in her children. At seven, I was reciting "The Prisoner of Chillon" at Miss Clifford's Friday programs, alternating with Shelley's "Skylark" or something from Longfellow.

Much later, as a sophomore, I spent bewildering weeks in preparation for Sophomore Day recitation at Commencement time at Wesleyan. Mrs. Alice Culler Cobb, English teacher, assigned a heart-rending narrative poem called "Flying Jim's Last Leap" to me as my part of the program.

Mrs. Cobb belonged to an elocution school where everything was literal. If you recited "Curfew Shall Not Ring Tonight," you had to seize hold of the imaginary bell clapper, heave it across the stage and hold it to one side to demonstrate that it should not ring.

Such histrionics did not appeal to Mama. In fact, the gestures with which Mrs. Cobb assiduously primed me, Mama would not countenance. Every night, she rehearsed me through "Flying Jim," meticulously deleting the Cobb excesses of the school-approved version.

Came the great day, with young ladies dressed in frilly white and seated on the chapel stage with Mrs. Cobb, Dr. W. C. Bass, Wesleyan's president, and other notables. Facing a fes-

A LITTLE LADY—CIRCA 1870

tively arrayed and proudly expectant audience, my classmates rose and recited their pieces with starting eyes and flaying arms in the Cobb grand style.

Quite secure in the knowledge that Mama was right—she was always right—and undismayed by the shock in store for Mrs. Cobb, I rose to do "Flying Jim."

Confidently, and with what must have been amazing restraint compared with the other performers, I recited the story of poor Jim, the forlorn tramp, begging for a crust of bread at the door of the great mansion. He was turned away, and shuffled despairing, down the marble steps. But, lo! A little child followed him. The darling of the great house had watched from the window, her tender heart moved, and she ran out with food for the starving derelict. Jim thanked the child with a tremulous blessing, consumed the food and straggled sadly off to the woods.

I recited softly and clearly, my hands at my sides. Then I told with ringing clarity how poor old Jim heard the fire alarm in the town, followed the shouting crowds and arrived at the scene as the mansion went up in flame, how he heard that his little friend was trapped in the blaze, and how he broke through the stunned throngs to dash into the holocaust, rescue the little one, and leap with her through a high window. The child was thus saved and Jim died a hero's death.

I sat down, confident in my triumph as the applause rolled up from the audience. There was a faint smile on Mama's lovely face as her eyes turned to meet Papa's delighted look. Mrs. Cobb remained cold, non-committal, and stately through the presentation of the J. W. Burke Gold Medal—to Miss Eugenia Dorothy Blount.

Our reading was strictly supervised. There was an early diet of Abbott's histories, Louisa M. Alcott, the Schönberg-Cotter series, and later Hume, Macaulay, and Gibbon, with indulgent dips into Scott, Thackeray, Dickens, and Hawthorne as special treats. We read poetry of Poe, Bryant, Tennyson,

Byron, the Brownings, Shelley, and Keats, and of course always Lanier. Mama loved Lanier, not only for Brother Charlie's friendship with Sid and the long association of the Laniers and Wileys, but for his fine poetry.

"What are you reading, Daughter?" Papa would ask me, grave and friendly. And, when I showed him my book, "Well, let's talk about it a little." Talk about it we would, until he was sure that the child, and later the young lady, was duly edified.

Into my young ladyhood I was always docile at Papa's question, "What are you reading, Daughter?" If he found my choice less than elevating, he would say, "My child, that isn't good for you." And away went the offending volume with no protest from me. I was well rewarded for such denials in Papa's pleasure on such occasions as the one when he found me voluntarily reading *The Rise and Fall of the Dutch Republic.*

Jimmy, the roly-poly, blue-eyed, laughing charmer of the family, who attracted the most delighted attention from friends and onlookers, was liable not only to disrupt the dignity of the dinner hour with his sly clowning, but to confound the family with his disappearances. Once Jimmy was missing for several hours and couldn't be found anywhere, though the family and servants searched the house and grounds and runners were even sent out all over town. Finally aroused by the commotion, Jim emerged from under the parlor table, yawning and rubbing his eyes. He had retreated there hours before to read (at the age of nine) Gibbon's *Decline and Fall of the Roman Empire* and had fallen asleep.

Years later Jim enlisted in the Army as a volunteer in the Spanish-American War. Private Jim Blount was encamped at Griffin, Georgia, with other Macon boys. He was assigned to K. P. duty, and his companions-at-arms came home on leave with the news that he had acquired a new nickname, "Plato," because the erudite camp cook was often seen stirring with one hand a great kettle of soup and holding in the other a copy of Plato which he was reading in the original Greek.

A LITTLE LADY—CIRCA 1870

My brother Jim grew up richly endowed with a flair for letters and the intellectual graces which my parents cultivated in their children.

He graduated with honors from the University of Georgia and later studied law at Columbia University. Having returned home to practice law, he fell in love with and married Sallie B. Comer of Birmingham. Their daughter, Eugenia, was born in Macon.

Jim wrote a book about the Philippines which was a national success. He produced a law book, *Georgia Forms and Practices*. He contributed frequently to high class magazines, was a versifier of some ability, and became a popular after-dinner speaker. In addition to being a practicing lawyer, he also followed a military career in which he advanced from private to major.

His record at home as an attorney and scholar and his success as a soldier earned him an appointment from President McKinley as Judge of the First Instance in the Judiciary set up by the United States as a part of civil government in the Philippines. His gifts as a linguist qualified him for conduct of the court in Spanish. He became an authority on Philippine affairs, and in the political tradition of his father's view of the rights of another island people, Jim believed the Filipinos should be left in freedom to run their own affairs.

After returning from the Philippines in 1920, Jim opened a law office in Washington. He resumed his writing, contributing to *Harper's*, the *North American Review*, the *Atlantic Monthly*, the *Green Bag*, (national organ of the Bar Association) and other publications. His book, *American Occupation in the Philippines, 1898-1912* was a history of the United States' role in liberation of the islands and administration of their affairs.

The book received long and thoughtful reviews in all parts of the country, with especially favorable comment from the *New York Times*, the *Milwaukee Press*, and the *Philadelphia Ledger*.

Andrew Carnegie was so impressed with the book that he bought copies which he presented to every member of Congress and placed on every cruiser and warship in the United States Navy.

Thus celebrated and in good graces with like-minded Democratic President Woodrow Wilson, Judge Blount was appointed in 1921 to head a diplomatic mission to Santo Domingo.

Two years later at the outbreak of World War I he returned to soldiering. He volunteered his services to the Army, and was appointed to serve in the Judge Advocate's Division at Charleston, South Carolina.

Just before he was to embark for duty in France, Jim took a Sunday horseback ride in Central Park. He was crossing the Boulevard in front of a bus that stopped on a signal, when a speeding ambulance caused his horse to throw him. His head struck the stone curb and he never regained consciousness.

Thus, at 46, ended tragically the life of my brilliant, merry brother Jim.

Religion occupied a revered place in our family values. It was of a stern, Presbyterian variety, with inviolable Sabbaths, grace at every meal, and daily scripture reading before breakfast. Papa would open the great family Bible and read a chapter a day until his family and servants had attended the reading of the whole book. Then, he would start all over again.

We didn't have audible family prayers at great length. There were occasions to bow our heads reverently; but we had natural Presbyterian inhibitions about speaking out in meeting, even at home. We felt ourselves, in the Presbyterian way, as publicans and sinners, as humble supplicants. So, we were not prone to beat our breasts, pray aloud and tell the Lord how fine we were, nor to make long-winded demands upon Him.

We went to Sunday School of course. My teacher was Mrs. Warner Clisby, wife of the pastor. I was taken to church as soon as I could sit alone. I really can't imagine how I endured it.

A LITTLE LADY—CIRCA 1870

Dr. Clisby was a Presbyterian of the old school, who delivered deep theological sermons of an hour to an hour and a half.

I do know that much of the time I amused myself by watching Miss Minnie and Miss Leila Wood. Miss Leila was later Mrs. Joseph Bond and Miss Minnie married George Plant. They went to New York frequently and brought home beautiful clothes, especially lovely bonnets. As they sat in front of us (ours was Pew 57, where I still worship) I would imagine how they would look with their bonnets exchanged. Back and forth they would go from one head to another, helping me to while away the sermon hours. Also, with my hands close to my lap, I would make little movements with my fingers, imitating the preacher's. Thus, I endured the dreary discourse.

Week days after school we little Blounts would play in our yard with a goodly number of the thirteen children of Mama's older sister, Mary, and her husband, Charles Jenkins Harris. But on Sunday there was no such diversion. The only amusement was reading books we brought from Sunday School, and very namby-pamby things they were. The order of the day was to recite the 23rd, 19th, and other Psalms, the Ten Commandments, and the Shorter Catechism.

Sometimes I took a Sunday afternoon stroll with Papa to Rose Hill Cemetery at the other end of College Street, a three-mile round trip. Papa, at his conversational and forensic best, would read me the tombstone inscriptions and discourse on the dead with considerable pomp and oratory. This was a wild and wonderful treat on Sunday.

The social side of religion came to a spring climax with the annual Sunday School picnic, when all the little Presbyterians, Methodists, and Baptists, from Vineville to First Street, dressed in gala white, met downtown at the Confederate monument for a grand march to Central City Park, a mile or so away. As Presbyterians, we Blounts wore blue ribbons to distinguish us from the pink-ribboned Methodists, the green-ribboned Baptists, and the Vineville children with yellow ribbons.

Teachers marched with the children, led by the marshal of the day. He was a mighty Methodist, Mr. Duffus Clancy, and he rode a great black horse. It was a long, long walk. And how we dressed up for that march through the dust! None of us would admit the march was too long, too dusty, or too hot, for that would have been admitting we were too little for it. Besides, we wanted to show ourselves in all our splendor.

At the park the children played games, spoke pieces, made floral designs from wild flowers, and sang under direction of Mr. Clancy, a man of tremendous voice, in the best Methodist tradition. We vied, worked, and played toward a lavish climax of fried chicken and ice cream contributed by our mothers.

We would sing, "Many, many stars are in the sky, as old as A-adam; down upon your knees and kiss who you please, your humble servant Ma-adam." Then the boy in the center of the singing circle would seize the little girl of his choice to claim a kiss. But my brothers would never let anyone kiss me. When the time came, Joe or Jimmy would hit the little boy and drive him away.

This was not the only frustration I suffered from the stern dictates of the men of the family. There was the matter of bangs. Many girls wore them and Mama thought they would look sweet. But Papa was inexorably opposed to them. I longed for bangs with a passion possible only to little girls denied the privilege of looking exactly like everyone else; and, provoked to the extremity of defiance one day, I actually cut myself some bangs—with Papa's razor. I don't remember the details of the ensuing storm, except that the violation of Papa's razor was a crime even greater than my disobedience as to bangs. I do remember it was a very serious time, because of Papa's outraged authority.

But I was not often rebellious, and Mother took great satisfaction in my ready obedience. "Dolly," she often said, "never bemoans what is denied her, but always goes happily on to the next thing."

A LITTLE LADY—CIRCA 1870

As a bigger girl of twelve, I went for a time to school to Mrs. Margaret Snider Birch, who opened Macon's first coeducational school on the ground floor of her Magnolia Street home. She was very strict and systematic and discouraged any attempt at romancing between the boys and girls, who were going to school together for the first time. The children struggled through their lessons, with the usual spelling difficulties of a language whose phonetics are by no means accommodated to the Southern accent. Rock Rogers (who grew up to be a director of the Exchange Bank, a Wesleyan trustee, a pillar of the Mulberry Street Methodist Church and a stately man of many parts in Macon) left his desk to stand by the door and hold up his hand, for such was the ritual Mrs. Birch required of a pupil who wanted to ask a question.

"How do you spell nelly?" Rock wanted to know.

"Why, just as it's pronounced," Mrs. Birch answered. "N-e-l-l-y."

"Oh, no, ma'am," Rock protested. "I mean nelly like when you say, 'I'm nelly through.' "

For some years I suffered serious pangs from love and admiration of prankster boys. To my acute embarrassment I was accosted and tormented almost on my own doorstep by Mercer boys. When I was old enough to interest these campus cutups but too little to repel them with a young lady's dignity, I ran an agonized gauntlet to and from home.

Six decades later, I was pleasantly revenged. As Mrs. Walter D. Lamar, I received from Mercer an honorary LL.D., and was baccalaureate speaker to the class of 1940. I began my speech:

"Once upon a time there lived in a large white house with a square cupola atop . . . a little girl named Dolly. The house, since burned, faced Tattnall Square Park looking west. As a child Dolly disliked, nay feared, boys, especially Mercer boys. . . .

In her daily walks from the square to her prep school, she encountered some of these boys who annoyed her with comments or calls that terrified. They would, on seeing her approach, string out across the sidewalk, lock arm in arm, a solid phalanx, all the while calling out:

WHEN ALL IS SAID AND DONE

"Here comes Dolly! Ain't she sweet? Ain't she cute? She's my sweetheart! No, she's mine!" And so on, until the poor, frightened little rabbit of a girl would dash out into the red dust of the road and run breathless to her home where her mother would exclaim: "My dear, what is the matter?" To which the terror-stricken child would reply, "Oh, Mama, those horrid Mercer boys again."

"And what did you say, my dear?"

"Oh, I just pulled my sunbonnet down and did not notice them."

Time marches on! Revenge is sweet!

Today Mercer boys stand before the once persecuted female, at her tender mercies for as long as she may choose to pinion them. And in the whirligig of history, there appear in this graduating class 15 young women who with all the rights and privileges of Mercer men are equally educated for life as are the males of the class.

As baccalaureate speaker I did not choose to "pinion" the boys very long, for I was pleased to have so advanced from "being afraid to meet a Mercer boy on the street to becoming one of them with a postgraduate degree that exhales dignity and gives impetus to personal usefulness for and pride in the institution." I expressed my pleasure at being the first woman to deliver a baccalaureate address at Mercer, and at joining the illustrious company of Robert E. Lee, who was also awarded an LL.D. from Mercer in 1866.

CAMPAIGNS AND CHINQUAPINS

PAPA WAS AWAY FROM HOME A GREAT DEAL IN THE FALL OF 1872. He was, we children knew, campaigning over the Sixth District. When he came home from Rockdale County he always brought us a sack of tasty chinquapins. The delicious chinquapins are my most vivid recollection of the tense and terrible election year when Georgia's Conservative Democrats, fighting for survival, laboriously pulled their state further out of the prostration of Reconstruction.

Outside the serenity of the household that Mama maintained, with its quiet rhythm of school, backyard play, pleasant mealtimes, and stern Presbyterian Sundays, Macon strained every sinew against the oppressors. All Democrats, a few Liberal Republicans, loyal or re-converted darkeys, and everyone except black and white Radicals toiled in the tremendous political effort over the state to wrest Georgia's sovereignty from the hated bonds of the Grant administration.

At the Cincinnati convention of the Liberal Republicans in May, the party nominated Horace Greeley as president, and enunciated this pledge to the South: "We demand immediate and absolute removal of all disabilities imposed on account of the rebellion, which was finally subdued seven years ago, believing that universal amnesty will result in complete pacification of all sections of the country."

Greeley himself, Southern newspapers recalled, at the close

of the war appealed for peaceful return of the Southern states to the Union, with the same political rights they had enjoyed before (except for the strictures of the 13th, 14th, and 15th Amendments) and with Secession forgiven and forgotten. Also, hopeful Southerners remembered, it was Greeley who, with Cornelius Vanderbilt, gave bond for Jefferson Davis which released him from his two years' imprisonment at Fortress Monroe. This was a sharply persuasive memory for the South, still lamenting that the Confederate President had suffered the ignominy and torture of iron chains during part of his imprisonment.

Although they were reeling under Yankee military rule, Maconites were loath to vote Republican under any promises. The bitterest cup to swallow was the Radical insistence that they were insurgents and traitors, or conquered aliens to be punished for exercising the inherent right of Secession which every state had cherished and which many Northerners had invoked. Only 17 years before she began to arm her sons to prevent the South from leaving the Union, Massachusetts had announced that annexation of Texas would drive her and other states to dissolution of the Union. So, this violation of a treasured principle was more galling even than economic ruin, arrests of gentlemen and patriots on affidavits of illiterate Negroes, the near-anarchy of Federal rule, or taxes which took their property.

All in all, a platform of any party which offered hope of return to a just and honorable estate in the nation carried a fervid appeal.

Earlier, many Northerners were outraged at the venal and cynical exploitation of the defeated South. In 1871, John Quincy Adams expressed this growing sympathy in a letter of counsel to an Arkansas newspaper. Macon Democrats read with excitement a reprint of Adams' message in the local paper.

Adams expressed a decent hesitancy to advise the "subject states," and didn't doubt that "under similar circumstances I should be today an 'unrepentant rebel'—sore, angry, beaten and defiant." He agreed that "doubtless the tender mercies of reconstruction have been harder to bear than all the horrors of invasive war. "

"I should," Mr. Adams wrote, "have been galled by misgovernment, robbed by imported knavery of the pittance which the war had spared . . . cruelly condemned to hopeless impotence for imputed guilt of cowardly crimes I abhorred . . . holding my personal liberty at the nod of a mercenary carpetbagger or the whim of a military satrap."

Mr. Adams noted that the Union "is now held together by force" and wondered what chance there could be for free government if "the North is to rule the South." He warned that "such injustice threatens the freedom of us all."

Georgians who read Mr. Adams' letter were doubtless warmed and encouraged by such an accurate description and such a sympathetic Northern view of their suffering in the year 1871.

"You cannot be subject and we long be free," wrote he, affirming his belief in "local self-government of the States." As a fellow-citizen, then, he advised the South to accept "revolutionary changes forced on the Constitution . . . the new relation toward the emancipated class." He concluded that for unity and amity, "there must be sacrifice for us all and much self-control in the South."

In 1872, Georgians were to find themselves taking his advice. The state was this year able to see, with sanguine eyes, its way out of the worst days of Reconstruction. Whites, some of them Democrats turned Republican, to be sure, and others of more respectable record were struggling back into office. In Macon, W. A. Huff was mayor and his council was largely white. The list included at least one Negro, Ed Woodliffe, a literate freedman before the war and a Radical leader after. But there was a formidable array of old, respected, upperclass Democratic names among the aldermen.

Freedom from the usurpers was not to be easily achieved,

everyone realized. In desperation, my father and his friends discussed means of forcing or conniving at a November election which would give whites not disfranchised a chance to vote.

The *Telegraph and Messenger* reported that the election of 1870 drew about 2,200 votes in Bibb County, less than 100 of them white Democrats, and exhorted its readers to plan against a repetition of this calamity. All over Georgia where Radicals were in control, white Democrats had been crowded from the polls by apparently drilled and rehearsed freedmen who rushed the voting places.

Governor Smith, a white Democrat, was leading a General Assembly investigation against the former Governor Bullock, airing testimony of fraud and thievery, as Smith's campaign for re-election opened in the spring of 1872.

Representative Speer of Macon was in altercation with the mulatto firebrand, Jeff Long, former congressman and a leader of white and Negro Radicals in middle Georgia. The *Telegraph and Messenger* wondered if "jefflong" or "jephlong," as he was contemptuously called in print, was trying to turn "his white brother Speer out of office to take his seat in Congress."

Grant of course was nominated by Radical Republicans. Southerners planned for their Baltimore convention pondering uneasily the question of whether they should support Liberal Republican Greeley as the most practical and expeditious compromise for political rehabilitation.

In May, Editor Clisby of the Macon newspaper expressed local Democratic worries thus: "It is in the power of the Democrats, as the balance of Power, to elect Mr. Greeley in place of Grant. . . . Shall they do it, or hazard Grant's re-election in an effort to run a candidate of our own?"

A few days later he wrote, "Four years of bayonet law, four years in which Georgia has been kicked around like a football, four years of all personal and legal rights at the mercy of Grant's orders and proclamations, four years of vilification through all the organs of government, four years of hunting our people like dogs, as Ku-Kluxers, four years of steady Grant backing of every carpetbag rascal in every scheme to plunder.

"These are enough and more than enough. We can't stand any more. . . . There is no chance to be worsted by a change. The point, then, for us to accomplish is . . . the best change predictable."

There was a less emotional, more resolute, and dedicated editorial on May 16, which doubtless voiced the common decision of the country's upperclass whites. It said: "We are ready to support and vote for Greeley and Brown to defeat Grant. We also believe . . . [this is] a formative period in national affairs, when old issues, slavery included, have passed away and new parties and political affinities must be established."

In June, after the convention of Southern Democrats had thrown its support to Greeley and Brown, the paper opened its campaign of appeal and persuasions, which sharpened and intensified as the weeks went on to reach by fall a passionate pitch in urgency.

Said the *Telegraph and Messenger:* "To the South . . . overtaken by the tempest of Radical tyranny, robbed and trampled underfoot, her people at the mercy of Federal tax collectors and gleaming bayonets, here comes the nominee of Cincinnati, bringing the olive branch of peace and strong arms and stout hearts to the rescue, albeit they were once our enemies and persecutors. Shall we reject their sympathy and succor and sullenly hug our chains, and prefer defeat and ruin to such an alliance? We trow not. Let us rise above the atmosphere of ancient prejudices and feuds, and preserving our origin and identity as Democrats, strike hands with the Liberal Republican movement . . . and combine every energy of the country to defeat the dominion of the despotic Grant."

This resolve seems to have been shared by most of native Bibb County, excepting politically active freedmen, alien carpetbaggers, and Federal officials. Colonel Tom Hardeman, who had led Macon boys off to Virginia at the outset of the war, and back again to the greater distress of Reconstruction, was chairman of the Bibb County Democratic Executive Committee which now embraced the hopes and promises of the Liberal Republicans. He was also a delegate to the Baltimore convention of Democrats who endorsed Greeley. T. J. Simmons, a law partner of my father, was in the state legislature, as was Colonel C. A. Nutting, all backing the Greeley party. Papa, too, bowed to the exigencies of the times in voting Liberal Republican during Georgia's struggle for political survival.

Meantime, Radicals in the county were not idle. There were more arrests under the Enforcement Act, which provided that "if two or more band together or conspire to injure, oppress, threaten or intimidate any citizen to prevent or hinder free exercise of his rights or privileges . . . under the Constitution," such offenders would be guilty of felony. This act, implemented by suspension of habeas corpus, permitted Radical officials to arrest and imprison alleged Ku Klux members, disfranchised Democrats working for victory in the election, or any personal or political opponent on affidavits of Radicals black or white.

There was, reports the *Telegraph and Messenger,* a campaign of "wholesale arrests . . . instigated by jephlong." And Papa, who had never before run for office, was now considering the race for Congress against Radical Candidate Anderson. The young men and the worried, hopeful oldsters had discussed it with him, even as several of his friends, veterans of the early war days in Virginia, were arrested under the "Force Act."

As whites gathered their forces for the presidential fight, taking their stand with the Greeley party, Jeff Long preached to excited Negroes. While Macon whites met one hot and humid night in July at Ralston Hall on the corner of Third and Cherry streets to ratify the action of the Baltimore convention, Jeff Long conducted a mass meeting of Grantites at the City Hall where the Negro ex-councilman, N. M. Sellers, was secretary to the meeting.

The "incendiary" Long, the paper recounts, told his freedmen listeners that victorious Democrats would return them to slavery, or else their erstwhile owners would kidnap them and sell them as slaves to Cuban planters. Also, he warned, every former slave owner would be paid for his freed Negroes by taxes imposed on the Negroes. He recalled the nine o'clock curfew of slave days when "they drove you like sheep to your huts and hovels," and he promised return of the curfew with a Democratic victory.

"You're not free yet!" he cried to Negroes in the employ of whites. "If you vote as you please, you're driven from white plantations and farms to starve." On the other hand, he promised that a Radical victory would hasten the movement to send 30,000 freedmen to the West every year for education to "train you for equality and to assert your rights."

Long attacked Bob Thomas, Ben H. Hill, and General Wright, all Georgia congressmen and strong men of the slow counter-revolution against Reconstruction. He denounced Linton Stephens of the Georgia legislature, who had died within the week. A white heckler asked Long if he knew that Stephens was dead.

"You'll be dead before long," shouted the speaker, to an uproar of cheers and applause, "if you belong to the Greeley party!"

On Sunday, August 18, there was editorial mention of four gentlemen who had their hats in the ring for a Sixth District seat in Congress: Messrs. James H. Blount, A. O. Bacon, and C. A. Nutting of Bibb County and Mr. Reid of Putnam County. The *Telegraph and Messenger* supposed that "almost every Democrat in the county would be glad to vote for all three if he could and will regret the necessity for choice between them."

The new state election law had set the presidential and congressional elections on the Tuesday after the first Monday in November. So Georgia Democrats bestirred themselves mightily. The *Telegraph and Messenger* was exhorting patriots to vote and speechmakers were talking up Greeley. The "jephlongites" were raising an equal clamor on the other side, a Radical uproar considerably increased by drunkenness, lies, and demagoguery, the paper observed. Ben H. Hill, introduced by Washington Poe, talked to Maconites in support of the Greeley-Brown ticket.

We little Blounts were making dirt houses and mud pies or play-acting under the chinaberry trees on Tattnall Square with our Harris cousins, oblivious to the outside struggle. Yet even before Papa began to be away so much, we noticed that Mama had less time for reading and hearing our recitations.

I was only five that campaign year; so I don't remember anything extraordinary, except Papa's absences, the chinquapins, and his evening monopoly of Mama when he was at home.

Papa was as stern and jovial, as supreme and judicious as ever, when we saw him. Later, we were to measure his suspense and anxiety by the frequency with which he banished us, to talk to Mama. Older, stronger, and filling out to the robust stature which characterized his prime, Papa was absorbed not only in the state's crisis but also in the promise of his own political career.

Colonel Hardeman on September 12 called to order Bibb County's congressional convention to nominate a man for Congress and appoint delegates to the Sixth District convention in Milledgeville the next week. There was some dissension about whether the Macon convention should nominate a candidate, instruct delegates, or simply elect delegates to Milledgeville. The disagreement seems to have been resolved by the persuasions of Mr. R. W. Jemison, a Blount man, and also by the need to present a united front in every step of the crucial campaign ahead. The local Democrats voted Blount their nominee by a majority of 131 over Nutting, and named 12 delegates instructed to vote for Blount at the Milledgeville meeting.

CAMPAIGNS AND CHINQUAPINS

My father's nomination from the Sixth District was settled a week later at the old capital. The *Telegraph and Messenger* hailed "this gallant soldier and spotless gentleman" who won out against "all worthy men," and urged: "Let us rally to his support then, like the Clansmen of MacGregor to their loved chieftain." The paper also predicted that "Colonel Blount will carry the district if mortal man can do it."

Later the paper followed Colonel Blount's course as he stumped the district to "cover every inch of territory and meet his opponents," including some joint rallies with E. E. Beck, Esq., running for the unexpired term of Representative Speer who had died late in the summer.

Georgians were exuberant over the chance to have nine congressmen in Washington again and over their hopes to elect Greeley. But they saw that such good fortune would be won only by the most assiduous work: oratory with planning, speeches with close personal attention to constituents, and exhortations to vote coupled with careful techniques to get whites to the polls.

And in October, when hope was highest and the burden of Radical rule seemed ripe for the last strain and push that would throw it off, there came dire news from local elections in the North and neighboring states.

Radical victories, said the *Telegraph and Messenger,* were accompanied by "fraud in registrations, outlay of money like water, and the colonization of black voters from abroad." However won, the Radical victories were a grievous fact.

Late in October, the whole South was resigned to loss of the presidential election and the re-election of Grant. The Macon paper sadly and bitterly noted that widespread "hatred" in the North of anything Southern had hurt the Greeley cause, that Southern espousal had already beaten the Liberal Republicans.

The national defeat, however, seems to have bestirred Georgians to greater effort in their October elections of state officials. Governor Smith was opposing Bullock's candidate, Dawson

Walker, and almost every county saw struggles between Radicals and white Democrats for seats in the General Assembly.

As Papa campaigned for Congress, preparing for the November national election, Bibb Countians went to the polls in October to vote in the state elections.

In Macon, tense and determined whites went to the front entrance of the courthouse on Mulberry Street to cast their votes. There they found a mass of Negroes, whom they had expected to enter the rear door to reach their polling places, lined up and jamming the front entrances. Remembering the white voters' frustration in the last two elections, the Democrats expostulated. Special police, deputized by Mayor Huff, watched warily. There were angry scuffles.

Someone saw Dr. Appleton Collins fighting with a Negro. There was a shot from somewhere. And more shots. Jeff Long was heard from his place at a high window in the post office shouting to his people to stand firm. Later, others heard his shouted admonitions to the Negroes to run for their lives.

Mechanic William Corkle of the Macon and Brunswick Railroad, standing peacefully by and watching the fighting, dropped —shot dead by a stray bullet. Three Negroes were killed and an uncounted number were injured by gunshot and fist fighting. There were more white casualties among the wounded.

Whoever fired the first shot, the Mayor's special police or Negro voters, there was enough gunfire on the white side to disperse the Negroes. They fled to the City Hall.

There, Mayor Huff talked calmly to them. (He was a good friend to Negroes in Macon, and when he was first elected to office he was serenaded at his quarters in the Lanier House by a white band and a Negro band.) He urged the Negroes to return to the courthouse, line up quietly in orderly fashion, and vote thus without fear of interference or violence.

But there were Radical leaders and Negro speakers also on the City Hall steps, haranguing the black voters. "Go to your homes," advised Tillman Lowe, Negro candidate for the legislature. "You will be shot down if you try to vote." Another Negro leader, Pulaski Long, also urged dispersal.

Jeff Long was arrested, probably by city authorities on charges of inciting a riot, or whatever technicality came to hand. The details of his arrest are obscured in the scorn with which local journalists treated him, never deigning to dignify his doings with background details, but only recounting his more flagrant speeches with editorial comment.

The *Telegraph and Messenger* tells the election riot story largely through reports of the United States Commissioners' Court hearings of prominent Democrats arrested under the Force Act. It seems clear, even in the tangled and angry retrospect of those hearings, that the local whites after years of fruitless effort to vote, had resolved to exercise that right this October. They would fight fire with fire. Their program, which was climaxed in the bloody riot, was repeated in measures elsewhere over the state, where voting Democrats contrived to reclaim their land from the Radicals.

In Bibb County the successful effort cost at least four lives, many casualties and the arrest and imprisonment of at least 12 leading citizens. My family and their friends counted the results well worth the cost. Governor Smith was re-elected, and Colonel Beck was sent to Congress for the short term, defeating "jephlong." Also, Georgia's legislature was comprised almost entirely of white Democratic senators and representatives.

When the smoke had cleared away, the results showed 40 Democrats elected to the state senate, with but four Radicals, two of them Negroes. Of 145 representatives, 16 were Radicals and six were Negroes.

Now, as Papa pushed his congressional race against Radical Anderson, the reprisals broke loose from Federal officials in the post office. More than a dozen of his friends were arrested for intimidating Negroes at the polls, in what appeared to be a move to imprison the most zealous and politically active white Conservative Democrats in the county.

WHEN ALL IS SAID AND DONE

The *Telegraph and Messenger* reports daily hearings of a curiously assorted crew of accused, including Constable E. P. Smith, on trial for contempt of court, a charge brought after he arrested a man in the courthouse corridors when court was in session. Captain William H. Ross, George F. Cherry, and Matt Thornton were arrested among seven others on October 24 on charges growing out of the election riot and old Ku Klux accusations that were rehashed. Buck Plummer was arrested and tried on the affidavit of one Negro.

Mayor Huff testified that he had summoned about 60 special police from the Floyd Rifles, the Macon Volunteers, and the Zouaves, with George S. Jones as captain. He did not arm his police, and did not know where they got firearms if they had them. He said he had anticipated disturbance and had stationed the police outside the courthouse to avert trouble. The city charter, he pointed out, authorized special police for such service. He and other Democrats testifying recalled the experience of past elections.

Other witnesses, says the paper's account, testified that Jeff Long was "skulking in the post office during the voting and shooting, and was denounced by many Negroes for his "cowardly desertion" of them.

District Attorney Harry Farrow was in frequent altercation with defense lawyers, who were making themselves heard in the Federal building with a force and persistence unprecedented since '65.

Days later, the prisoners were released on bonds ranging from $1,000 to $5,000. Bonded were Captain Ross, C. J. Hancock, Theo W. Ellis, H. J. Peter, George W. Gustin, J. W. Burge, J. H. Able, D. D. Craig, and Henry Aderhold.

It was a time of crucial excitement for Macon, with some of its first citizens under arrest as felons or out on tremendous bond. Where the money came from in those meager times is as puzzling as the source of the guns with which Mayor Huff's special police armed themselves for the election, since most

CAMPAIGNS AND CHINQUAPINS

Confederates and Democrats had been disarmed long since.

Despite the tension the townsfolk—the excited ladies and outraged gentlemen—were careful to take it all with quietude and dignity. The *Telegraph and Messenger* observed at the time of arrest after arrest, and during the hearings at the post office, that "no one is excited; the city is quiet and calm."

It was, they decided, worth all the risks, violence, and death. They looked to Tennessee, where the notorious Maynard was returned to Congress. South Carolina, still helpless under the heel of Grant, had elected as lieutenant-governor, state treasurer, and four congressmen "sooty Negroes." Most of her state officials were black or white Radical, with the legislature "largely Negro Radical," the Macon paper said.

Louisiana was boiling with disgrace, misery, and outrage from the depredations of the Customs House Gang, seething to a New Orleans street revolution and an election scandal that availed nothing but several more years of bondage.

Whereas, Georgians had worked a long way out of their prostration. Said the *Telegraph and Messenger:* "Last Tuesday settled that white taxpayers should retain control of the State of Georgia four years longer."

On November 6, Papa defeated at the polls Radical Candidate Anderson by a majority of 3,787. Democrats carried seven of nine congressional districts in Georgia, with but two districts for the Radicals. Grant was re-elected, to be sure, but Georgia's Sixth gave Greeley a majority of more than 3,000. So, Bibb County's "gallant soldier and spotless gentlemen" (and a campaign charmer, to boot) was on his way to 20 years in Washington.

And my brothers and I happily crunched our chinquapins.

I was spared the strains and struggles of the crisis of 1872. I played, performed my duties, and continued to grow in the pattern set by my parents, undisturbed by the defeats and triumphs of that year. But the political concepts for which they fought in Georgia and the emotional impact of the effort were palpable in the air I breathed, the talk I heard without conscious understanding, and the strains that pulled beneath the ordered passing of my days.

Seventy years later, I followed in the footsteps of my father when I left the ranks of the Democratic Party to vote for Wendell Willkie. Later, in 1948, I left the party again to support the States' Rights Party candidate, Strom Thurmond. This was, to me, perfectly in the tradition of Southerners who voted liberal Republican in 1872 in an effort to save the sacred concept of States' Rights.

WASHINGTON CITY

PAPA'S GOING TO WASHINGTON AFTER CHRISTMAS IN 1873, to commence two decades of service in Congress, was an event in the family history which brought change and adventure to spice the quiet routine of family life in Macon.

During the three-months short term Mama usually accompanied him, leaving Joe, Jimmy, and me in the care of Grandmother Wiley. During the long term of six months, the whole family packed off to the capital to enjoy a glamorous stay of hotel living, Washington schooling, and friendships with men and women famous in the turbulent period of the brave and bitter rehabilitation of the South.

The perennial delights of the recurrent journeys to Washington are still fresh in my mind. There was the rumbling, grinding thrill of a Lynchburg, Virginia, stop, where the trains "changed wheels"—an operation still veiled in mechanical mystery to the feminine mind, but a thunderous milestone that the boys relished and I always anticipated with agreeable fright. Later, as we approached Washington we would see the Potomac sparkling through the suburban landscape; then the Capitol dome, and other landmarks as the train pulled into the city. In great excitement we would yell to each other from our windows to look at this and that wonderful Washington sight.

In our early days we boarded near the Capitol at the old National Hotel, where many congressmen stayed to avoid arduous transportation along the unpaved streets of the city. Papa had an office adjoining the family suite. I recall my mother's proud story of how Papa, early in his career, received a railroad magnate. The self-confident Western millionaire sent his card up to young Colonel Blount while Mama was in the office. Aware that his experience and influence scarcely warranted a call from such a personage, and suspecting something of his mission, the new congressman sent his wife from the office as he received the caller.

A man of few words, the tycoon went straight to the point. He offered Colonel Blount handsome remuneration in exchange for friendly treatment of railroad interests on the floor of the House.

"Get out of here, you scoundrel!" my father ordered in ringing tones of righteous indignation. "How dare you make me such a proposition?"

Unable to restrain herself, Mama peeped from the other room in time to see the urbane visitor, considerably ruffled, retreating before Papa, who stood with flashing eyes, his hand on a chair, ready to strike the caller who had so offended his honor.

Railroading in these Reconstruction days was one of the richest sources of graft and fortune-seeking in the national capital and in the Southern states. So in the Grant years of plundering lobbies, railroad interests were accustomed to joyful acceptance of favors among Scalawags and Radicals in the Southern delegations in Washington, and railroad officials blithely approached all potential friends in court.

Often by mail or messenger there came to my parents passes for railroad tours and lavish holidays, harbingers of propositions to come.

Fingering the bright folders and reading the suave and cordial invitations, Mama would exclaim: "Oh, Mr. Blount! How lovely! What a delightful and instructive holiday it will be for the children!"

"Why, Genie," Papa would protest, frowning at her naiveté, "can't you see that acceptance of such a proposition is unthinkable?" He would explain the political cost of such favors, until poor Mama was horrified at her innocent pleasure in the offers.

Early in our Washington years, we became six. Another son was born in 1873, a fair-haired, blue-eyed child they called David for Papa's half-brother and foster-father. This baby died in Washington in 1876, and his body was kept in the congressional vault until the close of the session, when the family brought it home for burial.

In 1879 the last baby came. She was Fanny, who, as the youngest, for some years went to Washington with Mama and Papa when we other children stayed at home during short terms. When Fanny was five, she contracted scarlet fever. The entire wing of the National Hotel was quarantined and my family's quarters were converted into a hospital, with Papa excluded to go about his congressional business while Mama nursed Fanny to recovery.

There was distinguished company aplenty at the old National, but we children were most vividly impressed with the vast Senator Davis, who regaled our mealtimes with the ritual of his approach to the table. An attentive waiter stood behind his chair, where hung his white bib. The waiter would assist the mighty Senator Davis to his seat, tie on his bib to protect his great paunch from the food that slipped 'twixt the cup and the lip, and take his order—to all of which the fat senator submitted with a docility that charmed us.

Mealtimes were also enlivened by the spectacle of the noted and eloquent Senator Joe Blackburn of Kentucky. He fired the Senate and served well the South with his oratory, and when he left the Halls of Congress he didn't stop talking. In fact, we children learned to anticipate with pleasure the garrulous gifts for which Blackburn was famed. His tireless tongue kept wagging whenever we saw him, and his perpetual talk intrigued us as much as Senator Davis' great avoirdupois.

Later the family moved to $4\frac{1}{2}$ Street, still nearer the Capitol, where we had rooms and board. Here lived also the famous

Mrs. Myra Clark Gaines, a noted lady whose legal difficulties in trying to recover properties of which she had been defrauded in New Orleans are told in Harnett Kane's recent novel *New Orleans Woman*.

She was a queer, preoccupied little old lady, who fared forth every morning with a black bag and umbrella to the United States Supreme Court to get about the case, which had become her *raison d'être*. She took a great fancy to Jimmy and they became fast friends, until one morning Jimmy, over-exuberant, ran up behind her and yelled "Boo!" Mrs. Gaines wheeled in fright and fury and chased the little boy down 4½ Street with her umbrella. He escaped, but that ended their friendship.

There were many sightseeing jaunts around Washington with Mama. I remember her proudly and scornfully zig-zagging down Pennsylvania Avenue to avoid passing under American flags, still faithful to the Stars and Bars of the Lost Cause and still stung by the sight of the Union flag and the outrages it had inflicted on the South since '65. No, we had not yet learned to love the flag in those first seasons in Washington. The wounds were so fresh, and the feeling so strong.

However circuitous our course through the city to take in the sights, sight-see we did, covering the monuments, shrines, public buildings, the Corcoran Art Gallery, and the Smithsonian Institute.

When I was too big for a nurse and too little to stay alone (I had my sixth birthday on our first trip to Washington), I often accompanied Mama to sit in the galleries of the House or Senate. In an early period of our Washington years, my mother was so absorbed in congressional debates that she could not bear to leave at lunch time. Equally excited was her friend, Mrs. John B. Gordon, wife of the Confederate general, Georgia Senator, and former Ku Klux Klan leader. Another rapt companion was Mrs. Anderson Reese, wife of Papa's secretary, who later became an owner and editor of the *Telegraph and Messenger* in Macon.

They sat, during the 1873 debates over the Louisiana election scandal, most days in the Senate gallery. Senators were to decide whether to seat Governor-Elect McEnery in New Orleans, elected by a coalition of Conservative Democrats with the notorious but now friendly Warmoth forces, or the Customs House Radical man, and his mulatto lieutenant-governor, Caius Caesar Antoine. The scandal exploded after Federal Judge Durell in New Orleans declared illegal the election count of the De Feriet returning board, and the Radicals set up their own board, to count Kellog elected, despite the McEnery majority. The U. S. Marshal and Federal troops took over the Capitol, to keep out McEnery and protect Kellog and Antoine.

All the South and much of Washington were scandalized at the forcible seizure of power and the Durell decision against the legal returning board. A wretched climax to Louisiana's Reconstruction disgrace and misery, it was accompanied by a street revolution in New Orleans, where the white citizens marched on the Capitol building held by Radicals, Negroes, and Federal troops, took over, and ensconced their duly elected governor, McEnery.

In Washington, Senator Carpenter almost persuaded the Republicans in Congress to accept the McEnery election. However, Radical Party Whip Morton persuaded his partisans to hold up any action until President Grant ruled in favor of the Kellog faction. With the arrival of three warships and fresh Federal troops at New Orleans, the state was returned to the Customs House gang for more years of pillaging and oppression.

Meanwhile, General Sheridan, military administrator of the "district," asked Grant for authority to deal with the insurgent whites of New Orleans as "banditti." This request recalled the earlier command of General "Beast" Butler, when he was occupying New Orleans. He ordered that ladies of the city who proudly and coldly scorned Federal officers—turning their heads and drawing aside their skirts as they passed—should be treated by his troops as "women of the town."

"Banditti, indeed!" Mama exclaimed. I recall so well her burning sense of outrage as Southerners in Washington received with horror the latest news of New Orleans and heard with anger the decision of President Grant. As she recalled, "We were in such a state of indignation we wouldn't have missed for the world the debates over Louisiana. They were the most bitter and exciting in Congress."

So, as the three ladies sat spellbound by the sound and fury, signifying so much to the rallying South, they forgot their hunger. And they forgot, too, the weary pangs of the wondering little girl who sat beside them.

Long after lunchtime they became hungry, but were too fascinated to leave. So one day they took crackers to sustain them. Crackers, however, crackled conspicuously and left crumbs. Next day the ladies brought fruit. That was too juicy and left them sticky. Peanuts aroused such a thirst they could scarcely sit through the debates. They finally settled on a quiet, tidy, and sustaining lunch of dried figs with poor me doomed to more long hours of sitting, so slightly sustained.

Like Presbyterian Sundays, the debates were so long that I wonder how I stood them. I suppose that being a Presbyterian little girl, I endured it with the conviction that what was to be, was just going to be, and had to be—and was. Now, I comfort myself with the conviction that I must have absorbed a great deal of parliamentary procedure which was worth years of study and fitted me for the office of parliamentarian which I have held in so many organizations.

Of course during these crises brought on by the raging disputes over a state whose rights were so frightfully violated, I absorbed a stronger respect for States' Rights.

Sons of the congressmen in these days were allowed the freedom of the floor of the House. While Joseph was at school at Ellicott City, Maryland, Jimmy roamed the floor with his friend, Percy Jones of Alabama. Percy, a rebel as unreconstructed as the Blounts, approached the notorious Radical, Ben Butler, and asked the former Union general for an autograph. The representative obliged with pleasure. Percy took his autograph home, decorated it with drawings of spoons and wrote on it the legend which was a familiar cry in Louisiana: "Hide your spoons! Butler's coming!"

Delighted with Percy's feat, which won some renown, Jimmy later approached Butler for an autograph. But the congressman had got wind of Percy's use of his souvenir, and gruffly refused to oblige another boy with a Southern accent.

A warm friend of Jim's in his boyhood days in the House was General Joseph E. Johnston, and he and Jim often discussed military matters, usually from ancient history. On one occasion young Jim demanded of his friend: "Don't you think, General Johnston, that the great mistake in Hannibal's career was not pushing on to Rome?"

This unfortunate reminder of Hannibal's Fabian policy, and of Johnston's own tactics for which President Davis had removed him from command, struck a sore spot in the General's memory.

"Certainly not," he replied to Jim. "There was no mistake in Hannibal's career!"

And poor Jim lost another friend.

Under Grant, the Blounts took no part in social activity that emanated from the Executive Mansion. My parents attended only one White House reception, the last one of the Grant regime.

"I did go then," Mama said, "to speed the parting guest."

Later we enjoyed the friendship of three First Families, Mama being on cordial visiting terms with the First Ladies: Mrs. Harrison, Mrs. Hayes, and Mrs. Cleveland.

Mama was especially fond of Mrs. Harrison, whom she found to be a very handsome and agreeable woman and with whom she made occasional trips from Washington. One such jaunt was for the dedication of a Union monument at Rochester, New York. It was the occasion for teasing on the Republican side, directed at my witty and resolute young mother from Georgia, a brand of teasing she learned to enjoy from many of her Washington friends who politicked on the other side of the fence.

En route, a young lady in the presidential party offered, jokingly, to present to Mrs. Blount a dignitary riding in the next car. He was the mulatto orator and Radical leader, Fred Douglas, of infamous reputation to Southerners.

"I told her," Mama said, still enjoying the situation years later, "that I wouldn't speak to Douglas if President Harrison himself introduced him!"

Bitterest cause of Douglas' ostracism from Southern circles and many Yankee groups too was his marriage to a white woman. It was not without a twinge of pity that Mama saw her at monthly presidential receptions, standing forlorn and lonely, shunned by everyone except her husband.

My family's personally friendly relations with Republicans in the blackest days of Reconstruction were an asset to the Southern program of reconciliation. But there were occasions when the raw wounds opened and throbbed. There was at least one party pleasantry which I remember Papa couldn't pass over lightly.

He was bidden to a stag dinner at the home of Secretary Frelinghuysen, where one of the gentlemen at table was General William Tecumseh Sherman.

After dinner, over cigars and brandy, the general turned genially to my father with the jocose remark, "I visited Georgia, Mr. Blount, not so long ago."

"Yes, General Sherman," Papa replied, "there is not a boy in Georgia over ten years of age who couldn't follow the course of your last visit by the blackened chimneys standing where once were homes."

In the next crucial four years, like other Southerners smarting under Reconstruction and laboring under grudging concessions of the North, my father learned patience and restraint in Washington. Grant was in the White House; Blaine was in the Senate to prod and stir up subdued war passions; "Beast" Butler, Pig Iron Kelley, and other Radicals in the House were always at hand to turn the knife in Southern wounds and rouse the vengeful feelings of Northern victors.

Young and old Southern statesmen schooled themselves in self-control, submission, and discretion, although there was, to be sure, an occasional stirring outburst from Ben H. Hill of Georgia, the great orator whose patience came hard.

The role of conciliator was perhaps easier for Papa than for some Southerners. His hearty and winning manners were an expression of his liking for people, whether political friend or foe. As a child, I was perplexed and fascinated to see that some of the Yankee gentlemen whom the ladies despised most hotly from their gallery seats seemed to be, after heat of battle, such jolly good friends of Papa's. After the most violent differences on the floor, the same men would be walking together a few minutes later on the outer rim of the House chamber, arm in arm, in the friendliest manner possible. Papa, particularly, seemed to recover quickly. I would see him with his arm around an erstwhile enemy's shoulder, laughing and talking.

In Washington my father learned much of restraint for the good of the South from the famed Lucius Quintus Cincinnatus Lamar. The gentleman from Mississippi was a cousin of our friends, the Henry J. Lamars in Macon, and was a frequent visitor to our Washington quarters on 13th Street, since his own home was nearby.

Whenever we were expecting Senator Lamar I would watch for him eagerly. We were on a slight rise of ground up the hill from the bus line which brought him, and I would run down the hill to meet him. He often had a little gift, a sweet, perhaps, for me. He was most charming and gentle with all children, and had such a winning and friendly way with him that the three of us loved him dearly. I love to recall his sweetness with children and his great eloquence, fire, force, and nobility before the Senate.

When we knew Senator Lamar in Washington he was married to his first wife, who died. Later, visiting in Macon, he courted Mrs. William F. Holt, formerly Hennie Dean, a sweetheart of his youthful days and the widow of a Georgia railroad magnate. Young Walter Lamar (later my husband) in whose home he visited tells the story of meeting his cousin Lucius on the street. Cousin Lucius stopped Walter's buggy and asked him for a ride.

"I want you to come along with me, Walter," he said, "and help me catch a Holt."

In Washington, everyone enjoyed a joke on the absent-minded statesman when he dropped a fifty-cent piece in the receptacle for his fare on entering a bus. A fellow passenger reminded Senator Lamar that the fare was only a nickel. With docility, he returned to the front of the bus and dropped in an additional five cents.

For all his gentleness and counsel of forgiveness and restraint to the younger men, Lamar was very strong in denunciation of what he didn't like. He made one of his most famous speeches in a strong reply to Senator Hoar during the amnesty debate in 1876. Southern congressmen had devoted much time and strategy of patience in support of the bill to extend amnesty to all former Confederates, without which the South could never hope to recover politically. Under this amnesty, Confederates who had served in the war with Mexico would be eligible for pensions.

My mother and Mrs. Gordon were in the Senate gallery, rejoicing that the long-desired victory was almost won in an atmosphere of generous and reconciled agreement in both houses. Then rose Senator Hoar of Massachusetts with a stinging amendment to deny amnesty and pension to Mexican War Veteran Jefferson Davis, who, he proposed, should be excluded as a traitor.

WASHINGTON CITY

This provoked Lamar to a reply refuting the treason charge. It was a masterpiece for its description of the place of the New South in the Union. He recalled that Colonel Davis had saved the day at Buena Vista and bore a record of valor for his entire service in the Mexican War. As the Georgia ladies thrilled to Lamar's response, he declared that most Southerners were as responsible for the Secession as Davis. Davis, Senator Lamar reminded, had endeavored to prevent Secession, but after it came he, like other Southerners, had risked his life and fortune in the Cause.

"I speak as a Union man," Lamar said solemnly. "The Confederacy is dead. But the South is here . . . to remain."

Turning to Hoar, he concluded, "The Senator, I believe, takes rank among Christian statesmen. He might well have learned a better lesson even from the pages of mythology. When Prometheus was bound to the rock, it was not an eagle, but a vulture, that buried his beak in the vitals of the victim."

On another occasion Lamar, with a soft sharpness more effective than the bellowings of his opponents, crossed words with Roscoe Conkling, the blonde, giant leader of the Radicals, whose handsome face and leonine head of gold hair I well remember. In a debate on the Army bill, Conkling loosed a bitter personal attack at Lamar, who replied in terms that brought rebuke from the presiding officer. Lamar apologized in words famous in the annals of the Senate. He admitted his language had been harsh and unbecoming, "such as no good man would deserve and no brave man would endure!"

One of the highlights of my mother's Washington memories was the senator's defense of the venomous Sumner, arch enemy of the South, as he lay dying and friendless in a Washington Hotel, scorned by Democrats and Republicans and deserted even by Radicals at that point in his political fortunes. Lamar eulogized the forgotten talents and virtues of the South's worst persecutor, and concluded with an appeal for amity: "My countrymen, know one another and you will love one another."

WHEN ALL IS SAID AND DONE

My Washington encounters with another Southern hero were less endearing than my little-girl friendship with Mr. Lamar, but interesting enough to remain very vivid. We frequently visited the revered Alexander Stephens, congressman, former vice president of the Confederacy and later governor of Georgia. His quarters at the old National Hotel were a gathering place for the Georgia delegation. The frail "Little Giant" would receive callers cheerily for long sessions of talk, seated in his wheel chair, always attended by his body servant, Alex, who stood just behind him.

I was impressed with his thin piping voice and pleased that the great man so beloved by my parents and their friends would take me on his lap.

"But, Papa," I would protest later. "I would like Mr. Stephens better if he just wouldn't kiss me."

Mr. Stephens' brilliant mentality and his nobleness of soul and kindness of spirit impressed themselves indelibly on my child mind, although even then I felt the strong contrast between these qualities and the physical ills that marked him. Smallness of stature was accentuated by his emaciation and his thin, quivering voice; yet the flash of the eye in verbal contest, or the glow of kindness in gentle courtesies, especially to women and children, won respect and love from all who came within the radius of his magnetic presence.

Weighing only 90 pounds, always a sufferer, he did not allow his physical disabilities to affect his power of initiative, his will, or his courage. He was a member of the House of Representatives for sixteen years ending in 1859. He was elected to the U. S. Senate from Georgia, but was not allowed to take his seat because of the bitter feeling of Reconstruction times. When, however, he was elected to the lower house of Congress he served from 1873 to 1882. At the age of 70, he became governor of Georgia (1882), and in March, 1883, he died in Atlanta and was buried at Liberty Hall, his home at Crawfordville. There a noble monument to the great Little

WASHINGTON CITY

Commoner bears some words of his that might well be the aim of all public men: "I am afraid of nothing on earth but to do wrong."

A visitor to Crawfordville asked a white-haired old Negro if he knew the Master of Liberty Hall and the Negro said: "Yas-suh, Ah knowed Marse Alex mighty well. He wuz kinder to dogs 'en mos' folks is to people."

On one public occasion the ruthless and excitable Bob Toombs unfeelingly flung out: "Why, that little chap—I could swallow him whole and never know the difference!"

"If he did," observed Stephens, "he'd have more brains in his stomach than in his head."

Looking back on the Recontruction days in Washington, I realized in later years that it was not only Papa's penchant for making friends and his political gifts which enabled him to step across the issues that meant life and death to Georgia. It was the new, practical Southern spirit of reconciliation by which our congressmen hoped to rescue their section from ruin. Long before Henry Grady made his "New South" speech, they had sounded the note of reconciliation. They offered their amity with dignity and self-control.

When I was in my teens, with a young-lady status, Papa was on friendly terms, personally, with such Republican colleagues as Thomas B. Reid of Maine, Joseph Cannon, and other big names of the Washington period. Even Pig Iron Kelley, the Radical who preached to Washington of the Negroes' intellectual superiority over whites, seemed to enjoy Papa's company when the members gathered on the outer rim of the chamber.

One of Papa's favorite stories was of his meeting with his friend, Speaker Reid, who told Papa with much pride and no compunction about one of the puns for which he was famed. Reid told of a tenacious dullard who overtook him as he walked near the Capitol and asked, "Surely, Mr. Speaker, you remember me? We had a long chat on the boardwalk at Atlantic City."

"Yes," replied Reid with acid enjoyment, "I recall that bored walk very well."

Another warm friend of my father was John G. Carlisle of Kentucky, at one time Speaker of the House, later senator and then Secretary of the Treasury under Cleveland. He was an unswerving adherent to the President's gold standard policy. I was frequently invited to receive with Mrs. Carlisle at their Washington home, and I remember Carlisle himself, tall, thin, gaunt with sunken cheeks in a young, keen face. Papa considered him a forceful and capable man.

Capable Carlisle was given to occasional sprees, during which he'd disappear and couldn't be found. When all else failed, Mrs. Carlisle, an Amazon of a woman, would calmly make the rounds of the saloons until she found her errant husband. She would resolutely fetch him home, put him to bed, and hide his clothes until his thirst had passed and he had sobered up. Then he would return to affairs of state as clear-headed, forceful, and capable as ever.

Governor Joseph E. Brown is a notable figure in Georgia's history. Sometimes he appears as a son of the soil with a self-made heroic career in war and Reconstruction years. In other versions he is a craven governor who knifed the staggering Confederacy in the back and turned shamefully Republican during Reconstruction.

Be all that as it may, his political approach seems always to have been practical, as when he tried to lead Georgia to Secession from the Confederacy in 1864. It took more than one visit of Jefferson Davis, Bob Toombs, and other do-or-die Confederates to Macon and other communities to oppose Brown successfully and keep Georgia in the war in its last days.

Whatever my parents felt about this Georgian, they welcomed him to Washington when he was appointed to the United States Senate by Governor Colquitt. Mama took Mrs. Brown under her wing, as both families were staying at the National Hotel. They found the Browns very plain spoken and plain looking and considerably in need of help around the intricately patterned social whirl of Washington.

On the occasion of their first White House reception Mrs. Brown, nervous about her costume, asked Mama to help her dress. The big hurdle, it seems, was application of a "Thompson wave," fashionable false tresses to adorn the front of the hair, sometimes also called "transformations." Mama arranged the wave so that it parted properly in the center of the head, its ends brought back to form a chignon. The Senator was wearing his first dress suit. He had been, Mama reported, much concerned about catching cold if he wore black broadcloth; so he had his evening coat made of beaver cloth. Thus the Browns set forth, Mrs. Brown Thompson-waved, and Senator Brown with his stiff tails sticking out behind.

All seemed to go well at the White House, until Mama glimpsed the teetotaling, straightlaced, and demure Mrs. Brown standing in a corner with the Senator. Her aspect was thoroughly tipsy. It was, however, only the Thompson wave which had slipped sideways and created the abandoned effect. Mrs. Brown was so quietly and happily enjoying the party, unaware of her disarray, that Mama didn't spoil her evening by telling her.

A graceless, earnest man, Brown had occasion to dispute on the Senate floor with a brilliant, dapper, and sometimes cruel colleague, Senator Ingalls of Kansas. I recall Ingalls as nimble, quick, and waspish; his appearance made one think of a little grasshopper that we used to call a devil horse. Brown had a curious habit of continually kneading his hands in conversation or debate. Ingalls seized on this mannerism to irritate him in the Senate thus: "Look, there he stands, the Uriah Heep of American politics, forever laving his hands in invisible soap and never cleansing them."

Shocked at Ingalls' personal venom, we assumed that the insult would preclude any affability between the Ingalls and the Browns.

However, that very afternoon, it being senatorial reception day, Mama and I called at the Ingalls home to pay our respects according to the Washington custom, and there was Mrs. Brown in the receiving line!

Brown seems to have served Georgia well enough in the Senate, for all his hand-laving and social stolidity. My girlhood impression of the homespun pair of Georgians is that they didn't find much joy in life, and didn't know how to have fun.

I do remember Mrs. Brown as a lady, simplehearted and as good as gold. In quiet conversation she was often entertaining, and made many witty remarks. She was always at her husband's side (the famous couple's attachment is portrayed in bronze in a statue of the governor and his lady on the Capitol grounds in Atlanta) and was noted in Georgia and Washington for her devotion to her husband. The Senator had a curious and happy faculty for rest. He would say, "I'm going to sleep for five minutes." As Mrs. Brown warded off disturbances he would indeed lie down and fall asleep, for just five minutes.

Mrs. Brown was a genuine personality and we liked her cordially.

Our friendship with the Grover Clevelands in my young ladyhood was a whole-hearted pleasure, politically and personally, for both families. I admired Mrs. Cleveland with a *jeune fille* pleasure in the full-blown splendor of an acknowledged beauty. Much younger than the President, she was always handsomely dressed. I recall him as a stout and pleasant gentleman, somewhat overshadowed in my young eyes by his lovely wife.

Mrs. Cleveland often invited young girls from congressional families to "stand behind the receiving line," a coveted honor for belles in the capital. I was frequently asked to "stand," and there I basked in the eminence of my position just behind the glamorous First Lady, where I happily bowed and smiled to less fortunate friends attending the monthly White House at-homes.

WASHINGTON CITY

Mrs. Cleveland was charming as well as beautiful. Her favorite costumes were of plush, and she wore a bustle and train, according to the mode of the day. Those who felt unkindly about her used to say she was draped like a parlor sofa.

As a young lady, I was sometimes entertained in the lavish household of the amazing Mrs. Leiter. This dauntless millionairess came out of Chicago and in the eighties opened a grand establishment in the capital and became a famous hostess.

In the days of her social invasion Mrs. Leiter became known as a regular Mrs. Malaprop. Chatting once with a guest, she said, "Senator, I want to show you my spinal staircase."

"Indeed, ma'am," he replied gravely, "it must be a back staircase."

I remember with delight Mrs. Leiter's remarkable daughter, Mary, who was considered the most beautiful girl in Washington, and was extremely charming and beloved. She was gracious, accomplished, and a notable linguist. This celebrated beauty enjoyed several seasons as a favorite in Washington and married a young attaché of the British legation, one Curzon. Young Curzon made his mark in time, and became Viceroy of India. So Mrs. Leiter's beautiful daughter reigned as Lady Curzon, Vicereine of India, with greater splendor than the Queen of England.

Before my entry into Washington society, Mama came home from a dinner at the White House with a story which amused the family greatly. She had sat beside a South American diplomat who, enjoying his soup course, asked her what it was. She replied that it was terrapin stew.

"Oh," replied her dinner partner with a sigh of relief, his dark eye cocked on the black bits of terrapin in his soup, "I thought eet was leetle neegar toes chopped up!"

I remember a famed bright spot in a House debate on the enormous Pauper Pension Bill, which Republicans in the eighties were trying to pass over President Cleveland's veto. Every man in the house was allowed five minutes in which to express himself pro or con.

Representative Bourke Cochran, the sound of whose voice was like the roaring of the Bull of Bashan, used his five minutes, as did John R. Fellows, another noted orator, both of New York. They made a great deal of noise, taking up their time without any arguments of value.

Then a witty Virginian, Sullivan by name, took part of his allotted time to tell a story which left the whole weary House convulsed with laughter and cut short the spread eagle oratory. Obtaining the floor, Sullivan said, "Mr. Speaker, the remarks of the two members from New York remind me of a man taking a heavy wagon load around precipitous curves in the Virginia mountains, in a terrible storm with dark descending. His wagon broke down and he tried in vain to repair it, amid claps of thunder and brief lightning flashes. Finally, he dropped to his knees and prayed, 'Oh Lord, give us a little more light and a little less noise!'"

The fabulous John B. Gordons are still bright and exciting in my Washington memories. I enjoyed a girlhood friendship with the daughters, Fanny and Caroline, during Mama's long Washington attachment to Mrs. Gordon.

The general himself, dashing hero of Antietam (where he was five times wounded), Manassas, and other battles, a leader of the Klan in the days of its glory, and a stirring speechmaker after the war, was ever a hero in the South. He was handsome, compelling, and magnificent on a horse. He had a cross scar on his cheek, one of the Antietam wounds, which by no means detracted from his appearance, making him, in fact, even more attractive.

Mrs. Gordon was tall and handsome, and touched with the same romantic charm as her hero husband. She was intensely devoted to him and was with him everywhere, it seemed, at home, abroad, in political caucus. Her wartime devotion to him has a legendary quality, but is quite factual. In the Virginia campaign, she followed him from battle to battle in a phaeton or on horseback. After Antietam, she told Mama, when surgeons despaired of his life, she nursed him through his shattering wound, sitting beside him in his tent day and night. His whole side was raw and torn from the injury. She told my mother how she saturated him with arnica and attended his burning agony until he recovered. Of course he always recovered—his charmed life was celebrated—and went back to fight some more.

Their daughters were like both of them, tall, graceful, gay, and attractive. They did very much as they pleased, with a lighthearted freedom that was most engaging to more restricted and conventional girls. Often we would see Fanny on her bicycle alone, blithely peddling along the avenue as unconcerned as if she were traveling in a fine carriage. Fanny married Burton Smith, son of the Secretary of the Interior under Cleveland. Caroline married Orton Bishop Brown of Berlin, New Hampshire, a lumber merchant on the Androscoggin River. General Gordon resigned from the Senate in 1876 to make way for former Governor Brown of Georgia. Gordon was then appointed counsel for railroad interests, a very lucrative post, although he had no experience in law or railroading. Despite this questionable shifting of position, Gordon was still our hero of Antietam, our Great Reconciler, idolized by the South and a great public figure over the country.

His daughters remained my friends for decades, and Caroline and I in later years enjoyed occasional happy reunions on the Stratford Board of Directors.

The four daughters of General Joseph Wheeler were also close friends of mine. With them, the dashing Gordon girls, and Laura Lester, daughter of Representative Rufus Lester of Savannah, I often went dancing and partying.

"Little Joe" Wheeler, the great Confederate cavalry leader,

was the hero of a brief epic poem with which Confederates sang his valor and military genius:

> Little Joe Wheeler
> He's no fool
> Ef he can't git a horse
> He'll steal him a mule.

General Wheeler and his wealthy wife regaled Washington handsomely at their regular at-home parties. Representative Wheeler and Mrs. Wheeler took a mansion on Massachusetts Avenue, and held open house for the whole world. And the whole world came and cleaned the platter.

In those days when the public was invited to congressional at-homes, the Wheeler parties were tremendous. The girls, Annie, Birdie, Caroline, and Julia, were lovely. They were not beauties, but they achieved such a delightful, oldtime Southern atmosphere in their home that everyone who went there was pleased. You were always made to feel that the Wheelers were happier to see you than anyone else.

Since my friends and I were very fond of dancing, a favorite spot for us was the Navy yard. Young officers often invited us there to dances. There we heard the Marine Band rehearse its concert music under Conductor John Philip Sousa. He was a promising young musician, who later toured Europe, and endeared himself to Southerners by reporting that in the European concerts with the Marine Band he found that the tune "Dixie" aroused more enthusiastic reponse than any other air that he played.

One of the most highly prized experiences of Washington life for a young girl was a visit to West Point at commencement time. My father was one of the congressional members of the Board of Visitors to West Point and I was privileged to go with him to the Academy at graduation time in the middle eighties. I suspect Mama persuaded Papa to accept the assignment in order that his young daughter might enjoy the military training school under such delightful circumstances.

WASHINGTON CITY

I formed a lasting friendship at that time with Laura Hoadly, whose father, Governor Hoadly of Ohio, was a Presidential appointee on the Board. Laura and I, meeting at West Point, became attached to each other and later I visited the Hoadlys in Cincinnati. Of course at West Point we were special honor guests at all social and military functions with our dates pre-arranged for us: a cadet for certain hours and an officer for hours when mere cadets had to be on duty or in barracks.

One of my cadet beaux invited me for a horseback ride, and as we ambled along, he began to make love to me, boring me greatly. So I gently pricked my steed with a hatpin, giving the cadet a wild chase—a drastic, possibly dangerous, but effective way of changing the subject! Different cadets took me around Flirtation Walk, each escort holding, as we strolled, my fluffy parasol—over himself.

Laura and I exchanged experiences at table and so intrigued my father that he said to me, by way of teasing, "My daughter, I would like to see this Flirtation Walk you girls talk about so much." Taking him at his word, I marched him around the circuitous path high above the river, going at a rapid pace, pausing at Lover's Leap to explain that this was the spot where cadets would say quite seriously: "If you do not love me, I will leap from this rock as did the Indian long ago." That was when hearts were young and gay.

REBEL AT WELLESLEY

I CAN'T REMEMBER THAT I PARTICULARLY DISTINGUISHED myself at Miss Lipscomb's school, Waverly Seminary, in Washington. I studied there during the long term Washington stays, one of the younger students at that combination preparatory and finishing school for young ladies from the South.

After preparatory work alternating between Miss Lipscomb's in Washington and Mrs. Birch's in Macon, I stayed home for a while to finish Wesleyan, and was graduated at sixteen. I boarded at the college when the family left for Washington long terms.

My freshman year at Wesleyan in 1879 was enlivened by a three-way contest as to my sorority membership. Philomatheans vied for weeks with Adelpheans, each society seeking to make Miss Blount its own. Papa resisted both, insisting that "Doddice," as he often called me, should wait until the sophomore year to join a society.

After school, a shirt-waisted delegation of young ladies from both factions would walk to the Blount home to overwhelm my mother and me with their respective blandishments. I was concentrating on getting Papa's consent; so I was not thinking about which sorority I should join. My best friend, Ruth Smith, was a Philomathean, but Mary Lou Bacon (later Mrs. W. B. Sparks) and Stella Hunt (who married Campbell King) were notably persuasive on behalf of the Adelpheans. Mama, too, was not concerned so much with which society as with Papa's permission for my membership.

Finally, both groups despaired, convinced that they could not move the adamant Colonel Blount. At this point, the Adelpheans regained their hope with a new plan. They switched their strategy with a downtown attack.

About a dozen of the prettiest, most eloquent Adelpheans descended on my surprised Papa at his Mulberry Street office. And the usually impregnable colonel went down under a wave of pretty pleas, ruffles, arch importunings, smiles, braids, hair ribbons, and teen-age oratory.

So, the issue was decided for me. Papa had perforce consented. Since the Adelpheans turned the trick, I joined them.

Later my vanquished parent inquired: "Well, my daughter, this is a literary and not a secret society, I suppose?"

"That, Papa," I replied, "is a secret."

I may have shown more promise at Miss Lipscomb's than I remember, for one of the teachers, Miss Claire de Graffenreid, persuaded my parents to send me to Wellesley for a year of postgraduate work. A Macon girl herself, Miss de Graffenreid was a young friend of Mama's, and one of the best informed and most intelligent women of her day. She was sent abroad in later years to study European working conditions for women, à propos of labor legislation in this country.

Alumnae of Miss Lipscomb's remember Miss de Graffenreid with great affection and respect, but I recall the fascination I felt at the lady's heedlessly uncorseted avoirdupois. In a day when all ladies, great and small, well fleshed and scrawny, were armored in rigid corsets, the free-breathing and unabated fat of the brilliant and unconventional Miss de Graffenreid was a source of amazement to me—and still is. She was the first woman I ever saw dressed without a corset.

In the fall of 1883, I was packed off to the considerable adventure of a year at Wellesley but only after Mama had written to inquire whether the female college accepted Negroes. She was assured that "Wellesley has never had a Negro student."

Papa took me, then sixteen, to the New England school

along with a Fort Valley girl, Stella Harris, who was to be my roommate for our year of broader cultural horizons. Poor Stella, more of a home body, soon languished in the bitter climate and alien atmosphere, grew homesick, and returned to Georgia.

Papa met the authorities and accompanied me to my dormitory room. After inspection, some grave admonitions, and cheering pleasantries, he announced: "My daughter, it is time for me to leave." We parted bravely enough, but my heart failed me when he was gone. I fell sobbing on the strange bed, already bereft and homesick.

After a while, there was a knock at the door. Red-eyed and weeping, I opened it. It was Papa! He explained to me, now radiant and smiling, that he had missed the bus. He took me in his arms, comforting away my pangs, and stayed for a last, heartening visit. When he departed, I was in permanent good spirits.

It still isn't clear to me whether Papa actually missed his bus, or bethought himself of his frightened sixteen-year-old and passed up the bus to return and reassure me.

A few days after I started my classes (I was taking a special scientific course), I saw a Negro girl sauntering along the campus, her books under her arm. To Miss Blount from Georgia, this was a shock and circumstance which jeopardized my whole year at Wellesley. I could scarcely expect my family, who had suffered through black rule in Georgia, to allow me to pursue studies on equal terms with a Negro.

I felt a sudden and dramatic indignation (the kind of righteous impulse which often affected Papa), an urge to invade the office of the famed and formidable Miss Alice Freeman, Wellesley president, and voice my protest. I would also announce my departure from Wellesley, I planned.

Troubled, I pondered the matter for a while. I inquired as to the girl's status, her quarters and her classes, and found that the Negro was at college on a Greek scholarship, taking a classical course and living in a campus cottage. I, studying science and living in a dormitory, thought the likelihood of encounter very small. So I let the matter resolve itself since there was no contact or association with the innocent offender. Later, my parents approved my discretion.

The Wellesley year is a vivid memory to me of hard study, all-girl parties, boating and ice skating, the continued agonized pursuit of music somewhat encouraged by membership in the Beethoven Society, the Spring Daisy Chain and a procession of impressive lectures from popular great minds of the day.

I had my close friends and the usual college admiration of a Wellesley glamor girl, Edith Tufts, a senior, president of the Beethoven Society, and at that time, the most beautiful, wonderful person in the world.

I also remember a relentless round of sweeping and dusting imposed on the young ladies, whether to cultivate our moral quality with unpleasant chores or actually to teach us domestic skills, I can't say.

Appearance of the Negro student was a little crisis of conflicts for me. But it was a trivial distress compared to a later, greater challenge to my Southern loyalties.

Miss Morgan, the ethics professor, took occasion one day in chapel to pay a tribute to Abolitionist Wendell Phillips, a hated name in the South. To emphasize her admiration of this creature, Miss Morgan even read an excerpt from one of his bitter attacks on the seceded states.

Miss Morgan's glowing praise of the old enemy and her relish over his diatribe was too much for me. Outraged to a frightful display of courage, I rose from my seat. I left, swishing my skirts ostentatiously, and walked haughtily down the center aisle the vast distance to the door, with my head in the air. I had on new shoes which squeaked with every step, and when I left, I banged the door behind me.

I returned to my room, with a thumping heart, and my blood

still a-boil. I felt no regret, firm in the conviction that I had behaved properly in the face of public insult to my loyalties. But I was considerably apprehensive.

Next day the following note confirmed my disgrace: "My Dear Miss Blount, it seems necessary to remind you that a student who has withdrawn without permission during any exercise conducted by a College authority transgresses the simplest laws of courtesy, if she fails to present her excuse at the earliest opportunity. As I was away from College last evening, I think you may have called during my absence. I will receive you at 1 o'clock at No. 30 Stone Hall. A. E. F. Morgan."

I did not call on Professor Morgan. Late the same day came an even more formidable communication:

"At an official meeting of the House of Deputies of Wellesley College . . . the following motion was unanimously carried: Moved that the continuance of Miss Eugenia D. Blount as a member of Wellesley College be made dependent upon her making such reparation for her recent disorderly conduct in the classroom as the professor in charge shall deem suitable. No future attendance at recitations will be expected of you until this condition is fulfilled. Louise M. Hodgewick, Secretary of the House of Deputies."

An informal written message from H. W. Tuttle informed the culprit—now quite cornered by the assault of notes from official quarters—that "Miss Freeman would like to see Miss Blount as soon as possible."

Righteously firm and defiant as I was, I didn't refuse to see Miss Freeman. I called, and found that lady grave and stern, with a faint suspicion of a twinkle in her soft brown eyes. That pleasant light vanished, however, as Miss Freeman explained that Miss Morgan expected and was due an apology.

The weight of my transgression settled grievously on me—the more grievously because I felt justified in leaving a room where the South was insulted. A capitulation would be unthinkable, a cowardly violation of my integrity.

Practically, I pondered the rashness of the expulsion so close to the end of the term, the waste of time and money and work without credits. Girlishly, I considered the colorful festivities just around the corner, the Daisy Chain, the awards and honors, the parties, and everything I expected to enjoy so much.

I thought and worried, and gave a little under the pressure. Then I snapped back to my former resolution. After all the sufferings of a cornered Confederate in a Yankee camp, I triumphantly hit upon an apology that would placate the stern authorities without violation of my own principles.

With pride and care, drawing profound comfort from the prospect of its delivery, I composed this apology: "To the young ladies present at the lecture in Ethics, April 22, 1884: I, Eugenia Dorothy Blount, do hereby tender an apology for yielding to the *principle* which prompted my discourteous withdrawal from aforesaid lecture."

It was grand, I felt. Brief, firm, and adroitly unrepentant. It demonstrated with dignity and force that I was goaded to withdrawal by insult to my native land, provocation no young lady of courage and honor would ignore, but that I apologized for the *necessity* of withdrawal with mere lip-service to the authorities.

I waited eagerly for the hour of my triumph, when I would read the "apology" in chapel. Before the assembled student body and waiting faculty, the professor in charge approached the dramatic moment. She announced the reading of the apology of Miss Eugenia Dorothy Blount. I waited, my head high, to be called to the front, as the girls listened, their excited buzzing stilled by the climax.

Then, the professor, after announcing in ringing tones that she had received my apology, mumbled and garbled the text of it so rapidly and so low that no one could hear it.

I was thus mumble-mouthed out of my triumph. But the crisis was over, at any rate.

We seemed to work as hard keeping Wellesley tidied as we did improving our minds. Such chores pleased none of us, but they were done. "Miss Blount," says one note in my scrapbook, "Please sweep the second floor East instead of the 1st floor during recess. L. A. Dennison."

"Dear Miss Blount," says another, "The gym looks very nice if you will take away a collection of stockings, match boxes, and hymn books that are on the stage ! ! ! We will sweep tomorrow. Miss Dennison will find us some girls."

Another note instructs me in "cleaning the machinery" in order to have everything ship-shape for next year's opening.

In addition to this general cleaning, which would have called for a huge staff of Negro servants at home, we also kept our own rooms and took turns waiting on table.

Matthew Arnold, a literary idol of the day, was one of the speakers served up to Wellesley students in 1883-84. He was doubtless intellectually impressive, but I was most struck with his long, tall, and limp aspect and his loose-jointed swing from his notes on the desk to a stance facing the audience. He resembled a human windmill and rhythmically kept up this swinging performance throughout his lecture. I later discussed him with Mama, who recalled meeting Arnold at a supper party with his daughter, who was touring with him. A butler passed some hot batter cakes to the pair, and Arnold advised his daughter, "Try some, Maria; they ahn't hahf so nahsty as they look."

More personable in the lecture hall was Phillips Brooks, noted Boston divine, whose magnetic voice, beautiful diction, and thrilling message instinct with religious conviction were more gratefully received than Arnold's platform eccentricities.

Social life at Wellesley had its gala occasions, without, however, the benefit of young gentlemen. That omission was no loss to me as Papa would not permit me to go in Macon society until I was through school. So, when most of my contemporaries were making débuts at home, I was improving my mind—and doubtless my biceps, too, what with the burden of Wellesley domestic duties.

There were visits to Boston, duly chaperoned, for museums, matinées, Boston Symphony Orchestra concerts, and meetings with friends. There were quite festive and exciting affairs of the Boat Club which I joined. Dressed in dark skirts, white flannel blouses, and caps with green ribbons, my club rowed a little craft called "The Undine" on the campus water course, Wabun Mere. In winter, the girls skated on the frozen lake and I became expert at this exhilarating sport. When I returned to Macon and a young gentleman invited me to go roller skating at Ralston Hall, I accepted with much pleasure, expecting to cut quite a swath amongst the home provincials. But I soon learned, when my heels went up and my head went down, that roller skating is by no means the same as ice skating!

Sometimes the girls at Wellesley would have a party where half of them would dress as gentlemen. Bidden to such a George Washington Leap Year party by my friend, Helen Morgan, I planned to masquerade in knee breeches, silver buckles, and powdered hair. I replied to her invitation:

"Ye Sir Eugene Blount gratefully accepts ye kindlie offer. Ye shall not long tarrie in ye outer hall, but shall be righte welcome to the best of all ye morn of ye 22nd of Feb., ye 1884, A. D."

Contemplating this archaic bit of girl foolishness, I recall how very hard we tried to have a good time!

My record at Wellesley was unremarkable, but adequate. I was not noted for anything but being a rebel.

DEBUT IN THE EIGHTIES

I WAS HOME FOR MY FIRST SOCIAL SEASON IN 1885, AND duly delighted with the company of young gentlemen, my first balls and dances, Sunday afternoons at home, my evening décolletages and trains, and particularly the attentions of the older beaux of the town.

Among these were such dashing gentlemen as W. H. Felton, John Baxter, Azel Freeman, Stuart Jones, Cullen Battle, John Salisbury, and W. B. Sparks—a coterie of sophisticates, mature and worldly wise beyond the experience of swains nearer my age.

My first big party was a german at Volunteer's Armory on Mulberry Street early in the season. With great trepidation and excitement, I donned my first grownup evening dress, a white surah silk with low neck, short sleeves, and a long train lined with canton flannel. I was escorted by Cousin Tracy Baxter, that tormenter of my childhood, grown tall and suave and amazingly polite; but Joe claimed the first dance as he did ever after during my young ladyhood in Macon. I had a triumphant and heady evening, surrounded by the older blades of the town, dancing the night through with my train held grandly over my wrist.

It was a dazzling winter, after the intellectual rigors and girlish festivities of Wellesley. There were more balls, more new frocks, roller skating, horseback riding, and Sunday afternoon at-homes, when a girl who didn't have forty callers was a failure.

DEBUT IN THE EIGHTIES

The parties of the 1880's marked the beginning of my long young ladyhood. It was long, at any rate, for a Southern belle, most of whom were out at 15 or 16 to dance, first, and be courted for a few seasons before choosing a husband.

But in the leisurely and happy course of the next few years, whenever I seemed most interested in a serious suit, it was time to go to Washington for another six months. There were suitors, though, in Macon and in Washington.

In my childhood, Papa and Mama had worried a good deal about Sister Mary. Things weren't going well at the Haddock Place. Tom Bowen, her husband, was a well-born, hard-drinking, fascinating ne'er-do-well in the eyes of his troubled in-laws. Papa had long pondered the problem of Sister Mary and her children, at the mercy of a husband and father who was by no means discharging his family responsibilities. His latest scheme was to sell the Bowen mansion at Haddock and leave Georgia. Appalled at the prospects for his wife and children, my father made his brother-in-law a lucrative offer.

He would buy Belmont Farm, as the Bowen place was called, if Bowen would deed a share of the property to his wife. My father would add the rest of its considerable acreage to his holdings in Jones County. The lovely Pratt-built house should be Sister Mary's for her lifetime. Colonel Blount's price was more than acceptable to Mr. Bowen, even with the stipulation that he depart from Georgia for good, and leave his wife and children in peace. Brother-in-law Tom seemed as pleased to shed his responsibilities as my father was to take them over. So, off he went to Texas, and there he died.

After my parents' stay in the Sandwich Islands in the nineties, Mama named the Haddock place "Hale Nui," which means "Big House," as the Negroes always designated their owners' residence on the plantation. We took over the place after Aunt Mary's death.

The country quiet of our summers at Haddock was frequently broken by vacation trips to watering places and mountain resorts. Society page reports of my vacations and other social appearances provide a gay and nostalgic picture of summer doings in the late eighties and nineties, and of the society writers' glamorous view of every young lady in the news.

The *Macon Telegraph* in a story of "Doings of the Smart Set" says: "The Cumberland Island correspondent of the *Atlanta Constitution* has the following mention of Macon young ladies: Miss Dorothy Blount, the bright and charming daughter of Hon. James H. Blount, has been spending a month at Cumberland. Her fine intelligence and affable manners have added much to the social life of the Hotel Cumberland. She has won a host of gentleman friends and has been in demand for every possible function in parlor and pavilion and for every kind of frolic from an oyster roast to a turtle hunt."

Again: "Of Miss Eugenia Blount, one of Macon's favorites and an acknowledged belle in Washington City, Mr. Claude N. Bennett of the *Atlanta Journal* writes: Miss Blount of Georgia, by the way, who learned to ride in Macon, where schools of this kind are unnecessary, is considered one of the bravest and most graceful equestriennes in Washington. She rides with a dashing fearlessness which could only be exhibited by a Georgia girl, and sits her steed under all circumstances in a manner which would prove an inspiration to the patrons of the riding school."

Washington Correspondent Bennett missed one circumstance, however, when Miss Blount failed to sit her steed. I was riding with Billy Butler, the charming blonde son of Senator Marion Butler of North Carolina—such a pretty boy, as I remember. On Pennsylvania Avenue, riding side saddle, of course, I was feeling very chic in a long, tailored habit and a new silk hat trailing a fine gauze streamer, when we encountered the uproar of an Emancipation Day parade. The horses became excited as we turned the corner into 15th Street. My horse slipped, reared, and I was hurled from the saddle.

Billy dismounted in great alarm to see what injuries the lady in his care had sustained. But I picked myself up, in great concern over my beautiful new silk beaver hat. It, too, was uninjured; so we repaired to a nearby tailor shop across 15th from the Treasury Department, for a dusting off, and then proceeded with our ride.

Billy confided later that much of his distress over my tumble was concern over his sailing for Europe the next day. He had feared my accident might change his plans. He laughingly explained that he had even planned to rush me home, deposit me safe and unconscious on a sofa, and quietly escape for an undelayed sailing.

Another society page bouquet, tossed me without even the provocation of a party appearance or a summer trip, says: "Among Macon's brightest and most talented young ladies, none take precedence to Miss Dolly Blount. Her sparkling originality, in conjunction with her gracious and elegant manners, make her a delightful figure in society."

This "delightful figure in society" remembers earlier moments of gaucherie. There was an occasion when Mary Ellen Johnston, who later became mistress of her parents' famous Italian villa mansion on Georgia Avenue, came to Washington for a season under the chaperonage of Mama.

Invited to a large embassy tea for the next day, we received as callers two young men at the hour of 4 P.M. Sitting primly, with ankles crossed properly under long ruffled skirts, we inquired conversationally if the gentlemen were going to "the tea."

"Which tea?" asked one of the young men, exchanging an amused glance with the other over the innocence of two girls who fancied that Washington society confined itself to one tea an afternoon.

We soon learned better, in a whirling season of balls, dinners, teas, and receptions, and many a visit to the White House. I remember our popularity at dances by the condition of our feet when we arrived home to Mama after midnight. Sitting with the exhausted members in pans of cold water, we would relate to her the triumphs and excitements of the evening out.

Back in Macon for another season, I was bidden to a ball at the W. B. Johnston house, where a party was always a great occasion even for a young lady launched at the capital. The Johnstons always entertained lavishly and impeccably, and above all systematically. The music, the dances, the refreshments at the close of the party were so scheduled that each item rolled off like clockwork. Everything was just so; if one dropped a crumb, a butler would appear at one's elbow to sweep it up immediately.

Escorted by Stuart Jones, I was borne thither in a stable carriage, in company with another couple, with the driver high up outside, the proper means for getting to a fine party.

It was a brilliant evening in the Johnstons' great ballroom. When the party ran its gay and stately course, the musicians were dismissed and the guests went outside to leave. And they saw in the clear white moonlight—snow! Only such a rare phenomenon in Middle Georgia could disrupt the schedule of a Johnston party. The leave-taking was definitely upset, because wires, sleet-laden, had snapped and fallen on the carriages, tangled harnesses, and trapped horses. It became apparent that it would be a long time before the guests could leave, with only one carriage free to bear them away.

So, we were bidden back into the house, the musicians were recalled and the party started over again to last until dawn. By morning, the one carriage had, in relays, delivered the last of the guests home.

The Johnstons were up against the elements, and extraordinary elements at that. All their system availed them nothing, when snow fell on Macon!

Surprise parties were much in vogue in the eighties. A group of friends would send word that they were coming to call, and descend in dozens for a "surprise." Mama never seemed to mind at all, and always managed to have a party ready when a throng of couples came in.

DEBUT IN THE EIGHTIES

The Theater contributed excitement and glamor to the local social scene. The performances of Booth, Jefferson, Salviati, Modjeska, Rhea, Bernhardt, Frederick Ward, or perhaps Billy West's Minstrel Show, were occasions for full dress, as debutantes and escorts, fashionable married couples, and oldsters turned out in silks and satins, kid gloves, top hats, and tails. There were no movies, no telephones, no radios. Yet, to the mystification of young people today, we had a wonderful time and were never bored.

Among the few gifts a gentleman might send a well-bred young lady were long-stemmed American Beauty roses, books, opera glasses, riding crops, or slim perfume bottles of cut glass used as accessories to evening dress. A favorite perfume vial in my collection was of crystal and silver, long and about an inch in diameter.

My later career as a public speaker, writer, and civic leader is presaged in an account in the *Telegraph and Messenger* of my young ladyhood:

"The beautiful parlors of Mr. Calder Willingham's home on the hill were the scene of a brilliant gathering last evening, the occasion being the first meeting since last season of the Athenaeum."

The club had under consideration Percy Bysshe Shelley, and the program was embellished with songs by Misses Georgia and Virginia Hopson, Mr. Hope Polhill's essay on the poet, Mr. Cosby Smith's study of Shelley's poetic nature, Mrs. Tindall and Mrs. Edwards in an instrumental duet, and Mrs. Leila Legg's recitation. There were also "a few words from Professor Derry," and Mrs. Dasher read "The Cloud."

"Miss Eugenia Blount then read in a rich, clear, melodious voice a very fine paper on the friendships of the poet." Reflecting on this performance today, I venture to say that I was quite unaware of the nature of some of Shelley's friendships.

"This club," the account concludes, "was organized by Dr. A. J. Battle and is an ornament to Macon, bringing together as it does some of the most refined and cultured people of the city." The Athenaeum later languished, and some years later was revived in my Georgia Avenue home.

There are few social milestones in my life so memorable as the last visit to Macon of Jefferson Davis and his family. The aging leader of the Confederacy, beloved as a symbol of the Lost Cause, came as a martyred hero, all the differences of the war years forgotten by the townsfolk who welcomed him.

Of his five Macon visits, two came in wartime. The other three I remember. I was a little girl when he stopped in Macon in the middle seventies en route to Savannah, and Papa presented him. On his arrival, Mr. Davis appeared for a brief greeting on a high balcony of the old Terminal Station on Broadway, on the site of the present Happ Brothers Factory and just across the street from the old Brown House.

I remember well the tall, slim, gray-haired hero's emergence on the balcony with Papa. The crowd in the street below was wild with expectation, so that my father could scarcely attract their attention when Mr. Davis did appear. Finally, with both arms outspread, and in a mighty voice, Papa shouted, simply, "Boys, here he is!" And the crowd roared its welcome.

On still another visit not long after, Mr. Davis addressed a crowd at Central City Park, where he was again introduced by Papa. I was permitted to slip behind the speakers on the platform, to touch Mr. Davis' hand. I felt that my hand was forever consecrated!

In the middle eighties, Mr. Davis came again and was the guest of the Marsh Johnstons in their Victorian mansion on the slant of Coleman's Hill on Georgia Avenue. With him were Mrs. Davis and their daughters, Winnie and Margaret.

Macon planned a great welcome for the revered guests. Veterans in gray would form their lines of march downtown, ascend the rise of Mulberry Street to Georgia Avenue and there greet the President of the Confederacy with formal military ceremony.

DEBUT IN THE EIGHTIES

My brother, Joseph Blount, was selected Marshal of the Day and on horseback led the parade to the Johnston home, as crowds lined the way cheering the aging veterans and the handsome young marshal. Soon, the men saw Mr. Davis waiting for them on the balcony of the big house, halfway up the grassy hill.

I stood with other girls in a group on the lawn, and saw the old man stand quietly smiling at the men who had fought in the Cause he had led. He seemed deeply moved as he stood high over the grounds, looking into the street, pulled out of his usual aspect of utter exhaustion.

There was a pause, a vibrant uncertainty in the street, and a sudden confusion in the ranks of the parade. The line of march broke. With cheers, shouts, and tears the men in gray poured from the street, up the hill, and over the iron fence around the grounds, each one drawn by love and memories.

The great lawn was filled with gray-clad men, swarming over the grass and up to the house—packing around the balcony. The President waved and smiled and bowed, his hands outstretched in pride and affection, for perhaps half an hour. Then, shrunken, white, and spent, he turned, and waved again and again as he slowly retired into the house.

I remember most vividly the complete emotional exhaustion of his appearance then, which emphasized "the President's" natural gentleness and quietude of manner.

There was a dinner party at the Johnstons that night, but Mr. Davis was too tired to attend. I sat by Daughter Margaret Davis, who confided the first of several Davis stories to me—intimate glimpses of the man and his family which I have cherished through my lifetime. This personal illumination of Mr. Davis increased my interest in him as a statesman, which grew through some decades to color my leadership of the Daughters of the Confederacy. Margaret and I, chatting together, began a cordial friendship which lasted for nearly forty years of occasional correspondence, long after she became Mrs. Hayes.

Margaret told me that while she was at a convent school in France during the War Between the States Père Hyacinth addressed the students on the affairs of the Confederacy, and took occasion to revile its President Davis, who he said should be "put in chains as a traitor to his country." Margaret left the classroom, as a gesture of furious dissent. Her punishment was confinement to bread and water for several days.

She scarcely had need to embellish the story to me, whose milder experience at Wellesley prepared me for acute and indignant sympathy. So, I was tremendously cheered by the dénouement of the French episode which Margaret related to me.

Some years later, Pére Hyacinth visited the States. When in New Orleans, he asked permission to call on Mr. Davis, who was then a guest at the home of the Charles E. Fenners, a characteristically Southern mansion, its grounds enclosed by an intricate wrought-iron fence. The penitent Father was rewarded with an unequivocal refusal by Mr. Davis, who gave as his reason Margaret's experience at the Paris convent.

Many years after our talk at the Johnston party, I visited Margaret Davis Hayes at her home in Denver, where I heard another story of the Davis ladies' loyalty to the Confederate leader, a loyalty firm against blandishments from high places.

President Teddy Roosevelt, who had written inimically and inaccurately of Davis in one of his books, on the occasion of the Confederate President's death in 1889, wrote to Mrs. Davis that he would like to attend the funeral and pay his last respects to a hero and a gentleman. Mrs. Davis remembered that Teddy had written that Jefferson Davis, as Governor of Mississippi, had repudiated state bonds, in addition to charging him with treason. Davis wrote to Roosevelt to correct him with the information that he had never served as Governor of Mississippi, and asked that the impossible charge be retracted. Roosevelt's third-person reply was: "Theodore Roosevelt desires no communication with Jefferson Davis."

Mrs. Davis was unmoved and unconsoled by belated graciousness from the President of the United States. She wrote to him, "The family prefers that Mr. Roosevelt not attend the funeral."

However, as Mrs. Hayes recounted, Mr. Roosevelt, determined to behave as usual—thinking when he attended a wedding he was the bride and when he went to a funeral he was the corpse—sent a handsome floral offering from the White House.

PARAMOUNT BLOUNT

IN 1892 MY FATHER LOOKED BACK ON TWENTY YEARS OF service to the South and the nation in Congress, and decided to retire. He had worked hard and well for rehabilitation of his section and the common interests of the Union, and he left Washington with profound satisfaction in the role he had played in re-uniting the states and helping to protect and advance their welfare as Chairman of the House Foreign Affairs Committee and many other committees of importance.

Papa was fifty-five years old—not an old man, but tired enough to turn to rest with happy relief and a growing zest for life and work ahead of him at home. For some years he had looked with proud and longing eyes toward his great land holdings in Middle Georgia, and now he was returning to the good red earth to pursue the farming of his fathers.

He owned 13,000 acres of land, portions of it planted in cotton, peaches, and other income yields of Georgia. The Blount land hunger had moved him for several decades to buy up nearby property in Jones County, adding to his inherited interest in the Blount estate. One Negro tenant, the son of a family slave, said years before: "Marse Jim, he buy any lan' dat jine his'n." And so he did.

Mama, too, looked happily toward a quieter life in Macon with summers at Hale Nui, a more settled social life for me, a rooted home for Jim, and an open door for Joseph when he wanted to come home. We cherished the stirring days in the capital, the history of which we had been a part, and the friendships with the nation's great personalities which we had enjoyed. With a pang or two, Mama sighed over giving up her twenty-year attendance at the more important and exciting congressional debates. It had been her longtime duty to read the Congressional Record to keep Papa posted.

So, we left Washington for good. On February 4, 1893, Papa went to the House alone, while Mama stayed at home attending to chores of packing and departure. This day the House resolved itself into a Committee of the Whole to pass on the Diplomatic and Consular Service appropriation of more than one and a half million dollars, just submitted by Representative Blount.

The House voted unanimously to make this huge appropriation (phenomenal for those days), and Papa settled back to attend to the next business before the House. Then rose Representative William S. Holman of Indiana, to launch a tribute to the retiring Georgian, an act unprecedented in the annals of the House. Republicans and Democrats followed Holman to express their regret at my father's retirement, to praise his ability and integrity and to emphasize his devotion to duty above partisan and sectional interest.

Holman recalled in glowing terms the "prudence and judgment" with which my father as foreign affairs chairman had met last year's crisis in the matter of the Venezuelan border.

Republican Floor Leader Robert R. Hitt of Illinois paid this tribute to a Southerner:

"I will mark, most of all, that patriotism above party that inspired him in this House when, last year, leading a great committee to consider the affairs and interest, not of a party, but of a whole nation embroiled in sharp dispute with a foreign power, he rose to the occasion and proved himself first and altogether a patriot, an American, so that a foreigner looking down from the gallery upon this hall could never have told whether he was a Republican or a Democrat, but would have known that he was in every fibre an American."

Holman added:

"I wish to congratulate the gentleman from Georgia, as well as the distinguished gentlemen composing his committee on foreign affairs, with having brought into the House a very important appropriations bill which is so perfect in all its details as to receive the approval of the Committee of the Whole House. It is generally unusual for [such] a bill, even after the most severe examination . . . to escape criticism . . . but the House has become accustomed to pass bills reported by Representative Blount without controversy . . . it is taken for granted by the House that a bill reported by him has undergone the severest scrutiny and that no consideration whatever has been taken into account but the interest of the public." Non-partisan praise of "one of the most able, careful, laborious, and upright legislators known to our time" was echoed by Bland of Missouri, O'Neal of Pennsylvania, Springer of Illinois, McCreary of Kentucky, and others.

Papa's composure wavered as he rose to reply, and to recall the contributions of Speaker Samuel J. Randall of Pennsylvania, Mr. Holman, Republican Hitt, and others to his service in Congress.

"If I desired fame," he said, "if my heart were filled with ambition, in this presence I wish to say in the past few moments there has been written a chapter in the history of this House that brings to the wife and children at home and to the friends who have followed me through these years a sense of its consequences that will outlast and outweigh any office in the gift of the State or Federal Government."

The love feast concluded, with long applause, in an atmosphere of affection and respect which crowned the twenty-year career of this Georgian who labored for recovery of the South and re-union of the States.

At home, Mama was torn between gratification and dismay that—of all the sessions she had attended in two decades—she missed this triumphant conclusion to father's career for which she had lived and labored so faithfully and zestfully for twenty years.

Congress, just before we returned to Georgia, was much concerned over the Hawaiian treaty. A revolution, of obscure inspiration, as far as Americans could tell, but approved by American commercial interests, had overthrown the island queen, Liliuokalani, and set up a provisional government with some American officials. This government proposed that the United States annex the islands. Three weeks before President Harrison was to turn over his office to Grover Cleveland (elected for his second term) commissioners of the provisional Hawaiian government called on Harrison. This commission was headed by Lorrin A. Thurston, chairman of the new Protectorate and friend of Americans. President Harrison approved their annexation treaty and sent it to the Senate for approval.

Many congressmen and a disturbed public disapproved the treaty, fearing such territorial expansion and the demands it would make on the U. S. Navy. Cleveland and most Democrats wanted to delay ratification of the treaty, as opposed to Republicans, who traditionally favored the big business viewpoint of commercial interests, and who approved U. S. possession of islands so rich for exploitation. Democrats sought to delay ratification of the treaty. This Democratic opposition delayed treaty approval until Cleveland got into office, and the country waited for his decision.

Late in January we arrived at our Tattnall Square home, rejoicing in the homecoming. We were all together, except Joseph, who was on tour, and we relished our plans and anticipation of the full years ahead of us. We retired our first night, each to his own high-ceilinged, upstairs bedroom, to sleep and rest secure in the knowledge that we would live in the normal routine of home for the rest of our lives.

Next day our peaceful prospects were shattered by a summons from Washington. President Cleveland, my father's old friend, with an urgency that brooked no protest, informed Papa that he was appointed "Commissioner Paramount" to the Hawaiian Islands. He was to leave immediately for Hawaii to investigate the revolution, the attitude of Queen Liliuokalani and her subjects, and the possible role American sugar planters might have played in the revolution. They were suspect, Democrats figured, as wanting Hawaiian territory annexed in order to admit sugar to the States duty free.

Papa himself had long been troubled by the oppressive aspects of the American commercial faction in the revolution, and his States Rights' convictions inspired in him a sympathy for the plight of the Sandwich Islanders whose self-government he feared was usurped by sugar planters.

So, with disappointment, but a growing interest and concern in his assignment, he prepared to leave for the West Coast, and thence to sail to the Islands. Mama, of course, accompanied him.

News of Papa's mission was received with indignant outcries from the Senate, as President Cleveland withdrew the treaty and recalled the United States minister, John L. Stevens, a friend of the revolution.

The *New York Herald-Tribune* led the hue and cry and Republicans angrily denounced "paramount Blount," who they claimed had been endowed with autocratic and arbitrary powers by a hostile president. It was all very undemocratic and un-American, to send a "Commissioner Paramount" to investigate, with powers to nullify "a people's revolution," they argued.

When my parents arrived at Honolulu, the paramount Georgian immediately ordered the American flag, which had been raised by Stevens, lowered from the government buildings. Thus he pursued his investigations without any feeling of pressure from a *fait accompli* upon the Hawaiians. He established himself in an office and began to hear evidence from both sides: Queen "Lil's" supporters, common natives, and the revolutionary faction which included natives, American officials, and notable pineapple executives and sugar planters.

While Papa investigated, weighed, appraised, and judged, Mama was busy acquainting herself with the sights to be seen on the island, meeting and talking with natives and members of the provisional government. Her informal and friendly contacts with these individuals and factions of course assisted Papa in his investigation.

No sooner had Commissioner Blount lowered the American flag, "to give the people back their government," than a chorus of alarms rose in Republican circles in the States. The Blounts had been warned by American officials and business men at Honolulu that great distress, violence, and bloodshed would result if he lowered the flag and returned such a "savage people" to power. But no such disasters followed.

From sightseeing, conferences with Queen Lil, and contacts with both sides, my parents derived quite a different notion of the "savage" Hawaiians.

"They were," my mother often recalled, "a pleasant, peaceable people, extremely kind and submissive. There was absolutely no just reason why their government should have been taken from them."

Charmed with the friendly attitude of my parents and their open-minded and sympathetic disposition, a band of natives marched to the Blount cottage at Honolulu and serenaded the visitors with the most apt and fitting music they knew—"Marching Through Georgia"!

Early in the summer of 1893, my father, as commissioner, returned the islands to Queen Liliuokalani and her subjects, deposed the provisional government, and reported to President Cleveland. Papa's report said he had found the revolution was instigated and fomented by pineapple interests and sugar planters, in connivance with the American minister, Mr. Stevens, and implemented considerably by the presence of United States Marines who provided effective intimidation to resistance factions. (Stevens had ordered 140 sailors and marines to land from the USS Boston to "protect American interests.")

President Cleveland withdrew American claims to rule and to any territorial acquisition in the Hawaiian Islands. He dispatched this government's apology to Queen Lil, and proposed that she should be enthroned by force, if necessary.

The outraged queen, however, was unwilling to forgive and forget. She imposed terms which included revenge on her enemies, and refused them amnesty. Her attitude gave pause to Congress, and neither house acted on the President's proposal.

In Honolulu, Papa awaited Congressional action to confirm his restoration of the native government. And, when Congress balked and waited, he deemed his mission accomplished as far as possible, and notified the President that he wished to return home. Cleveland, however, ordered him to stay.

But my father judged that he had completed his mission; so he put Admiral Skerrit in charge and sailed for home.

"He was," Mama explained, laughing, "so paramount that he ignored the appointment."

"Paramount Blount" succeeded with his mission. But the victory developed into another Lost Cause. The following May, a Republican Congress, urged by pressure from pineapple and sugar interests, passed a hands-off resolution which returned the islands to their status at the time of the so-called revolution. Queen Lil never regained her throne. She abdicated in July of 1894, and a republic was established which lasted until 1898.

At home again, Papa supervised the cotton fields, peach orchards, and timber lands of his Jones County property for a fruitful and gratifying decade. He saw me happily married and launched on civic and social activities in which he took pride. He felt blessed in Jim's marriage to Sallie B. Comer. His first grandchild, Jim's daughter, Eugenia, was a great joy in his later years.

Mama and Papa perused the Congressional Record as closely as before, and kept up with national and world affairs; while

Papa, as a retired statesman, lent his counsel in state and local politics.

It was a happy life in the nineties and past the turn of the century. Then an undefined malaise began to distress Papa recurrently—dizziness, heat, and weakness. In 1903 he took to his bed. His sickness was probably high blood pressure, not so readily diagnosed in those days. On March 8 he died at his home on College Street.

The death of my father, recently famed as Paramount Blount and always remembered as a low tariff champion, was national news. It was recorded with eulogies in the South and in many Northern papers. Some newspapers, like the *New York Tribune,* wrote obituaries reporting objectively his Confederate war service, his congressional career, and his work as an attorney and planter after retirement. But these stories bore a tinge of the old Republican anger of 1893.

The *Tribune* recalled his "inscrutable mystery" at that time which "he did not discard until after his return to this country the following August" and "presumed" that, after lowering the United States flag, the Commissioner "found it easier to pursue his investigations." But, the story complained, "he remained as much a mystery as ever to those with whom he came in contact." Another reporter recalled that "compared with Commissioner Blount, the Sphinx was a chatterbox."

There is a painting at the Capitol in Washington which the family likes to view. This pictures shows my father among those present at the meetings of the Electoral Commission which decided the contest for United States President in favor of Hayes against Tilden. Each face is finely portrayed in the huge painting that hangs at the entrance to the Senate gallery. Besides my father I recognize and remember James G. Blaine of Maine, Samuel J. Randall of Pennsylvania, John G. Carlisle of Kentucky, Pig Iron Kelley and Quay of Pennsylvania, L. Q. C. Lamar of Mississippi, Ransom of South Carolina, John A. Logan, John B. Gordon, and many more.

There are also many ladies in the throng of spectators depicted. Mrs. Gordon is quite prominent, as is the famous Reconstruction days beauty, Kate Chase Sprague. Mama, who had attended the commission's session every day with Mrs. Gordon, until she became ill, is not in the picture. On the day of her absence, the artist sketched in the faces of those present, a happen-so I have always regretted.

JAMES H. BLOUNT

MR. AND MRS. JAMES H. BLOUNT

COURTSHIP AND MARRIAGE

ONE YOUNG GENTLEMAN — WALTER LAMAR, THE QUIET, patient one—continued his suit throughout my young ladyhood, apparently undisturbed by my frequent goings and comings and my reluctance to settle down.

In the summer of 1896, I found myself entertaining some unexpectedly pleasant and serious reactions on the occasion of his periodic proposal. His gentleness and patience became more appealing, he looked a bit more handsome, his manner seemed more charming, and his occasional slow, dry witticism was more amusing than I had previously thought. Walter was gaining ground.

One October night when he called (Mama and Papa were at Hale Nui with Joseph, who was ill), he seemed less patient. In fact, I was quite excited by his suggestions that we marry, drive to Haddock, and confront the family with a *fait accompli*. Of course I, dutiful, would not consent to such a drastic plan; nor was I quite decided what to do.

Quite properly, I banished him for a week of prudent consideration, and then wrote to him:

My dear Walter,

When you pleaded your cause so earnestly last Friday . . . I was more impressed than ever before with your true worth and superiority over other men of my acquaintance and I determined to give the subject more consideration. . . . It became necessary for me to consult older and wiser heads than my own, . . .

Therefore I deemed it wise to lay the case before those to whom I am dearest, my Father and Mother, and so I sent them a letter some days ago telling them of all that passed between us last Friday. Now they have under consideration the letter I wrote, although of course I did not tell them of your plan to surprise them at Hale Nui.

I expect them home today. I can not doubt your sincerity and earnestness after all these years, and we will settle this matter finally. Wishing for you a successful trip and assuring you of my sincerest friendship, whate'er betide.

Just before Mama and Papa returned from the country to Macon, Mama wrote me that the decision was up to me, with, of course, a few parental reservations. The reservations were quite proper, but (as it seems now) devious. Papa professed to know nothing of Walter's business ability, but to know him only "as a courteous gentleman." Mama wrote insistently that I must decide for myself, at the same time making it quite clear that my acceptance of Walter depended entirely upon Papa's consent. It was a nice, loving letter from a prudent set of parents.

Later perusing the letter, I was amused at their insistence that the decision was freely up to me, while Mama reminded me several times over that "you must make no arrangements with him until he has consulted your father," and that "if then your father consents, you will be free to make your own plans with Walter."

When Walter returned after his week's banishment he and I sat as usual before an open fire in the dining room, while Papa read in his study across the hall. In undertones, we discussed Walter's trip into the study. Finally, he arose, left me, and went to confront Papa.

He stayed so long that I became faint-hearted, and wondered if Papa were refusing my hand to Walter. Finally, Walter emerged, patting his damp face with a handkerchief, and resumed his place beside me.

"Well?" I asked.

"Well," Walter faltered, "I just didn't get around to asking him. We were discussing the Cuban War."

COURTSHIP AND MARRIAGE

"That," he added, frowning at the embers in the grate, "is the hottest fire I have ever felt in my life!"

Later, having cooled off and being resolute again, he returned to the study. He came back shortly, wreathed in smiles and almost limp with relief.

"Whew! That's over," he reported, beaming.

We were engaged, with Papa's consent.

Walter had been a patient lover and a docile suitor, but when he won me, he "took over." With our engagement, he began to make the decisions and give the orders—quietly, courteously, and firmly. No, there wouldn't be a long engagement; he had already waited long enough. It was already November when Papa said yes, and Walter intended to be married in December.

No, we wouldn't live with his family, or mine. It was generous of both families to want us, but the Walter Douglas Lamars would have their own home. In fact, he had already rented a sizable house on Rogers Avenue, a pleasant, tree-lined street in the up and coming suburb of Vineville.

Yes, we would have a wedding trip to New York. He would like for us to view the sights of the great city with the Gay Nineties in full tide. Yes, he approved our decision for a comparatively quiet church wedding and a small reception at home.

It had been a nice long courtship, with no hot-headed wild-hearted nonsense about it. Then there was a short engagement, with stacks of letters from far and wide, numbers of parties, and happy evenings with Walter by the fire.

From November 9, the betrothal date, to December 16, there were parties. Among them was a euchre party given by Mrs. Lee Ellis at her home at the corner of Georgia Avenue and Orange Street, one of the first affairs beginning the era of daytime card games for ladies. Also Mrs. Ed McLaren, who was Walter's sister, Valeria, entertained us with a reception and dance at her home in Vineville.

Mama and I were busy assembling a quick trousseau of fine lingerie. There were of course matching sets of chemises, pantalets, and corset covers, with puffs, insertion, ruffles, and lace edging. There were five petticoats for each dress, the top one edged with five ruffles!

There were also the requisite number of gowns with bustles, leg-o'-mutton sleeves, and elaborate shirtwaists worn with billowing skirts, a silhouette to enhance the twenty-one-inch waistline of the bride of that era. For sentiment's sake, my trousseau included an outfit remodeled from one of the trousseau gowns Mama never wore. It was green silk with moss roses in the beautiful plaid pattern, worn with a shirtwaist of maize colored grass cloth.

I was at this time finding my in-laws very dynamic people. They lived in Vineville in a great spreading white house on what is now school property, a block or so from the Rogers Avenue home Walter had selected for us. The place sprawled over twenty-two rooms on one floor, with several parlors and more rooms upstairs.

Walter's mother was a witty and talented woman who played the piano with great skill and a touch of genius. She also played Lady Bountiful to a number of needy protégées, many of them old women who enjoyed her friendship as well as her charity. It was a common occurrence for callers at the Lamar home to find the lady of the house in the parlor playing her piano to a group of shabby old ladies from the other side of the tracks, rapt as they listened to the concert.

Mr. Lamar was a benign, bearded gentleman with a fine face distinguished by what I call the "Lamar nose," a generous, spreading, but not unpleasant family mark. Like Walter, he didn't talk much, but he always said something when he did.

There were seven children in the family—Valeria, Henry, Fannie, Alberta, Jack, Wileyna, and Walter.

I do not know enough of the personal characteristics of the ancestors of this interesting family to account for the interchanging frenzy and poise of the varied individuals of which it was composed. Suffice it to say that through the storm and

COURTSHIP AND MARRIAGE

stress of such a vigorous and intense family, they were in their childhood and youth devoted to each other.

All the Lamar children grew up as independent thinkers and doers of their theories. Their doings, which today seem tame by comparison with current behavior, were once sensational. For example, my first recollection of Valeria and Fannie was their early violation of all the prejudices against makeup. They appeared at a party rouged without stint, long before any respectable woman in town had the courage to do so. There was a great furore of excitement when the two of them were seen at the famous home of the Bonds on the Hill with lavish makeup—and furthermore, sipping champagne.

The betrothal of Walter and me was favorably received by both of our families. From numerous and far-flung kin of Blounts and Lamars came cordial and sentimental letters, reflecting pleasure in the union of families long associated in social, civic, and political ties.

Not long before our marriage, Papa (for all his reluctance about giving me away) confided to me with a smile as we walked in Tattnall Square Park, "I've really been surprised, Doddice, that you haven't accepted Walter long ago."

I was married on the night of December 16, 1896, in the First Presbyterian Church.

The towering lines of the old church seemed to reach up in beneficent grace, transformed by flowers, candlelight, organ music, and the happy, expectant hush which precedes a wedding. The grim Presbyterian rigors of my early devotions that night melted and mellowed to memories that sweetly enhanced the familiar setting.

I wore heavy white satin with bouffant sleeves and a short train, and a veil of tulle caught by a coronet of valley lilies. My bouquet was of Roman hyacinths—blooms with which Walter greeted me ever after on our wedding anniversary.

Cousin Mamie Wiley (Uncle Charlie's daughter) was maid of honor, and John Hoge was Walter's best man. The three bridesmaids were Eva Chamberlin of Atlanta, Mattie Nutting, and my sister Fanny.

It was not very grand or very large, as weddings went in the nineties. But after I had promised to love, honor, and obey, and Walter, to cherish, the occasion was pronounced as touching and happy a wedding as fashionable Macon could want to see.

We left the church in the most brilliant moonlight that ever shone, returning to my home in Tattnall Square for a small reception. Scheduled to leave immediately for New York, we eluded the wags and jokers by spending our first night at my home. We slipped off quietly to the train next day, escorted by best man Hoge in a fine livery stable carriage.

In New York we put up at the old Fifth Avenue Hotel way downtown, and repaired thence to sight-see, attend the theater, dine at famous places, and do some shopping for our new home. Happily we selected ornaments, lamps, some furniture, and a most enchanting set of Japanese china, eggshell painted with purple pansies.

Highlight of our honeymoon was to be Christmas Day, when Walter had planned a full round of celebrations. But on Christmas morning we received a telegram notifying us of the sudden death of Walter's father in Macon, and we left for home Christmas afternoon.

After several weeks at the Lamar home on Vineville Avenue, we moved to our house on nearby Rogers Avenue. I was delighted with my first fling at housekeeping. Thrilled, I devoted myself to chores which I considered proper for a wife. I had, for instance, always heard that wives darned their husband's socks. So darn I did. I always sat late in the afternoon just where Walter could see me, dutifully occupied when he came in. For some weeks he endured this uxorious display.

"You know, Dolly," he finally ventured to remark, smiling, "I really don't like to wear darned socks."

I was as relieved to abandon the chore as Walter was to leave off wearing his lumpy, repaired socks. It was a happy

COURTSHIP AND MARRIAGE

agreement which presaged many more, leaving me free from distasteful duties to pursue the work, studies, and achievements for which I was fitted, and of which Walter was always most affectionately proud.

Once, soon after we were married, Walter, seeing me downtown just ahead of him, hurried to greet me, calling, "Miss Dolly, oh, Miss Dolly!" I turned and laughed, reminding him that now I was his wife he might make bold to call me just "Dolly."

Established on Rogers Avenue, I joined a cooking club of earnest brides and young matrons who sought, thus pleasantly, to improve their household arts. We studied and exchanged recipes and talked of cookery, as if the very existence of our lords and masters depended on our slaving in the kitchen.

However, about the only occasion on which we stood over a hot cook stove (wood burner, of course), working our fingers to the bone, was at the weekly meeting of our cooking club. Then, each of us would bring the ingredients of a dish to be prepared and served at luncheon, and repair in solemn excitement to the kitchen, to burn our hands and use up every available pot and pan. The rest of the time, we rested from our club labors to gather strength for the next meeting, collecting recipes, planning the next meal, and dividing the club chores betimes. And expert Negro cooks reigned competently in our kitchens.

Walter was made executor of his father's estate. After a few months, affairs of the Lamar drug business took us to Atlanta for a three-year stay.

So, my fling at housekeeping was short-lived. In Atlanta we boarded with Miss Flora Fitten at her elegant home on Linden Avenue, a choice establishment which housed and served meals to select "paying guests." It was a congenial household and a happy interval for Walter and me.

Atlanta launched me into new associations and activities which helped prepare me for my busy career of club leadership, literary pursuits and friendships, and purely social activities.

I met Mrs. John K. Ottley, celebrated Southern clubwoman, who remained my friend for several generations of service, and together we later weathered some sharp controversies in the Georgia Federation of Women's Clubs. Through Mrs. Ottley, one of the most brilliant, remarkable women I have ever known, I first became interested in Mrs. Lipscomb's North Georgia mountain school for white illiterates, an interest which helped to establish the famous Tallulah Falls School under auspices of the Federation.

A fast friend of those days was Isma Dooley, one of Atlanta's first well-known newspaper women, then a reporter on the *Constitution*.

One of my most entertaining memories of my Atlanta stay was an evening in the home of Mrs. Ed Brown, where Miss Dooley, Mrs. Ottley, and I were invited to meet Corra Harris, the Methodist preacher's widow and author of *The Circuit Rider's Wife* and other novels about rural and small-town Georgia.

Mrs. Harris brought to her friends at Mrs. Brown's home the literary problem of a wife with a philandering husband, tangled figures in the new book she was writing. Mary, it seems, busy in war work and good deeds, was distressed to find her John slipping—in the direction of an unattached lady with time on her hands. How, Mrs. Harris wondered, would Mary lure John back to her arms?

The young president of the Atlanta Woman's Club, Mrs. Ottley; the brilliant journalist, Miss Dooley; the gifted beauty, Mrs. Brown; and I, all bent our heads to the problem.

Boldly, the lady of the city suggested a lipstick. Aghast at first, but finally emboldened, Mrs. Brown said Mary might rouge her face to entice the errant John. I, clothes-minded and trousseau-clad, suggested a "ceinture."

COURTSHIP AND MARRIAGE

"Whatever," cried all the ladies, "is that?"

Worldly wise, what with a New York honeymoon and so many Washington seasons, I explained to the fascinated provincials that a ceinture was a wide and seductive sash, and that Mary would do well to get herself up in white satin with a bright blue ceinture to retrieve John's roving eye.

Mrs. Harris pondered all our suggestions, returned to her manuscript, decked Mary in rouge, lipstick, and white satin with a bright blue ceinture and recovered the wandering John for a happy ending.

In 1901 we returned to Macon, to open house again, this time on College Street, next door to the old Wiley place, my mother's girlhood home. We were just in time for our fifth anniversary party and the welcome-home festivities proffered by friends in Macon.

IX

A DAUGHTER
OF THE CONFEDERACY

IT IS THE MISSION OF THE UNITED DAUGHTERS OF THE Confederacy to look into the past of the South to bring to the present the lessons of Confederate history. Herewith it becomes the joy of a Daughter of more than 60 years' standing to look into the past of the U.D.C. and count the steps and milestones of a great patriotic program.

Such a trip into the past will show the sacrifice and the devotion which have adorned and changed the very face of the land with bronze and stone records that will keep alive the spirit of the Confederacy for ages to come; the living memorials in that army of boys and girls who have been educated through U.D.C. gift and loan scholarships, and the study, corrections, and interpretations which have clarified the truth of Southern history.

Indoctrinated from my youth with the Bill of Rights as provided in the ten original amendments to the Constitution, and especially revering the principle that *"the powers not delegated to the United States by the Constitution, nor prohibited by it to the States, are reserved to the States respectively, or to the people,"* I early realized that the Daughters of the Confederacy looked to this, the Tenth Amendment, as their guiding star. For this reason I have given U.D.C. a lifelong devotion. It is small wonder that profound conviction and undivided service to the principles upon which this republic was founded should be the motivating force in my service to U.D.C.

A DAUGHTER OF THE CONFEDERACY

In November, 1897, I attended my first General Convention of the United Daughters of the Confederacy in Baltimore. Mrs. Billups Phinizy and I were delegates from Athens and Macon, chaperoned by Miss Mildred Rutherford of Athens, a leading spirit in the early organization of Georgia Daughters.

I recall nothing of business proceedings, but the ardor and spirit of this early General Convention are fresh in my mind. Most of the delegates were women rounding the half century in age, and over the sessions there was a dark shadow of grief for fallen heroes as well as a high zeal for Confederate ideals.

The crippling loss and deep sorrow of the South three decades after the war were symbolized for me at that convention by the preponderance of widows in black gowns, coronet bonnets, and long crepe veils which were thrown back during the sessions. The mourning of those women was deep and unmistakable.

I was elected to the presidency of the Georgia U.D.C. in October, 1911. This year was a banner one for Georgia Daughters of the Confederacy, whose achievements are recalled to me by our delegation's strength and importance at the fall convention in Richmond and by wide commendation of the year's report, submitted by me as Division President. This was my first tenure of office; I was twice elected to serve two-year terms as head of the Georgia U.D.C.

The year 1911 was a busy time for me, since I functioned in the triune capacity of Division President, Macon's Sidney Lanier Chapter President, and Chairman of the Woman's Auxiliary for the United Confederate Veterans' Reunion scheduled for May, 1912, in Macon.

At the Richmond Convention the Georgia delegation, with its strength of 212 votes, was the largest next to Virginia, and far ahead of third-place South Carolina with 139. So our role in the convention achieved the prestige of numerical strength as well as of accomplishment. We proudly elected Miss Mildred Rutherford of Athens Historian-General and Mrs. L. H. Raines of Savannah, Custodian of Crosses.

Miss Rutherford was highly esteemed over the South for her valuable lectures on Southern history and her courageous attacks on myths which had obtained. A picturesque and commanding figure, she appeared on many a platform in hoop skirt and all the appointments of a lady of the sixties.

She left a monument of vital import in 57 volumes of Southern history which she gave to U.D.C. General. The collection of rare, invaluable, and out-of-print books is now in the Georgia Room at the Confederate Museum in Richmond. U.D.C. General has appropriated funds to index, document, and edit books and papers in the Rutherford collection, and the work is now in the hands of an able committee.

During my state presidency, I was privileged to witness from the speaker's platform, as the aide of the U.D.C. President-General, Mrs. Daisy McLaurin Stevens of Mississippi, the unveiling at Arlington of a magnificent monument to the Confederate dead. The occasion is memorable for the significance of this first honor to Confederate valor in the national cemetery for American heroes. Mrs. Stevens presented the monument to the United States, and it was accepted for the nation by President Woodrow Wilson. The President said in part: "I am not so much happy as proud to be a participant on such an occasion, proud that I represent such a people. . . . The generosity of our judgments began when, soon after the great struggle was over, men came and sat together again in the Congress and, united in all the efforts of peace and government, . . . worked again to lift the burdens of mankind and show the paths of freedom to the world."

The following day, with the President-General, I enjoyed a study of the monument in detail under the tutelage of Sir Moses Ezekiel, the Confederate-veteran sculptor, who had been among 225 V.M.I. cadets who marched the 100 miles into the jaws of death at Newmarket.

The monument of bronze stands on a foundation of dark gray granite surmounted by a figure of the South holding a laurel

A DAUGHTER OF THE CONFEDERACY

wreath and wearing a wreath of olive leaves. At her side is a sickle and a plowshare, and on the base is written: "They have beat their swords into plowshares and their spears into pruning hooks." Below this appears a circle of 23 life-size figures illustrating the spirit of the South when the tocsin of war was sounded. Among them are soldiers marching and an officer taking leave of his family. There is a gigantic figure of Minerva trying to support herself on the shield of the Constitution. The inscription reads: "Not for fame, not for place, not for rank, not lured by ambition, or goaded by necessity; but in simple obedience to duty as they understood it, these men suffered all, sacrificed all, dared all—and died."

As one of the younger daughters who were achieving leadership in the U.D.C. in 1915, I was gratified to learn that my work was to be rewarded with nomination by the Georgia delegation for President-General. It was an experience most complimentary to a young woman to know that the Georgia Division Executive Board and others of my delegation wished to see me national leader of U.D.C., and to learn also of support from other states which made my election almost certain.

In those days an election was far from settled before convention time, but we felt that the Georgia delegation had enough support to assure victory this year. I had been put forward by Miss Rutherford, the revered Georgia Historian-General of U.D.C., who said that she herself did not intend to let her name be presented for Historian-General again.

Shortly after I was approached and had accepted the candidacy, I learned that Miss Rutherford had changed her mind and would run for re-election in this important office at the coming convention in San Francisco. In addition to this, Mrs. George Baker of Savannah, Corresponding Secretary-General, was this year entitled to re-election. My election as President-General would, then, give Georgia three officers in U.D.C. General.

I had pronounced views on such a number of officers on the

General Board from one state, feeling that no Division should take the lion's share of honors, eliminating a wider and more democratic representation in top councils of U.D.C. I greatly admired Miss Rutherford, who had served Georgia and U.D.C. for many years, and I recognized Mrs. Baker's right to serve her second term as Corresponding Secretary. So, I decided to withdraw my name.

It was amusing at the time to consider the advice which I received and which was tendered Miss Rutherford by U.D.C. friends. For instance, Mrs. Lawson Peel of Atlanta, my mother's friend, said to me very firmly: "Dolly, you ought not to let the Juggernaut of Millie Rutherford's ambition run over you; she has had her day." On the other hand, some, like Mrs. A. C. Campbell, told Miss Rutherford, "You should not be intimidated by Mrs. Lamar's youthful ambition"!

Relinquishing the certainty of the ranking office in U.D.C. was a disappointment to me, but I had the satisfaction of feeling that I had acted fairly, and the additional gratification of a warm commendation signed and made public by officers of my home chapter.

In 1915 I assumed the chairmanship of the Jefferson Davis Highway Committee, appointed to promote a thoroughfare from the East to the West of our nation, traversing historic Southern cities, two capitals of the Confederacy, and other points of significance and historic interest.

The country needed more and better highways, and I felt that enough monuments were already erected, or were in the process of being built, to permit the Daughters to turn their attention to an ocean-to-ocean highway memorializing Davis. In this way practical patriotism might put forth a worthy blossom. Thus U.D.C. might demonstrate its four-fold purpose— Memorial, Educational, Social, Historical.

I urged all Daughters to study the topography of their states, their claims to historic distinction, and to put such claims before the Jefferson Davis Highway Chairman of each state for pres-

A DAUGHTER OF THE CONFEDERACY

entation by the General Committee at the San Francisco Convention in the fall. Each state chairman was also to request her Governor to form a state committee to cooperate officially with us and promote publicity in the press.

Through several years I promoted this project, and then because of a long illness gave it up to my successor, Mrs. J. L. Woodbury. Her brilliant record as chairman of this tremendous work is outstanding in U.D.C. history. In fact, the Jefferson Davis Highway, completed in 1947, is one of the greatest accomplishments of U.D.C.

Daughters of the Confederacy on several occasions have reached hands across the sea to erect memorials to Southern ideals as exemplified by leaders of the Confederacy. We have established memorials in three foreign countries which recall and extend our ideals by monuments.

To the Swiss government was given by U.D.C. a portrait of the great Naval hero, the first and only Commander of the Confederate Navy, Raphael Semmes, and this portrait was accorded the most desirable location in the Hall of Alabama at Geneva.

On the shores of France in the cemetery at Cherbourg sleep several sailors of the ill-fated ship, *Alabama,* whose bodies were washed ashore after the ship had perished in the waves of the Mediterranean. Each grave is marked, "A Sailor from the Alabama, CSN."

A bronze bust of Robert E. Lee was installed in England at the military school at Sandhurst with solemn and beautiful ceremonies. This memorial was provided through the generosity of Mrs. Lewis Burnett of West Virginia.

In 1924 there was unveiled at the Military Training School for officers of the French Army at Saint Cyr, near Paris, a similar bust of the great Lee. I was on a foreign tour that summer and had the good fortune to attend the Saint Cyr presentation. A large and representative delegation of Americans took part in these ceremonies.

WHEN ALL IS SAID AND DONE

On October 10, 1931, the U.D.C. with Sons of Confederate Veterans unveiled a boulder at Harper's Ferry honoring Heyward Shepherd, a free Negro who refused to be a party to John Brown's Raid, and, in fact, fell defending the property of his employer. He was the first victim in the Brown insurrection.

A dramatic and unexpected incident shocked the audience. Pearl Tatten, a Negro music teacher, who directed the singing of the Stover College Choristers, rose and announced: "I am the daughter of a Union soldier, and not of the black mammy type, but a modern Negro. . . . John Brown was the champion of my race and fought and died for our freedom."

This unpleasant injection was followed by a strained silence. Then the chorus began to sing "Standing in the Need of Prayer." The unhappy statement made the atmosphere congenial for the masterly array of facts from Dr. Matthew Page Andrews, whose address followed and recalled the actual happenings of John Brown's Raid and presented a sound interpretation of Brown's lawless outrage.

Several years later, in 1934, my functions as Historian-General included work with this valued friend of U.D.C., Dr. Andrews, again a propos of John Brown. We sought to stop a congressional appropriation to name a national park in honor of the infamous fanatic. Alerted by Dr. Andrews, our President-General enlisted me in the effort to influence congressmen to deny this measure. The House had already appropriated money for this purpose.

We sent out a dozen or more letters to picked men in Congress, and learned in the course of our correspondence that this measure was slipped through the House of Representatives without the knowledge of Southern members. We received assurance from our friends in Congress that such a bill would never become law, and that the matter would be handled in sympathy with U.D.C. This duty of my office impressed me anew with the fact that eternal vigilance is the price of success in such work as ours.

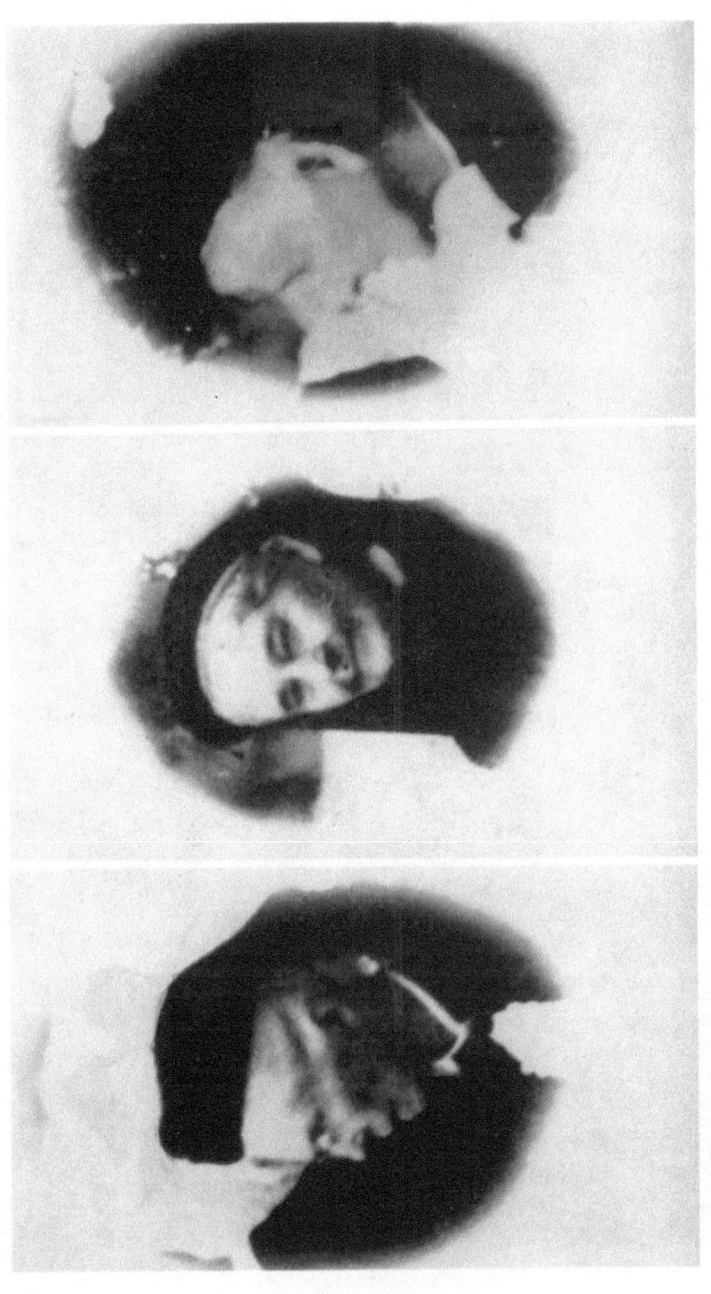

MRS. C. HELEN PLANE MRS. JOHN B. GORDON MRS. JAMES H. BLOUNT

JUDITH GAMBRELL WILEY

A DAUGHTER OF THE CONFEDERACY

U.D.C. was a young organization (just fifteen years old) when it first espoused the cause of Major Henry Wirz, Confederate commander of the prison for Union captives at Andersonville, Georgia. Georgia U.D.C. in 1907 resolved to erect a monument to him at Andersonville, declaring the truth about his imprisonment and execution. The monument was erected in 1909 at Andersonville with a ceremony which was attended by Major Wirz's daughter, Mrs. J. S. Perrin, of Mississippi. I furnished inscriptions for all four sides, recounting for the world the truth of the Wirz story and his martyrdom.

I feel it to be a singular fact that I, who hate a brawl and love peaceful consideration of all questions, should have become involved in so many matters where differences of opinion were intense, where I was vehemently opposed while actively engaged in combatting or espousing a cause.

One of these embattled causes was the award of U.D.C. Crosses to women of our Armed Forces who were lineal descendants of Confederate soldiers. I launched this movement in the late twenties, not long after U.D.C. bestowed its first Crosses on male descendants at the Washington convention in 1923. My determination to reward heroic women of Confederate lineage was inspired by the valor and devotion of my dear friend and kinswoman, Judith Gambrell Wiley.

Judith Wiley's entire life, in war and in peace, has been given in service to others, to friends and family between wars and to fighting men in wartime. The selfless, spirited, and cheerful ministrations she has given to family and friends are not part of her qualifications for U.D.C. award, but my intimate knowledge of her character and spirit certainly spurred my efforts toward recognition of her war work, and that of other women deserving the honor.

Mrs. Wiley's father, Dr. J. B. Gambrell, served as President of Mercer University for four years beginning in 1893. His influence among Southern Baptists was such that he was called the Pope of the Baptist Church. From Macon the Gambrells moved to Atlanta, where Judith was married to my cousin, Sidney Wiley.

Intensely grieved by her young husband's death in 1902, five years after their marriage, Judith entered Johns Hopkins Hospital in Baltimore in 1906, as a student nurse. After several years' training she went to Dallas, the original home of the Gambrells, where she was soon made superintendent of Baylor Hospital.

Later, Judith cut short this promising career to return to Macon at the behest of her father-in-law, Colonel Wiley, to nurse his daughter, Mamie, who died of cancer after a long illness. The next years Judith spent keeping house for and nursing Colonel Wiley himself until his death in 1927.

At the outbreak of World War I, Judith volunteered her services as a nurse, and went to Camp Wheeler at Macon to brave the frightful epidemic of influenza, pneumonia, and meningitis which were claiming soldiers by the hundreds. It never occurred to her to consider her own safety in those deadly days, and she was unmoved by the pleas of friends that she spare herself the dangers of the plague-ridden camp.

Judith applied for overseas service as a Red Cross nurse in 1917, and in January of 1918 she left New York aboard a French troopship to serve at U. S. Army Hospital Number 3 in Paris. After a short while in service she was put in charge of repatriated children in France.

For 17 months Judith lived, worked, and fought like a soldier. She bore the exhaustion, the hardship and fears and risks of war as surely as did infantrymen, though her fight was to save French and American lives rather than to destroy enemy soldiers.

She saw duty with a Paris hospital for base, and was subjected to German bombardment from the air. She frequently left Paris with teams of doctors and nurses for temporary evacuation hospitals at the front, to tend the wounded from nearby trenches under fire. Later she served as head nurse at U. S.

A DAUGHTER OF THE CONFEDERACY

Hospital Number 12 at Paris. Such daughters of Confederate heroes should be entitled to our Military Cross, I was convinced.

I thought awarding crosses to heroic women descendants was a matter of simple justice, and had no expectation of such intense opposition as met me. Objectors seemed to feel that opening the honor to women would result in its being cheapened and held lightly. Leaders of the opposition reasoned that if U.D.C. changed its rule to admit women inducted into the Army and Navy as nurses, every Southern woman who rolled a bandage or looked pretty in a Red Cross veil (or thought she did) would claim the right to our decoration.

I had ascertained, however, that the Cross would be rarely awarded to women, and was convinced that those who gave and dared so much proved themselves true heirs of the Confederate tradition for sacrifice and courage, and must be rewarded as surely as men. In 1931 I brought to bear the formidable opinion of three incontrovertible authorities, and my opponents laid down their arms in the face of my strongest arguments. I presented letters from General John J. Pershing, Judge Advocate General Blanton Winship of the Army, and Major Julia C. Simpson, superintendent of Army Nursing Corps, testifying that women in our armed forces in wartime deserve such recognition, being as much an integral part of the Army as men.

Finally the Daughters voted to amend the rules so as to include women in the award of our coveted Cross.

At the General Convention in Memphis in 1932, I was happy to bestow the first U.D.C. Cross of Service upon a lineal female descendant of a Confederate soldier. Judith Gambrell Wiley, graceful and erect in her nurse's uniform, received the Military Cross on her own valiant record and that of her father, James Bruton Gambrell, C.S.A.

I assumed with much pleasure my office of Historian-General of U.D.C. at my election in 1934. I knew that the office carried many arduous duties and close attention to detail and accuracy, and that it would not be an easy one. However, in importance, it is the second highest post in U.D.C. combining in its work all four cardinal points stressed in the U.D.C. charter—Memorial, Educational, Social, and Historical. And, while the work is heavy, it is a most gratifying channel for furthering the cause of truth in Southern history.

I doubt if any Historian-General ever brought to the office greater love for her duties and stronger desire to establish historical truth. My interest in this work was so whole-hearted that during my entire tenure of three years I felt compelled to pass up many of the social privileges and enjoyments attendant upon the office, to dispatch thoroughly and properly the work of research and promotions. While this decision caused me occasional disappointment, I felt rewarded for my assiduous attention to my duties.

I began my service as Historian-General with emphasis on Jefferson Davis, believing this to be one character whose study would convey to the uninformed the reason for, the spirit of, and the ends to which the Confederate government was established.

So, the program theme for United Daughters of the Confederacy for three years was the study of Davis, with some variations and emphasis on Sidney Lanier, to further our promotion of the Southern poet for the Hall of Fame, and other Confederate writers whose works might enrich chapter programs.

My 1935 program was built around a "Southern Cavalcade" theme, in which I marshalled, month by month, a program study of each sovereign state in order of her secession. This was a framework for the Davis study, as each state was shown to have some connection with the Confederate President—scenes of his birth, schooling, young manhood, his work and goings and comings in the years of the sixties. Reference books were rare for such information; so I was often obliged to search my own rare volumes and send out information and studies to the different divisions for distribution.

The "Cavalcade" continued into 1937, with emphasis on

"Things of the Spirit in the Army of the Confederacy," with much attention to Davis, Lee, Jackson, and other military leaders who made religious contributions to the Confederacy. I used war poems, many Lanier extracts, and Southern pictures from the movie "Gone With the Wind" to add interest to the studies. I drew largely on "Christ in the Camp," a rare and valuable volume on Confederate Army religious life which I found in an old bookshop in San Antonio.

Program planning is a major duty of the office, but response to requests for information seemed an even heavier chore. I was busy for the three years answering questions about the Confederacy and the work of the Daughters, most of such queries coming of course from chapters and divisions. Questions ranged from flag history and etiquette to Jefferson Davis's status as a citizen after the war.

In my second term as Historian-General I launched the work for the re-publication of Davis's *The Rise and Fall of the Confederate Government*. This reprint was financed by interest on the U.D.C. Jefferson Davis Historical Foundation, a fund of $30,000 gotten together by the Daughters under the direction of Mrs. John F. Weinman of Arkansas for historical purposes and approved by U.D.C. in convention assembled.

Re-publication of the two-volume edition of *The Rise and Fall of the Confederate Government,* a memorial edition, was the great U.D.C. achievement of the year 1939. I was especially happy to see the work published during my presidency, since I had launched it when I was Historian-General. It has proved to be one of the most valuable assets of the organization.

Daughters of the Confederacy have taken up arms in several states at different times against school histories which misrepresent the Confederacy. We believe it of basic importance for our Southern children, particularly, to learn from unbiased textbooks their country's history and the struggle of their own section for its rights.

WHEN ALL IS SAID AND DONE

In 1936 I appeared before the Georgia Textbook Commission as Historian-General of U.D.C. and as a citizen interested in the education and welfare of Georgia children to state the objections of my organization to Muzzey's *History of the United States*. I was received most courteously and sympathetically at the hearing, but I learned to my regret that the objectionable history had been already selected and printed on the book list. However, we U.D.C. do not count such seeming setbacks as failures, for we know that any articulation of our viewpoints, even though it may not prevail immediately, is a voice heard for truth and its effect is felt and will bear fruit.

A thrilling experience of my tenure of office as Historian-General was a trip with Mr. Lamar to Petersburg, where I attended officially the re-enactment of the Battle of the Crater. In April of 1936 with other U.D.C. officers we saw Virginia Military Institute boys as Confederates fighting Marine troops as Union forces. Dr. Douglas S. Freeman, as narrator, clarified the battle movements for the spectators. The occasion, frighteningly realistic, made a lasting impression on all who heard the perfect diction and magnetic voice recounting the battle as it was re-enacted.

In 1937, as Historian-General, I addressed the Convention of Georgia Daughters in Macon, recounting the achievements of my office in memorializing Jefferson Davis and setting forth a program of further study and interpretation of the great leader.

Thinking of the integrity, sacrifice, and devotion of Davis, who served the Union in two wars and served as a Senator and as Secretary of War, I contrasted his early record with that of Lincoln. The two men were born in the same state in similarly humble circumstances, grew up resembling each other physically, both achieving fame and knowing tragedy as leaders of opposing sections of the country in the War Between the States. Historians have often compared and contrasted their careers,

A DAUGHTER OF THE CONFEDERACY

and both the parallel and the great divergence in their lives struck me, lending force and feeling to the concluding words of my speech in praise of Davis.

"Let the world know," I ended my peroration, "of the wisdom, the kindness, and the justice of the great and only President of the Confederate States of America—Abraham Lincoln!"

I sat down and noted a curious silence, then a sound like a collective gasp. I wondered what was wrong. Suddenly, realizing what I had said, I rose smiling and remarked, "It was just one of those slips." I laughed, and laughter broke and rose in the convention hall. We enjoyed the *faux pas* and thought the matter closed.

I added the further explanation that the contrast between the two men, so clear in my mind, must have prompted the slip of the tongue. The mirth subsided, and we went on to our convention business.

However, the incident was good for more laughs, much conjecture, and extended talk far beyond Macon, Georgia, and the confines of the old Confederacy. Next day my slip hit the front pages of papers, North, South, East, and West, and was in the next issue of *Time Magazine*. With my picture, under the caption "Slip of the Tongue," *Time* said:

> If a Daughter of the American Revolution should end a Fourth of July oration in a burst of praise for George III her audience would be justifiably startled. Last week in Macon, Ga., Mrs. Walter D. Lamar startled a convention of the Georgia Division of United Daughters of the Confederacy with an indiscretion no less dramatic. Climaxing a rhetorical eulogy of famed Rebel Jefferson Davis, Mrs. Lamar said: "Let the world know of the wisdom, the kindness, and the justice of the great and only President of the Confederacy—Abraham Lincoln."
>
> The Daughters of the Confederacy gasped. Said Mrs. Lamar: "It was just one of those slips."

The Georgia Daughters laughed over the slip and the national publicity. Many friends and U.D.C. colleagues wrote me teasingly. The most interesting letter I received was from Margaret Mitchell in Atlanta. She made the interesting observation that some thirty years of work had failed to do what a simple slip of the tongue had achieved: i.e., bringing to national attention the name and attributes of Jefferson Davis.

So, we forgot at last the amusing and resounding incident, but it came up again, for international notice. I had never expected to be the object of observation by disciples of Freud; but the Davis-Lincoln *faux pas* landed me squarely in the middle of a treatise on psychological significance of slips of the tongue, written by the great master himself and incorporated in the collection, *Basic Writings of Sigmund Freud.*

I was astonished to find that the father of psychoanalysis, in the devious way of the Freudians, had attributed my slip to a subconscious belief in the superiority and rightness of Lincoln! This learned nonsense I have found as amusing as the celebrated incident itself. I still defy the psychiatrists to find in the depths of my subconscious any hidden or repressed conviction that Lincoln was the superior of Davis in any particular.

At any rate, the incident, regaling my friends and the newspaper readers for some time, did indeed serve to turn the public eye to a new appraisal of the long-neglected and maligned Davis. And my mistake thus reached a happy ending. My good husband commented: "My dear, I have willingly accepted Lee and Davis, Jackson and Lanier, as your affinities, but I cannot take on Abraham Lincoln!"

In the fall of 1937, for their General Convention hundreds of Daughters from all parts of the country went to Richmond, the city so redolent of the ideals we would perpetuate, a Confederate shrine which wears its Southern monuments and manners with the pride and charm of a great lady. The Richmond convention was thus a happy prospect for all, and particularly important for me, for I was elected President-General with no opposition. In fact, Daughters from many other states had already signified a desire to see me President-General before convention time, and my election was a foregone conclusion.

At this convention Dr. Douglas S. Freeman conveyed to us a message from General DeWitt of the Army War College, requesting U.D.C. to present the College with a portrait of Robert E. Lee in Confederate uniform. We were happy to have this opportunity to honor Lee.

There were presented at this convention the famed U.D.C. Crosses of Military Service to latter-day soldiers descended from Confederates, notably on this occasion to First Lieutenant Carter Glass, Jr., U.S.A., Retired. Lieutenant Glass's venerable father, the distinguished Virginia Senator, was present and participated in the presentation.

Historical prizes for essay winners and other awards by which we largely measure our work in telling the true story of the Confederacy were also made.

I spoke briefly on "Their Heritage," a tribute to soldiers of World War I who fought with the ideals handed down to Southerners from the days of Thomas Jefferson and on through the Confederacy, marshalling these beliefs as a present-day bulwark against threats of Fascism. I recalled also the soldiers of the Spanish-American War and the Philippine Insurrection who inherited from Revolutionary and Confederate forebears courage of conviction and loyalty to the principles of America.

After I was installed as President-General I announced as a cardinal phase of my administration plans to further honor Jefferson Davis. The Daughters were already committed to, and working for, a monument to the Confederate President to be located at Montgomery and also a memorial edition of his *Rise and Fall of the Confederate Government.*

During the wholly harmonious convention, a harsh note intruded from without, which, while it shocked and aroused us, rendered us more united than before.

It was during our convention week that Gertrude Stein's *Everybody's Autobiography* was published, with considerable publicity, especially in Richmond. The Richmonders were intrigued and offended by some of her comments on their city —at least by those portions from which they could wrest any gleam of sense. It was apparent, even in the turgid obscurity of Miss Stein's strange style, that she didn't think well of the present-day aspect of the capital of the Confederacy.

What was more stunning and shocking to the Daughters was her extraordinary and unprecedented opinion of Robert E. Lee. We read in the local papers these curious and meandering excerpts from her book:

". . . And there I was in Richmond and I had always thought about General Lee and I did think about that, and I had always thought not thought but felt that Lee was a man who knew that the South could not win of course he knew that things how could, a man who was destined by General Scott to succeed him in command of the American armies who knew all that how could he not know that the South could not win and he did know it of that I am completely certain, he did know it but and that is why I think him a weak man he did not have the courage to say it, if he had had that courage well perhaps there would have been not just then and so not likely later that Civil War but if there had not been would America have been as interesting. Very likely not very likely not."

On went the confusing prose to tell the story of the Charlestonian who quoted his father-in-law as saying Lee was "a great man a great man and we all love him" but that he would not want Lee visiting all day of a rainy Sunday.

So, Miss Stein, the expatriate writer of books even her publisher did not pretend to understand, damned Robert E. Lee as a coward—and a bore.

Defense of Lee was scarcely necessary in view of his loyalty to his state, his self-immolation at secession, his valor and genius at war, and his superbly Christian spirit of forgiveness and patriotism after the war—attitude and achievements which have made him the idol of the South, the ideal of all Ameri-

A DAUGHTER OF THE CONFEDERACY

cans, and an inspiring figure to literate people all over the world. When I was approached by reporters for comment, I simply said: "Gertrude Stein is woefully ignorant of anything about General Lee or the history of the Confederacy."

Our convention time was also the time of the annual fall meeting of the Stratford directors, who had invited the Daughters to motor from Richmond for a tour of the estate and a reception. So the convention activities ended with our pilgrimage to the tradition-hallowed birthplace of Robert E. Lee.

In January, 1938, I was invited to Savannah for an official visit to the Savannah Chapter of U.D.C. There was an evening historical program where I spoke on Lee and Jackson and was honored at a reception following the meeting. State officers and past Division Presidents also came to Savannah for my first official visit, and the dignitaries, the entertainments, the meetings with old Savannah friends and co-workers added to my pleasure in the visit.

On April 26 I made the Memorial Day address in Augusta. In my speech I called for leaders of the caliber of men who had led the South during the war. I pointed out the strength in the faith of Confederate fathers, and hoped for a revival of this faith to cope with current problems.

In response to the request of General DeWitt at the 1937 convention, the presentation and unveiling of the Lee portrait at the War College took place in May, 1938. We were not only happy to place Lee in the War College, but also gratified to realize that our efforts to interpret Lee and, through him, the Southern Cause had resulted indirectly in this sign of high esteem and appreciation from a Federal agency. Lee had indeed come into his own.

The Lee portrait, on an easel and draped with a Confederate flag, stood on a platform in the War College auditorium beside an American flag. Dr. Bolling Lee, General DeWitt, and I were seated near the Secretary of War, Harry Woodring. General Marlin Craig, Chief of Staff of the Army, was among the guests.

I expressed our appreciation for the opportunity to present the portrait and declared that such ceremonies serve the nation in "putting before the youth of today the highest type of American citizenship, the kind needed to solve the world's problems."

After the presentation, the young Lee descendants, Mary Lee and Hanson Ely, grandchildren of General Lee, unveiled the picture. General DeWitt accepted the gift for the nation and expressed thanks to U.D.C. He traced the military career of Lee, emphasized his American patriotism before and after the war, and gave us a soldier's view of Lee as a military genius.

After farewells, we emerged happily from an atmosphere of gracious hospitality and went sightseeing about the grounds of the War College.

Suddenly, we were on the grounds of the arsenal prison, transported in imagination back to July, 1865, when a spectral picture rose to view and intruded vividly and horribly on our happy mood. There on that smooth greensward of what is today the War College appear four gaunt gallows, gibbets from which once dangled the bodies of three men and one woman.

The men hanged there testified to the innocence of the woman, and asserted her ignorance of the plot to assassinate President Lincoln. Priests sought a change of sentence, and her own testimony and that of her attorneys as to her innocence were incontrovertible. But all to no avail. Mary Eugenia Surratt suffered death by hanging.

Her wraith—so vivid to me on that happy sunlit day on the scene of her shameful death—cries out forever to deaf ears: "Why did President Johnson sign an unread petition? Why did Secretary Stanton vent his spleen upon my innocent head?"

This stain upon our nation's escutcheon can never be effaced. I never felt it so bitterly, nor with such protest, as on the day we had our happy ceremony at the War College and I stood upon the scene of this frightful injustice to an innocent woman.

An early duty of my 1938 tenure was a summer trip to

A DAUGHTER OF THE CONFEDERACY

Washington to lay a wreath, an annual tribute, before the bronze statue of Jefferson Davis in Statuary Hall of the National Capitol on the birthday of the President of the Confederacy, June 3rd. The District Children of the Confederacy and the Major Charles M. Stedman Chapter, U.D.C., of Washington arranged the anniversary wreath-laying. Senator Walter F. George, Georgia's senior senator and a sympathetic aide to U.D.C. projects, spoke at Statuary Hall, which had been reserved for this occasion, the general public being excluded.

From Washington I went to Baltimore and addressed the Baltimore Daughters on "Jefferson Davis, the Constitutionalist," an aspect of his career and political genius to which I have devoted much study, and which phase of Davis's life, when properly considered, clears him and the entire South of any charge of "rebellion," "treason," or action against our country.

I emphasized that the North, imposing its idea upon the South, violated the Constitution and Bill of Rights, a solemn covenant under which the states banded together, with clear assurance that rights not expressly delegated to the Federal government remain with the states. I developed the idea that if there was "rebellion" in the sixties, it was on the part of the Northern states which rebelled against this agreement and took up arms, actually, against the Constitution to prevent the Southern states from withdrawing from the Union to preserve their state sovereignty. In support of this I quoted the son of Harriett Beecher Stowe who so believed and so expressed himself.

Late in 1938 I learned that the original copy of the Constitution of the Confederate States was for sale. The Constitution had been purchased in July of 1883 by Mrs. G. W. J. DeRenne, grandmother of Wymberly DeRenne and mother of W. J. DeRenne, founder of the famous DeRenne Library at Wormsloe in Savannah. This was the permanent Constitution of the

Confederate States of America, not to be confused with the Provisional Constitution in custody of the Confederate Memorial Society at Richmond. As President-General of U.D.C. and also as a Georgian, I was concerned lest the hallowed document leave the state, or depart the South altogether. Other officers of U.D.C. shared my interest and concern.

The University of Georgia in 1938 purchased the DeRenne Library and also secured an option on the Confederate Constitution. The University was already acting as custodian of an incomplete original draft of the Provisional Constitution; therefore, we expected that the Regents would be most anxious to add the original permanent Constitution to the valuable collection.

However, we communicated with Mr. Marion Smith, Chairman of the Board of Regents, hoping that when the University's option expired the U.D.C. would have a chance to purchase the document and that the cost would not be prohibitive. At the 1938 Tulsa Convention I was empowered to negotiate with owners of the DeRenne papers for a U.D.C. option, and later conferred at Athens with Mr. Wymberly DeRenne, visited Mr. Marion Smith in Atlanta, and discussed the option chances for U.D.C. with Dr. S. V. Sanford, Chancellor of the University System of Georgia.

In August of 1939 I heard from L. R. Siebert, secretary of the Regents, that the Board had authorized "the purchase of the permanent Constitution of the Confederate States."

So the matter ended with my letter to Mr. Smith: "As a Georgian, I am happy to hear that the Constitution of the Confederate States will remain in Georgia at the University. But, as President-General of the Daughters of the Confederacy, I regret that our organization did not have the privilege of saving the venerable and revered document for the South."

In 1937 I undertook to strengthen the prestige and significance of the U.D.C. Cross of Honor, coveted award for present-

A DAUGHTER OF THE CONFEDERACY

day military men who are direct descendants of loyal Confederate soldiers. I used the weight of my office as President-General and what personal influence I could bring to bear on a latter-day tendency to hold the Cross lightly, and to tighten up regulations governing the awards to keep them from any but absolutely qualified applicants.

As I reported to the 1938 convention of Daughters at Tulsa, it was an unpleasant but necessary duty in the course of the year to deny a number of applicants. I was obliged in some cases to refuse registration papers, where the record of the ancestor proved that he was a deserter from the Confederate Army and took the oath of Allegiance to the United States Government before surrender.

I was asked, "Who would not take the oath to the United States Government in order to get out of a Federal prison?"

Despite my natural sympathy with the sufferings of those prisoners and the hardships which impelled them to take the oath for relief from their incarceration, I emphasized that the Daughters originally devised the Cross to honor men who endured all that war and imprisonment had to offer, and remained faithful to that end, whatever their suffering. The Registrar and Recorder, too, sympathized as I did, and honored the loyalty of these men while it lasted, and regretted that they were disqualified by later conduct, so that their descendants could not be given the award. We were forced to remind the applicants of other Confederates who had suffered, rotted, and died in Northern prisons rather than sell their loyalty and conviction for freedom from imprisonment.

I stressed anew at the 1937 convention the dignity and significance of the Cross of Honor and called on every Daughter to guard it.

At Annapolis the previous June, a Daughter came to greet me, wearing like a piece of costume jewelry a Cross of Honor.

"I suppose," she said, "I ought not to have this on."

I stated my objections to such misuse of the Cross—that it

WHEN ALL IS SAID AND DONE

was for war heroes of today descended from Confederate heroes of the past—and indicated most clearly my disapprobation.

One Daughter took me to task for my attitude and insisted that U.D.C. should change its rules governing bestowal and use of the Cross. To this I replied, "I cannot change my views. These rigid rules indicate the reverence with which the Cross is protected for its true mission, the reward of valor earned by a Confederate soldier and emulated by his descendants in service."

There were many social and memorial occasions during my 1938 Presidency which refreshed me after the rigors of desk work and administration. Among the most memorable, colorful, and stirring of these was the presentation of U.D.C. annual awards to distinguished graduates of the United States Military Academy at West Point and the Naval Academy at Annapolis.

Late in May I started from Macon for Baltimore to meet a group of Maryland U.D.C. officers who would attend the June Week presentation of U.D.C. binoculars to the outstanding math student in the graduating class at the Naval Academy. At Annapolis I was assigned an officer who escorted me to the parade ground to a place on the front row of the reviewing stand.

Looking directly ahead across the carpet of green turf that stretched to the water's edge, one thrilled to the beauty in the softly rippling waters of the River Severn, glimpsed through the tall poplars growing along its bank. The scene was enlivened by the flitting of white sails up and down the stream in the bright June sunshine.

Soon there marched across the field the army of Naval cadets in full dress uniform, white-topped caps and swords gleaming in the light. After a perfect drill, and music by the Navy band, the outstanding members of the class were ranged in front of the stand. The significance of this moment of award was emphasized by a table containing all the prizes to be presented to the cadets standing before us. There I presented to Joseph Paul Arezzo the Matthew Fontaine Maury Memorial Award of U.D.C.—the traditional binoculars and accompanying citation handsomely gotten up and stamped with the U.D.C. insigne.

In 1935 U.D.C. had been annoyed by a protest from the 31st Ohio Regimental Association, whose members objected to the Daughters' award of the Lee sword each year to an outstanding West Point graduate. The information came to my attention from the president of the New York Division, Mrs. H. W. Rayner.

The secretary of the protesting Association had sought to prevent the presentation of the Lee sword, terming it "The Sword of Treason." It was the old story of die-hard opponents of the Confederacy seeking to slander its leaders forever as rebels and traitors.

West Point commandants had been troubled previously by such incendiary appeals against this presentation. But our award became the best evidence of a fine record at West Point which a boy can receive. The young man who wins it should always be supplied reasons why he should prize it above all else. To this end, it was recommended at the 1936 convention that the Historian-General be empowered to formulate a statement of the purpose and spirit of the award and this statement was to be given the winner with congratulations upon the honor he had earned.

The recommendation was adopted, and the 1937 winners at West Point and Annapolis received this statement and congratulations, explaining the memorial intent and the patriotic spirit of the award.

At the Military Academy we were allowed to "preview" the U.D.C. sword, which was sent directly to the Academy by the jeweler. We were thrilled at the splendor of this Robert E. Lee memorial, bearing the name of the winner, John Robert Jannerone, and the insignia of the United States and the Confederacy.

WHEN ALL IS SAID AND DONE

I am happy to have had the privilege of making these awards, particularly that of the fine Lee sword. Shortly thereafter, in deference to the practicality of the times and symbolic of changes in warfare, U.D.C. discontinued its award of a sword and gave instead a typewriter to the West Point graduate winning our award. Something of romance and grace was lost in the change, and something of honor and courage in war as symbolized by the sword, but the Daughters felt that their award would carry more weight if it were practical rather than symbolic. Later the award took the form of a $100 check from U.D.C.

In April of 1939 I was invited to Athens, Georgia, to make the Confederate Memorial Day address. I spoke for "a more Southern South."

I have long felt that the strength and charm of the South and its hope for the future lie in its conservation, its cherished attachment to traditions of our forebears, and its predominant Anglo-Saxon racial integrity. I have applauded industrial progress and business growth to a large extent, but I have also deplored alien innovations which our more radical and prosperity-bent progressives would inflict on us in the name of plenty and industrial development. Our forefathers achieved the finest flower of civilization, grace, morality, and integrity under an agrarian system, and I have always felt that this traditional Southern way of life is the soundest, most certain way to our well-being. I expressed this in the Athens address on April 26. I appealed for "a Southern South as old-fashioned as you please."

Newspapers generally, exhorting the communities to bring new industry to the South, disagreed with me editorially. But I found eager support from friends and strangers who wrote me from all parts of the country.

Another stirring duty of my office as President-General was participation in the Centennial Celebration of Virginia Military Institute. V.M.I. was 100 years old in 1939. It celebrated its Centennial with various programs throughout the year. On

A DAUGHTER OF THE CONFEDERACY

the anniversary of the Battle of New Market, May 15, 1939, I attended the ceremonies to pay tribute to the V.M.I. boys who were heroes of that great engagement. I spoke on Maury, the Southern Pathfinder of the Seas, and Jackson, one of our greatest generals, both V.M.I. alumni; and I thrilled with pride at the array of young cadets who marched out to honor those who had died on the field of battle.

My chief impression of my regime is that of long hours of desk work, letter-writing, arbitration, instructions, and a most assiduous routine of administration required by the office. Looking back, however, I can see that there was a great deal more of traveling, speechmaking, and public relations than I realized. I recall a round of appearances after my election, a strenuous program, which was nevertheless pleasant because of its social aspects.

Memorials are the chief business of United Daughters of the Confederacy, expressing as they do in permanent physical form the historical truth and spiritual and political ideals we would perpetuate, and it is a puzzle to me that every such enterprise seems to be accomplished only after a fight.

I cannot, in fact, recall any important memorial erected without contention and ofttimes bitter disagreement. Of course, U.D.C. "fights" over memorials are usually quiet and strictly internal, and of comparatively trivial origin, so that rifts are closed before anyone hears of them outside the organization.

The colossal and all-time example of such controversies was the prolonged dissension over Stone Mountain. Although the difficulties began outside of U.D.C., the organization was gravely divided over them.

Another sizable and newsworthy U.D.C. monument controversy concerned the memorial to Jefferson Davis on the Capitol grounds at Montgomery, where the Confederate President first took his oath of office. This memorial was in the making seven years before my two administrations as President-General. And in 1938, with $20,000 raised, the U.D.C. special commit-

WHEN ALL IS SAID AND DONE

tee prepared to select a sculptor and proceed to the erection of the long-planned statue.

After two years of planning, and attendant controversy, the dedication and unveiling of the monument took place in November of 1940 at the general convention in Montgomery. It was unveiled by Davis's great-grandson, Jefferson Addison Hayes-Davis, and Mrs. Hayes-Davis, dedicated eloquently by Dr. Francis P. Milton Bonner, legal adviser to Governor Dixon, who could not attend. The monument was a worthy one, true to the physical aspect and the spirit of Jefferson Davis, and U.D.C. seemed happy in our achievement.

As another generation of Southern children made its appearance in 1922, the Daughters organized the Children of the Confederacy, with aims memorial, benevolent, historical, educational, and social. The third vice president was named Director General, and groups of girls were organized into chapters over the South, and later in other sections where Southerners lived.

The Macon chapter was formed soon after, and to my gratification, it was named the Dorothy Blount Lamar Chapter. Of course my namesake chapter has increased my interest in work of the Children of the Confederacy here and elsewhere. My feeling about the Children of the Confederacy groups and my hopes for their achievements are expressed in a letter with which I greeted a new chapter in Johnson City, Tennessee, the Sidney Lanier Chapter. I wrote:

My Dear Young Friends,

The news of your organization for U.D.C. activities fills me with joy and impels me to write you this word of greeting and caution. It particularly heartens us who have grown gray in the service when young people affiliate with us, for thus only may our objectives be kept alive.

That we may honor our Confederate forebears, we must know the principles of their faith. We must know that Southern statesmen in declaring for secession made another Declaration of Independence, prompted by loyalty to the Constitution of the United

A DAUGHTER OF THE CONFEDERACY

States, which distinctly reserves to the States the right to regulate their own affairs in all matters not expressly delegated by them to the United States government. When centralization of power at Washington flourishes, the rights of the states are weakened and will soon degenerate into a totalitarian form of government.

Today by the side of every man and woman born to the purple of state sovereignty, there marches invisible a man in gray, and he is saying: "Watch your step, my child; be not led astray from loyalty to the rights of your state for which I fought in that fearful strife between brothers in the Sixties. Let all your aims be for your God and for your State. Thus and thus only may the Union of States be preserved and its power be strengthened without loss of honor to the citizen."

Remember, that the better Daughter of the Confederacy you are, the better Daughter of the Revolution you are, the better citizen of a Republic founded by the wisdom of your fathers. Let this be your guiding star that shall not change, call it what you will. Names are as shifting sands, but truths are eternal.

Never speak of the War of the Sixties as a Civil War, because a civil war is a war within a state. Therefore the correct nomenclature is the War Between the States. . . .

Daughters of the Confederacy for many years were disturbed by the inscription under the bust of General Robert E. Lee in the New York University Hall of Fame. Placed in 1901 by the New York Division, U.D.C., the memorial was inscribed with the words, "Duty is the sublimest word in the English language."

The "duty" quotation has been attributed to Lee since 1864, when it appeared in a "private letter" purporting to have been written by Lee and printed in the *New York Sun*. The letter since has been proved a forgery, but the spurious quotation lives on, and was even graven under the bust given by the New York Daughters.

This spurious quotation has clung persistently to the Lee memory and the Lee literature because it seems characteristic of the Confederate leader's life and beliefs. But the facts are that Lee never wrote this "duty" letter and all indications are that he never said "Duty is the sublimest word in the English language." It was purely in the interest of truth, to correct an absolute falsity, that I renewed the long effort of U.D.C. to have the tablet inscription changed.

I was not the first to appeal to the Hall of Fame for a change. Early advocates of this correction included Edith Pope, editor of the *Confederate Veteran* magazine and a scholarly Daughter of the Confederacy. Miss Pope, in fact, asked me to take the matter up when I was Historian-General, 1935-38. Petitions to change the inscription had been refused, I believe, because Hall of Fame officials and other people concerned felt that the quotation was so true to Lee and had become so much a part of the popular conception of the great General that it represented him as truly as any other quotation which could be authenticated.

In the disputed "private letter," published from a purported copy of an epistle from Lee to his son and dated 1852, the General tells this son, G. W. Custis Lee, that he is leaving for Mexico with his "fine old regiment." The letter is written from "Arlington." It was published as from Lee himself, without the name of the contributor of the document, and was for years accepted as valid.

In 1914 Professor Charles A. Graves of the University of Virginia Law School, after study and research, published a masterly paper which exposed the "duty letter" as a forgery. Professor Graves delivered his findings before the Virginia Bar Association, and with that body's approval published them in pamphlet form. The paper was also published in the *Confederate Veteran* of November, 1915, and in Richmond newspapers.

Professor Graves ascertained that in December of 1864, the *Richmond Sentinel,* a few years after first publication of the "duty" letter, re-printed it with a repudiation of it as a "Yankee forgery." The old Sentinel declared that its repudiation came from "a source entitled to know," which suggested to Professor Graves that Lee himself had initiated or sanctioned this repudiation. The *Sentinel's* anonymous "repudiation letter" points out that the style of this "Duty letter" is not genuine, that Lee never dated any of his letters "Arlington House," and that in April of 1852, he had never belonged to a regiment, and was never in his life in New Mexico. In the spring of 1852, the repudiation letter says, Lee was at Sewell's Point Flats constructing a fort near Baltimore, and was preparing to go to West Point as Superintendent of the Academy. All of which facts in refutation were substantiated by Professor Graves.

This exposure had been known to U.D.C., of course, since the time it was first published. Also, Daughters recalled that at the time they presented the Lee bust to the Hall of Fame they were not accorded their right of selecting the inscription. The Duty quotation was selected by someone else, probably the Hall of Fame officials.

Getting the inscription corrected was a long process, and was not accomplished until 1947. Hall of Fame officials, notably Dr. Finley, were cooperative, but leisurely, in negotiations. Naturally, Dr. Finley was anxious to see every scrap of evidence disproving the validity of the quotation, and assembling the proof for him took time.

I was also obliged to dig up records showing that the Daughters of the Confederacy had not selected, or approved, the inscription in the first place. Dr. Finley was under the impression that they had done so, since this was our prerogative. Such a circumstance, if true, would have lessened our chances of achieving the change.

After the officials had agreed to change the quotation, at U.D.C. expense, it was not a simple matter to select a new inscription. At last we agreed upon these words of Lee in reference to duty, taken from Lee's letter to Lord Acton: "There is the true glory and the true honor, the glory of duty done—the honor of integrity and principle."

But the Duty quotation still lingers on in the public mind, along with a persistent army of myths which the Daughters vigilantly attack. On January 19, 1950, Lee's birthday, commentator Edward Murrow paid a fine tribute to the Confederate hero and quoted him as saying, "Duty is the sublimest word in the English language"!

In October of 1939 Winston Churchill, First Lord of the British Admiralty, delivered himself of an eloquent and rallying address to hearten his country and France, then standing alone against the German conquerors who had half of Europe and were at war with England and France.

In the course of his speech, Churchill cheered his countrymen with the observation that: "Britain may take good heart from the American Civil War when all the heroism of the South could not redeem their cause from the stain of slavery, just as all the courage and skill, which the Germans show in War, will not free them from the reproach of Naziism with its intolerance and brutality."

The Churchill call rang, as usual, round the world, inspiring the Allies and thrilling the watching nations. But his observation about "the stain of slavery" in the South as comparable to Nazi "intolerance and brutality" fell with a raucous clank on Southern ears.

In Macon, I was preparing for a trip to Charleston to preside over the U.D.C. General Convention. So I inserted in my report a brisk protest against Mr. Churchill's comparison, to this effect:

"The gratuitous insult to the best part of America shows both ignorance and stupidity, ignorance of historical facts and stupidity in that it antagonizes a large part of the country he would least desire to anger, by comparing the Southern States with Hitler and his policies."

There was quite a clangor as my retort to Churchill hit the headlines across the land and overseas. I myself was almost inundated in a flood of eager and approving letters from Southerners at home and in the North.

Among the writers to Churchill were a Texas newspaper

editor, some Virginians of longtime Southern ancestry, some Alabama women, some Southern ladies transplanted to Northern cities, and Southern scions scattered over the country, protesting the stigma he attached to the Southern Cause. Each protestant sent me a copy of his letter to London, with a long outpouring of his own to commend me and interpret his view of the cause of the War Between the States. And many who didn't write to London simply addressed me, or the editor of their local papers.

Not all the angry expressions were pro-U.D.C. and anti-Churchill in this case. I received stern castigation from an occasional Northerner or Westerner, or a Southerner removed from home and its traditional sympathies, some angry at my terming the South "the best part of the country." In this correspondence were many viewpoints and angles for dissertation, including even a strong thread of anti-Semitism which found its way into the debate.

All in all, it was a most diverse and revealing correspondence, which produced a by-product of minor hysterical outbursts showing the distressed temper of the days.

Dr. Matthew P. Andrews, good friend of the U.D.C., wrote at my behest to Mr. Roger Macarness of the *English-Speaking World,* saying in part: "Mr. Churchill's analogy is very unfortunate and it should be brought to his attention so that the blunder will not be repeated by any officials of the British government. To illustrate, General Lee owned no slaves while General Grant did at the time of the American Civil War; and the 'Emancipation Proclamation' was a war measure issued for the same reason that Lord Dunmore in 1775-76 issued one at the time of the secession of the 13 American colonies from the British Empire. . . . President Lincoln's proclamation didn't free any slaves within the Union lines. They were specifically protected from its provisions, and the South could have come back in the Union with slavery intact . . . the vicious comparison of Mr. Churchill . . . is a serious reflection upon the people in one-fourth of the States in the Union and it will be resented as such."

Dr. Andrews had gratifying response from London, before the U.D.C. convention. He wrote confidentially to me that an "Englishman in a more or less official position" had replied to him: "Mr. Churchill, although probably the best orator in this country, and as such, of tremendous value today, has never been renowned for his historical accuracy in his speeches, and it is truly unfortunate that such a lapse should have occurred at this particular moment."

In another letter to me Dr. Andrews quoted from a British correspondent who had received a letter from Winston Churchill himself. The correspondent's remarks were as follows:

"Mr. Churchill felt pained and surprised at the interpretation which had been put upon the closing passage of his broadcast, as he assures me nothing was further from his mind than to suggest that there was any analogy between the cause and character of the struggle between the Confederate States and that of Nazi Germany in the present war. On re-reading his broadcast afterwards, Mr. Churchill sees that the words might easily bear this construction, but came to the conclusion that the least said the soonest mended.

"Mr. Churchill goes on to say that he has long been an admirer of General Lee and Stonewall Jackson, and that in the history which will shortly be published there will be found the account of the constitutional causes which led the South to take up arms, and conceived in a strain which he believes will be read with pleasure throughout the South."

Dr. Andrews, conveying to me this gratifying and gracious, if quiet, back-track, wrote that "I am making it clear to my British correspondent that I didn't expect Mr. Churchill to make any public retraction or apology. He couldn't very well do it. The sooner that part of the broadcast is forgotten, the better—my idea being to prevent the repetition of the statement by others."

A DAUGHTER OF THE CONFEDERACY

Dr. Andrews recalled that World War I found him correcting a similar blunder on the part of American writers. He was one of the "Vigilantes," 150 writers who volunteered to make the war issues clear to the country. Vigilante Booth Tarkington at that time wrote a pamphlet embodying "some such comparison" as Churchill's, Dr. Andrews remembered, and it was widely distributed among Americans, Englishmen, and Frenchmen. Dr. Andrews, however, enlightened and "called down" Tarkington, he said, and "headed off" further issues of the false propaganda brochure. He wondered in 1939 if Churchill had come by the Tarkington piece "thinking it good American material and sound history."

Meantime, the hue and cry set off at the U.D.C. convention bore fruit for all to see.

In London, by November 17, the First Lord of the Admiralty paused in his pursuit of the war on the seas to surrender in the war with the United Daughters of the Confederacy. His secretary issued a statement which was published in London and the United States to end the hostilities. Said he: "Nothing was further from my mind than to suggest that there was any analogy between the cause and character of the struggle maintained by the Confederate States and that of Nazi Germany in the present war."

Again, and most spectacularly, United Daughters of the Confederacy had won a victory in their constant, vigilant defense of the truth of Southern history.

MACON'S REUNION OF CONFEDERATE VETERANS

BY 1911 I HAD ASSUMED A BUSY PLACE IN MACON'S CLUB, civic, and patriotic work, and was well-primed for the tremendous and thrilling job which was assigned to me that year. I was delegated to attend the Reunion of Confederate Veterans at Little Rock, Arkansas, to invite the veterans to meet in Macon in the spring of 1912.

My husband and I were accompanied by a large delegation from Macon and in my invitation address I told the veterans about Macon's beauty, central location, and historic appeal. Our invitation was accepted and the veterans planned to come to our town in 1912.

There immediately began in Macon preparations for the great Reunion in May of 1912. Colonel Walter A. Harris was made general chairman and he appointed me to organize the Women's Auxiliary for the Reunion—leaving me uninstructed and uninhibited!

As chairman, I called in December a mass meeting of all Macon's interested women. U.D.C. members of course attended, but the city hall was largely filled with housewives, church workers, club members, and friends of our plans from all over town. I explained the tremendous work ahead of us—to open our homes to visitors accompanying the veterans, to lodge and feed thousands, to dress up our homes and grounds, and to raise, by canvass and benefits, our share of the cost.

MACON'S REUNION OF CONFEDERATE VETERANS

After Christmas I appointed district chairmen to lead Auxiliary work in every neighborhood of Macon, and spoke at meetings of women gathered in schools, churches, neighborhood halls, and homes. I felt, now, that I had inherited Papa's pleasure and gift for making friends, for I met women by the hundreds in all corners of the town and in all walks of life, and enjoyed each new contact.

I made repeated trips to the suburbs, the far reaches of Vineville, East Macon, South Macon, and downtown neighborhoods, conferring with new friends and committeewomen. And, like my father, who needs must buy wool socks for the whole family from a Twiggs County constituent, I spent uncounted sums for tickets to bazaars, suppers, recitals, and amateur plays. I tasted candy, bought cakes, acquired needlework. The effort and the expense were richly rewarding, however, in the friends I made and the zeal wrought for the Reunion cause.

There were big downtown benefits and enterprises which not only helped fill the Reunion coffers but kept Macon society busy and entertained nearly all winter and spring.

The Sons of Confederate Veterans staged a Queen contest, which aroused great excitement and raised a considerable sum, in the rivalry over which Georgia belle should be chosen Queen of the Reunion and crowned at a great ceremony. The Sons favored Miss Mary Scandrett, while the Daughters cast their influence to Miss Harriotte Winchester, a lovely favorite of young and older socialites.

It was about this time that the Dorothy Blount Lamar Chapter of the Children the Confederacy was organized at the home of Mrs. Duncan Brown, and her daughter, Louise Callaway, became their leader. So the little girls were organized to do their share in welcoming the veterans.

Bazaars, plays, concerts, suppers, and home-made carnivals enlivened the town for weeks. Nearly every night of the week before the Reunion, young and old were in evening dress, dancing, concert-going, or partying for the Cause.

All our benefits were not of local talent. We brought to Macon some distinguished artists, including a Russian symphony and the great diva, Nordica. An amateur opera troupe presented "Pinafore," quite in the professional manner.

I particularly remember Nordica whom I welcomed to Macon by calling on her in her hotel suite. Bearing a big bouquet, I rapped and was admitted by the famed singer herself. She smiled and her eyes traveled from my face to the floor. She pointed at the rug, shrieked, and stepped back. I, too, retreated in alarm.

"Your feet!" she cried.

"What is it?" I begged to know, afraid of a mouse, or even a rat.

"They are so *leetle!*" she cried, her hands spread and her eyes big with amazement.

I laughed, reassured, and explained that "all our feet are like that here in the South." That wonder settled, we sat down for a chat.

These were of course the days when we dressed in skirts so long and voluminous that our feet were not very apparent—when a lady's feet, as Sir John Suckling expressed it, ". . . stole in and out beneath her petticoats like little mice," for we had been taught to sit very carefully and cover very gracefully our feet clad in small satin slippers.

During our season of preparation for the Reunion, Woodrow Wilson, then making a campaign tour of the country as candidate for the Presidency, came to Macon upon the invitation of R. L. McKinney, editor of the *Macon News*. I asked Mr. McKinney to invite the distinguished gentleman, after the campaign speech, to come to the Volunteers' Armory where Macon women were holding a brilliant evening of pagentry, tableaux, and music for the benefit of the Confederate Reunion fund. About nine o'clock Mr. Wilson, duly escorted, arrived, but the crowd was so great at the doorway that Mr. McKinney sent word to me, as chairman, asking that I make a way for the

MACON'S REUNION OF CONFEDERATE VETERANS

visitor to reach the platform. Accordingly, I took the President-to-be by the hand and tandem fashion threaded our way to the stage. Mr. Wilson made a gracious speech suited to the purposes of the gathering and we felt that the occasion was the more dignified and unforgettable by his appearance.

In after years, when I was presented in Washington at a lawn party given in honor of William G. McAdoo and the daughter of President Wilson on the occasion of their marriage, I reminded the President of his visit to Macon with a remark which at first mystified, then amused him: "Mr. President, I am the only person who can truthfully say, I led President Wilson." On recalling his experience in Macon at the 1912 bazaar, he was amused at this recognition of his adamantine firmness.

The Reunion itself was a spirited, gay, and at times profoundly moving assemblage of the surviving heroes of our Confederacy. Various events—some spectacular, others comic, and still others fraught with pathos—stand out in my mind.

I recall the opening session of the encampment at Central City Park, and the sea of tents (furnished, as were the cots for the old soldiers, by the United States War Department). A huge frame platform was erected for speakers welcoming our guests. Long before the days of amplifiers and mikes, speakers had to prove their lung capacity to be heard by the thousands of aging men in gray who stood before them.

Since the whole crowd stood on level ground, I was not visible to many of the veterans when the time came for my welcome speech. So, Colonel Harris and one of his staff helped me to a table top, whence I addressed them. Many veterans came up to greet me after the opening meeting, and one gray-haired soldier complimented me thus: "Honey, I couldn't hear all you said, but you sho is got a pretty shape!" To this day, I am puzzled by the compliment; for that was the time when all ladies wore at least five petticoats—and any lady's shape was purely a matter of conjecture!

WHEN ALL IS SAID AND DONE

Fourteen bands from half a dozen Southern states accompanied sessions and festivities of the Reunion. A feature of the convention was the arrival of a troop of Boy Scouts from Dublin, Georgia, who hiked fifty-five miles to Macon, pitching camp en route, to do honor to the veterans. Macon was bulging with company, ringing with music and oratory, and stirring with parades, parties, and pageantry.

I recall the lavish coronation of Queen Mary Scandrett, high on Coleman's Hill overlooking the panorama of Macon. Townsfolk in festive dress, visitors, and the veterans in gray attended the ceremony where maids of the court from many states attended the queen. It was a real spectacle, described in the *Macon News,* in the hyperbole of that day, as "the apex of earthly human splendor."

Most moving event of the Reunion, and the real heart and spirit of all our work and realization, was the closing parade of veterans through the downtown district. I remember the assemblage at Central City Park, with some veterans on horseback and others afoot, and still others in wheel chairs, nearly all of them men over sixty, and some quite aged. As the parade formed, the band struck up "Dixie," and veterans, horses, and spectators were stirred and excited by the thrilling and nostalgic strains. The veterans broke into the old rebel yell as the parade moved out of the park and into the street toward Macon's downtown district.

The procession moved up town, with carriages and a few early automobiles decked with flowers and Confederate colors to add to the pageantry of the parade. As the procession reached the main streets of Macon, the veterans were hailed by throngs lining the streets, Confederate flags on lamp posts and office buildings, and cheers and band music.

How well—through the festive and affectionate uproar of welcoming crowds—I remember the scarred faces, the empty sleeves, the occasional old warrior on crutches, and the many veterans in carriages or cars, too aged or crippled from sacrifice

GROUP OF CONFEDERATE VETERANS ATTENDING THE REUNION IN MACON

Left to right: Col. R. P. Lake, Memphis, Tenn.; Col. Henry C. Myers, Memphis, Tenn.; Genl. Burnett H. Young, Louisville, Ky.; Col. R. E. Bullington, Memphis, Tenn.; Col. Harrell, New Orleans, La.

EXECUTIVE COMMITTEE, REUNION OF CONFEDERATE VETERANS AT MACON

Top row, left to right: John J. McKay, "Reb" Massenberg, Llewellyn Hillyer, Richard F. Burden. *Second row, left to right:*

to the Lost Cause to walk! And how well I remember the love, pride, and gratitude of the Southerners who lined the streets and cheered the men in gray as they passed, marching, limping, or riding, and responding to the tributes with waves and smiles. Symbolic of their valor were torn and smoked battle flags which led the ranks, the prouder for bullet holes and discolorations suffered in battles of the sixties.

One of the liveliest and most endearing of Macon's last Confederate veterans was Major General A. J. Wommack. He was very tall and slim, with keen gray eyes, thin, reddish hair and an alert and responsive air. He was a fine old fellow, although not always a model of sobriety, and he rejoiced in telling of his conversion to abstinence.

Arriving home once, well in his cups, General Wommack roused his wife, who got out of bed, knelt, and prayed fervently that he might get religion and join the Primitive Baptist Church. Her pleas to Heaven continued for a long while. After many months, General Wommack agreed that if she would cease praying aloud, he would join the church and renounce cards and liquor. But he would not give up his fiddle, although fiddle-playing was considered a great sin by Primitive Baptists.

Finally the church agreed to take him into the fold if he would not play his fiddle on Sunday. "I won't scrape the fiddle on Sunday," he vowed. But, he lamented, "My hands itch so for that damned fiddle that I can't enjoy the Sabbath."

General Wommack had been a fearless soldier, and all his life had a great contempt for a coward or a liar. When the Sidney Lanier Chapter honored a fellow veteran, on what the honoree said was his hundredth birthday, General Wommack was outraged. "It burns me up to have old man Hub git that cake," cried he. "He lied about being a hundred years old. He ain't even as old as I am!"

General Wommack had served the Confederacy as a private under my father, and was endowed with his title of Major General by the local camp of Confederate Veterans.

WHEN ALL IS SAID AND DONE

When this doughty old veteran, a great fiddler, died, many Daughters attended the funeral, which was an impressive one with military and civic honors and tributes from U.D.C. and the townsfolk. Mrs. Glenn Priest Maerz, a local artist at Wesleyan, played "the fiddle," accompanied by Mrs. Doris Jelks. General Wommack's casket was draped with Confederate colors, and a male quartet sang hymns. Captain D. C. Harris, National Guard officer, commanded the squad which fired the salute at the grave, and Vernon Miller sounded taps.

Hiram Van Zandt of Bibb County and J. J. Henderson of Jones County were the last surviving veterans in this community. Through the years U.D.C. entertained the veterans and their families at a luncheon on April 26, our Memorial Day. When these two were the last left to us, and unable to get about, Daughters visited them and took presents on their birthdays and at Christmas. Mr. Henderson lived to be one hundred years old, and Mr. Van Zandt was not far from the century mark at his death.

Despite our devotion to other veterans, we enjoyed General Wommack the most of our last "Three Musketeers," for his valiant spirit, his gaiety, his candor, and his own lively pleasure in our attentions. He relished appearances with his fiddle on all occasions, to play and hold court, and he was always happy, friendly, and perfectly at ease.

LOST CAUSE OF THE TWENTIES

THE DREAM OF A CONFEDERATE MEMORIAL ON THE GRANITE face of Stone Mountain, conceived to equal anything in the world in size and grandeur, and the dissipation of that dream in a tide of politics, avarice, and misunderstanding, combine to make a sad story in the annals of Georgia. A particularly bitter phase of the struggle was the treatment of sculptor Gutzon Borglum. His great art and craftsmanship conceived the memorial. He worked it out to the applause of the nation and many European observers, and started it—only to be dismissed from his life's masterpiece, to be banned from Georgia like a criminal, and to have his work blasted off the mountain.

With the limitless concept of the artist, Gutzon Borglum envisioned a memorial to the Southern spirit, to be carved out of the biggest block of granite in the world, Stone Mountain in Georgia. He envisioned Southern leaders at the head of a gradually diminishing army that would emerge around the curve of Stone Mountain, following Lee, Jackson, and Davis.

Steeping himself in the history of the South, in the lore of Robert E. Lee and the attributes that made Lee the idol of his people, Borglum came to love and revere the Southern story and its epic hero. He then overcame all natural and scientific difficulties that he encountered in the seven years of preparation for the great enterprise. Not a moment of that time was lost, not a source of help untried, not a problem unsolved. Every employee on the great task, fired by Borglum's vision and zeal, risked life and limb repeatedly to bring the stone to life, as did the great artist himself.

And yet the dream died, killed by the machinations and ambitions of smaller minds, meaner spirits, and uncomprehending usurpers.

Today Stone Mountain stands scarred by several attempts to create a memorial, doomed to remain a gaunt reminder of the death of Borglum's great vision.

Many Americans believe that the Stone Mountain dream died because of Borglum's incompetence, neglect, and temperamental difficulties. Because of this misconception, I tell my view of the Borglum-Stone Mountain Memorial Association controversy, in justice to a true artist and a man of integrity and vision.

Around 1915 William H. Terrell, an Atlantan of Confederate ancestry and sympathies, wrote a letter to the *Atlanta Constitution* proposing that a memorial to the Confederate cause be carved on Stone Mountain. The proposal received editorial comment and lively interest, notably from Mrs. Helen Plane, organizer and Honorary President of Georgia U.D.C. This widow of a Confederate soldier approached the Venable family, owners of the granite mountain close to Atlanta, who agreed to deed the 1,000-foot granite face of the mountain for a Confederate memorial and authorized her to make the offer to the Daughters of the Confederacy in general convention at Savannah in the fall of 1915. Three times Mrs. Plane offered the enterprise to U.D.C. and three times it was reluctantly rejected, for we could see no way to finance such a costly project.

In the meantime, anxious for advice and support in her ambition to see Stone Mountain become a memorial to the South, Mrs. Plane communicated with the celebrated Gutzon Borglum for his views on the feasibility of the monument. She invited him to Atlanta, and then called John Temple Graves, distinguished Alabama editor and Southern patriot, and me, as president of the Georgia U.D.C., to confer with her on the subject.

At my meeting with Mrs. Plane, I, too, was fired by her vision and faith, and was enthusiastic over the reputation, achievements, and ideas of Gutzon Borglum. I pledged my support to Mrs. Plane. Mr. Graves, a charming and persuasive personality, promised help.

Mrs. Plane's zeal finally resulted in organization of the Stone Mountain Memorial Association, incorporated before World War I, with a membership including the Daughters of the Confederacy, to whom the Venables wished to entrust the mountain, the United Sons of Confederate Veterans, and other patriotic groups and prominent citizens of Georgia, who agreed unanimously that Borglum was the man for the enormous job. Notables from other sections of the country were enlisted as founders, donors of $1,000 each.

Naturally the plan was in abeyance during World War I years, so far as fund-raising and carving on the mountain were concerned, although Borglum was not idle in working out his plans. In 1923, however, when Mrs. Walter Grace of Macon was President of Georgia U.D.C., the Association revived and re-engaged Borglum to hew the memorial.

He worked for more than a year, conceiving and mapping out a group which was to be one of the greatest monuments in human history. North and South were thrilled by the size and spirit of the Borglum concept, and the Daughters were overjoyed that the project was well under way, that they could devote every effort to its realization.

Borglum planned a panorama and a memorial hall. The panorama, to be carved in full relief for 1,350 feet across the cliff side, would show the Confederate forces, some 700 figures, following their leaders—Davis, Lee, Jackson, and others of the high command—on horseback, with Lee as the central figure of the group.

Beneath the panorama he would carve a recess in the rock, a hall with a central figure in tribute to the women of the Confederacy, and a background of thirteen columns and thirteen panels representing the seceded states. A lagoon below would reflect the figure and the columns of the hall. From the lagoon steps would lead up the rock to the recessed hall and its carved records of Confederate States heroes, women of the Cause, and leaders in the Stone Mountain Memorial movement.

As Borglum worked on his mighty plan, the Daughters and other organizations strove zealously to raise money for the immense undertaking. The Venables deeded the mountainside to the Association in 1916, the memorial to be completed in twelve years. The gift provided that the rock would return to the family, unless the memorial was completed in that time. Meantime, Federal cooperation was secured, while state and national officials hailed the plan as a glorious and unprecedented memorial.

School children of the state in 1923-25 were giving their pennies, nickels, and dimes; Southerners and others of Confederate ancestry were contributing as founders; and many U.D.C. chapters raised $1,000 for the cause.

The United States mint, with the enthusiastic approval of President Harding, and later Coolidge, turned out a silver half dollar stamped with the central Stone Mountain figures designed by Borglum. It was to sell for $1.00, so that the $500,000 issue would bring one million dollars, the profit to go to the Association for the monument.

There seemed at times to be friction between H. S. Venable, spokesman for the quarry-owning family which donated the mountainside, and officers of the Association headed by Hollins Randolph of Atlanta, but it was smoothed over. On January 19, 1925, the birthday of Lee, the magnificent head of the Southern commander was unveiled before a tremendous crowd at the mountainside, to the great satisfaction of Borglum and to the pride and joy of Georgia Daughters and all other spectators.

When about five weeks later, Mrs. Grace, as U.D.C. member of the Association board, with a small delegation went with

Borglum to view his further work and discuss his plans, the group was summarily notified on the mountainside that Borglum was dismissed for "temperamental disqualifications" and that Mrs. Grace herself, state president of U.D.C., was voted off the board. Her removal eliminated from the Association the Daughters, original custodians of the mountainside, and other early friends and sponsors of Borglum.

With that, the fireworks burst. Eight-column headlines next day announced that the sculptor was charged by the Association with malicious mischief for destruction of the working plans and models of his memorial. The committee announced his dismissal, voted several days earlier, with that of his superintendent of construction, J. G. Tucker, who was named in the mischief charges. Big news also was the Association's suit against Borglum for $50,000.

The stories explained that Borglum was discharged at an executive committee meeting attended by Mr. Venable who had left, however, before the vote was taken so that he might visit Stone Mountain with Borglum and Mrs. F. T. Mason, Mr. Venable's sister.

The same day Governor McLeod of South Carolina called on other Southern governors and U.D.C. to insure completion of the monument. Disturbed U.D.C., D.A.R., and other groups had asked McLeod for help in pushing the project, jeopardized as it seemed.

For some weeks a confused and excited public followed Borglum's flight with Tucker from Georgia, charges by the Association, and replies from the sculptor. The Association secured a temporary court order restraining Borglum or his agents from trespassing on Stone Mountain. Spokesman Randolph said a new sculptor could use the Borglum plans and model from records in possession of the Association. He said that Borglum had neglected his work, had been overpaid for his progress, had delayed the bronze design for the memorial coin, and had frustrated the enterprise with temperamental behavior.

"Neglect and virtual abandonment of his contract, inordinate demands for money not due him and delusions of grandeur" were among the complaints named by Mr. Randolph.

Two days later Borglum, a fugitive from the DeKalb County sheriff, was in Raleigh, North Carolina, where he told reporters, "I'll rot in jail before I'll give the key to my design to that committee." He explained, however, that he was working currently without a model, because of a flaw in the rock which had made the model useless for the present, and that he had destroyed nothing of use to the Association. Later, it was made clear that Borglum had Tucker destroy the discarded model, which could not be used because of the rock fissure, lest the Association proceed with it.

On February 28, the newspapers recounted that Borglum, arriving at Greensboro, North Carolina, with Tucker and their friend and host, Colonel Benehan Cameron of Durham, was arrested, but released on a habeas corpus. He departed for New York, and an extradition hearing was set at Greensboro for March 5.

In New York, the outraged and pursued artist wrote a story for the *New York American* expressing his belief in the "inalienable right of the artist to his own creation," announcing his readiness for "a fight," and charging that "The Association is trying to ruin the greatest expression of a people's faith ever put into permanent form."

Borglum also told the story of his work to raise Stone Mountain funds, his personal contributions to the expense of scaffolds, dynamos, machinery, and engineering for the job. He made some charges of his own, airing the suspicions of many worried Georgians: that the Association had collected $130,000 and spent $170,000, and $70,000 of that in the office. He declared that he was dismissed two weeks after he demanded an accounting of the Association's stewardship. He also wrote that he had paid an accountant summoned from New York $100 a day to audit the books, and had received no audit.

LOST CAUSE OF THE TWENTIES

News also came from New York that a group from that city was willing to finance the memorial if the present Association members were ousted, and that Borglum would fight extradition to Georgia.

On March 2, the Association sought an indictment charging Borglum with larceny from the house for removing several small models and destroying larger ones. This charge is a felony in Georgia. Some weeks later the sculptor was so indicted and thus banned from the state.

I learned later from Borglum himself that the "larceny from the house" consisted in his removal of a plaster model of a work of art which he had purchased himself and brought to Georgia for his own enjoyment.

The Greensboro hearing was postponed, and later called off when the charges against Borglum as a fugitive from Georgia were dropped at the request of the Governor of North Carolina —and strangely enough, also at the request of the executive committee of the Stone Mountain Memorial Association!

Thus was the affair aired in Georgia papers and over the country. Borglum was not without defenders, and voices raised against the Association's executive committee argued forcefully their approval of the zeal, integrity, and good faith of the artist and strongly rebuked the chicanery of his enemies.

The Atlanta Chapter, U.D.C., for one, demanded an audit of the Association books and a public accounting of money given by the public and spent by the Association; the chapter also asked that a committee of artists be called in to judge the progress of Borglum's work. Daughters in Atlanta, with Mrs. Grace, expressed entire satisfaction with Borglum's industry and progress. By this time, however, the U.D.C. had been evicted from the Association and from any share in the Memorial which the Venables had originally entrusted to them.

A published statement of the Daughters in Atlanta cites one instance which illustrates the methods of Mr. Randolph and his friends in taking over control. In April of 1924, Mr. Randolph came to the Association meeting for election of officers with eighty-six men, whom he declared to be new members of the Association on payment of dues of $1.00. The dues had been set recently at $5.00, but because of the secretary's illness there was no record of the change and Mr. Randolph declared the dues to be $1.00. He paid for and voted in the eighty-six new members, who promptly reorganized the Association, omitting all Daughter members except Mrs. T. T. Stephens, who was given the "unimportant office of second vice president," according to the broadside printed and distributed over the state by the Atlanta Daughters.

Mr. Venable, speaking for his family, also made a long and unequivocal statement to clear Borglum of any neglect, avarice, or inefficiency and to damn the Association. He recalled that Randolph had installed Eretus Rivers as business manager in March of 1924, when the Association had $443,000 in money and subscriptions and that by May the sum was increased to $480,000. In a year of Mr. Rivers' administration, Mr. Venable charged, only $17,000 was raised. He pointed out that the executive committee's function was money-raising, and contrasted the record of Borglum himself in raising $15,000 with the entire Association's record of $17,000 in that period.

He also recalled that in April an engineer's survey showed $18,000 due Borglum who agreed to accept only $10,000, which he was never paid. "Mr. Borglum," Venable complained, "and the mountain were turned over to the committee in trust, inseparable. The committee has discharged Mr. Borglum, has excluded the U.D.C., and should also dismiss the mountain."

He emphasized the fact that the memorial as planned was extending on to Venable property, and that the family would not deed another inch to the Association. Venable further wrote that "if the Stone Mountain Memorial Association will deed this property to the Daughters of the Confederacy, I will give them all the additional space and time [beyond the 12-year limit of the deed, then expiring] they may need for this work."

Mrs. Grace's report on Stone Mountain affairs at the Sandersville U.D.C. convention resulted in the Daughters' refusal to participate in the coin sale or to surrender U.D.C. Stone Mountain funds already in hand to the Association until the Daughters could ascertain that the Memorial would be completed.

Later, alas, Mrs. Grace's successor as Georgia President ordered the state treasurer to disregard this decision of the Division and to pay the funds in hand to the Association. Many Daughters in Georgia and elsewhere could not see the chicanery of the Association, perhaps being blinded by the original glory of the memorial concept and their hopes for its realization. At this time, upon the advice of Mrs. Grace, the Sidney Lanier Chapter, U.D.C., in Macon, wisely withheld their gifts for the Memorial, and today is still using interest on that fund for gift scholarships to Confederate descendants.

Before Borglum's dismissal in 1925, another sculptor had been selected by the executive committee of the Association, Augustus Lukeman, Virginia-born, of Confederate ancestry and certainly nationally distinguished, but lacking the fire, vision, and drive of Borglum. These, I felt, were very serious lacks.

Lukeman was employed, despite a letter from Mr. Venable written "in justice to the sculptor with whom you expect to enter into a contract" explaining that the Borglum plans which Lukeman was to use called for additional space on the mountain which Venable would not give "to your Association." He wrote, he said, to protect "an innocent or misinformed sculptor ... signing a contract that ... cannot be carried out ... and that your association knows it would be illegal to participate in."

Venable, a man with no interest beyond his profound concern with achievement of the memorial and justice to its artist and sponsors, concluded his protest thus:

"As you, Mr. Randolph, have a majority of the Stone Mountain Confederate Memorial Association and as every applicant for membership must be presented to your committee, I do not expect to attend the annual meeting on April 24.

"If they wish to elect you as president and Mr. E. Rivers as business manager and Roger Winter as Publicity Agent (who, with his wife, drew $8,000 a year of the Association's $17,000 in 1924), this committee must be responsible for their acts and not myself. They must be responsible to the public, because sooner or later the public will demand an accounting.

"As for myself, candidly, I would not vote for either one of you because I believe if the business manager had dropped dead the day he was appointed the Association would have been better off financially, and I am sure the books of the Association will bear me out in this assertion."

This protest, written to Mr. Randolph, was reprinted and distributed to friends of the Memorial throughout Georgia.

The state was startled and shocked by an encounter between Mr. Randolph and Clark Howell, publisher of the *Atlanta Constitution,* who held Mr. Randolph responsible not only for the Stone Mountain Association's tangled affairs, but also for Howell's defeat for the office of Democratic National Committeeman. This controversy, too personal and political for review here, caused a sensation over the state, and demonstrated sadly the ramifications in which our memorial was involved.

Suffice it to say that Mr. Howell, with Mr. Venable, accused Randolph of "seizing the memorial and using it for political purposes," and other charges embellished with sharp epithets. These attacks the publisher made through the columns of his newspaper and in a written circular which was widely distributed.

From this time on, Stone Mountain business was executed, or delayed, with complete disregard for public interest and for the right of all donors to know of and take part in decisions. With his reorganization of the Association in 1924, and his packing of membership for control, Mr. Randolph also had the mountain re-deeded to the new Association, so that the Venables and the public were helpless to interfere.

LOST CAUSE OF THE TWENTIES

After all this, the Association had the temerity to request of U.D.C. their cooperation in selling the Stone Mountain half dollars. To this proposal Mrs. Grace, as Georgia Division President, made her well-considered report to the Daughters at the Sandersville convention in 1925, asking them to take no part in sale of the coins. Clearly and emphatically she made the point that the Association was selling the coins at one hundred per cent profit, but that there was no assurance of how this money would be used. She read Mr. Venable's letter refusing further space on the mountain, unless U.D.C. and Borglum were returned to the enterprise.

However, Mr. Lukeman went to work on the doomed mountain, and in 1927 Mr. Venable announced in the papers that Borglum's splendid head of Lee was to be blown from the mountain, to make way for a new Lukeman design.

Up to now, I had no official role in the Stone Mountain project, beyond my early conference with Mrs. Plane, my work as a member of the U.D.C., my natural eagerness to see the magnificent plan realized, and my feelings of outrage and despair over the Borglum dismissal and general conduct of the Association. Of course I was personally concerned and further antagonized by the summary dismissal of my friend, Mrs. Grace, from the board.

Then, remembering the spontaneous, thrilled tribute from crowds who had stood on the roadside January 19, 1924, as the Lee head was unveiled, it seemed incredible to me that this work should be destroyed. I recall the rapt astonishment, the joy of recognition in the throng, the murmurs and shouts of approval, as people said to one another, "It is Lee! It *is* Lee!" Few of us had hoped for a living likeness of the head on such a vast area, for a portrait in thirty feet of granite that would capture the spirit and the lineaments of that revered face. But Borglum did this very thing.

I knew not whether my protest would deter Mr. Randolph and his picked committee, but I was unable to refrain from

WHEN ALL IS SAID AND DONE

writing him to ask that he keep intact the head of Lee now on Stone Mountain until the recently accepted (Lukeman) design should be carved. I pointed out that the position of the Lee head did not interfere with the new design, and need not be injured by future blasting. I appealed to him to keep the head until the Lukeman design was an accomplished fact, as a generous gesture which would be appreciated by artists, patriots, and financiers.

Evasively, Mr. Randolph replied to my letter, which was front page news in Georgia, that the Lee head had not been blasted off. I was not reassured or satisfied by this ambiguous statement. My fears proved sound, for the head was blasted away not long after to make way for a design which was never executed.

The extent of misunderstanding about the Borglum story and the U.D.C. role in withdrawing from Stone Mountain was brought home to me more than once after Borglum's dismissal. It was reviewed editorially in the *Macon Telegraph* on the occasion of the election of the First Vice-President General at the 1927 U.D.C. General Convention at Charleston:

> Mrs. Walter D. Lamar, who has been prominent for many years in U.D.C. work, was nominated by New York and other states for First Vice President, which no doubt would have given her the presidency a year hence. Under ordinary circumstances, the Georgia delegates to the convention would have performed the lady-like equivalent of throwing their hats into the air. The election of Mrs. Lamar was assured. However, a number of the Georgia delegation nominated ... Mrs. Oscar McKenzie of Montezuma, Past President of Georgia U.D.C., in opposition. Mrs. Walter J. Grace of Macon requested that Mrs. McKenzie's name be withdrawn, as the Georgia delegation, she said, had not known of the intention to nominate her. The supporters of Mrs. McKenzie refused, and she was elected by a majority of 400 over Mrs. Lamar.
>
> The significance of the fight is, apparently, that the national U.D.C. is drawing away from its fight on the present officials of Stone Mountain Memorial Association. Mrs. Lamar has been a consistent champion of Borglum and a persistent enemy of the present regime at Stone

Mountain. When the fight first began, the U.D.C. was unanimously against Mr. Randolph and his associates, who ejected Mrs. Grace . . . and other U.D.C. from the board and angered the U.D.C.

That the anger of the Daughters had cooled became apparent... at Charleston when the "cooperationists"—that is, those who are friendly to the Stone Mountain Memorial Association—won a victory over the "non-cooperationists" in the election of officers.

The editorial is an accurate account of the 1927 Charleston election, and my defeat. At that time it showed clearly that even those most concerned with Stone Mountain, Daughters of the Confederacy themselves, were deceived about what had happened.

It was not my defeat which grieved my friends and me, nor the election of Mrs. McKenzie, who filled the office well. We were distressed at the way the wind was blowing, the ascendancy of Daughters who would have U.D.C. cooperate with the group which was inimical to Borglum and which later destroyed his memorial.

It was a source of sincere regret to the Old Guard that Miss Mildred Rutherford deserted us and adhered to the Association. In a pamphlet issued by her, giving the history of the Memorial, before she turned to the Randolph clique, she emphasized essentials in our later stand against the Randolph group. She mentioned specifically the donor of the mountain, Mr. Venable and his family, Mrs. Helen Plane, the Press, and so on. "But," said she, "the monument would not be possible unless a genius capable to carve it, and willing to sacrifice much to attempt it, could have been found, and to Gutzon Borglum belongs the honor of the man of genius found." In support of her statement about the chosen sculptor, she quoted a letter from Borglum to her in which he said: "We have prohibited the phrase, 'I Can't,' in this work. No man is allowed here who thinks it."

Borglum's great vision died hard with him, as it did with most Georgians. There was a time in the late twenties when he was fired with hope by an Atlanta movement to get him back to the Stone Mountain job. But nothing came of it, although his belief in the memorial and his devotion to his art inspired most generous terms from him. He would have agreed to forgive and forget his persecutions, his financial losses, and the damage to his reputation, if Randolph and his executive committee were ousted.

Lukeman's plans, too, came to naught. Money gave out, and the engineering and designing difficulties were doubtless beyond his powers. In the opinion of many critics, his artistry was inadequate to the task. Ben B. Johnston, *Macon Telegraph* columnist, wrote:

> Even if the Association were a going concern, Lukeman's design (gargoyles and all) is a pain in the eye to me.... The mounted men on horses—let's call them horses ... approximate the equine about as well as the modern steeds on a merry-go-round. But they are not my horses....
>
> Let the mountain alone. Quit calling it a Confederate Memorial. Let it stand as a monument to the innate and incurable propensity of human beings to make themselves ridiculous in their most sacredly sentimental undertakings.

As late as 1941 there was another attempt to revive the Association, long since purged of its frustrating and self-seeking executive committee by time and by death of some of the members. However, this plan died, too, its end hastened by World War II.

Today, again, there is half-hearted talk of a Stone Mountain Memorial to the Confederacy, to be financed as a sort of business-tourist proposition by the Reconstruction Finance Corporation. I do not believe it can be achieved. The public has lost faith in the idea, after its betrayal in the twenties. It will take much more time and forgetting to erase the old failure of the great dream and effort. And we are not likely to see again an artist of the stature of Borglum, with his imagination, his faith, and his fire.

In 1925 I organized the Sidney Lanier Memorial Association

UNVEILING BUST OF SIDNEY LANIER, HALL OF FAME, NEW YORK UNIVERSITY, 1946

Left to right: Dr. Isaiah Bowman, Pres. Johns Hopkins Univ.; Sidney Lanier, grandson of poet; Mrs. John A. Wilcox, Pres.-Gen. U.D.C.; Mrs. Walter D. Lamar, Chairman of Lanier Committee, U.D.C.

UNVEILING BUST OF SIDNEY LANIER IN THE MACON LIBRARY

in Macon to establish a Lanier room or some sort of permanent memorial to the poet at our Washington Memorial Library. Representatives of all women's clubs in Macon comprised the Association and assisted in raising funds.

In 1927 we decided on a Lanier bust, with later hopes of making it the center of a Lanier room to be endowed with pertinent literature and what Lanierana there was to be found in this section.

Mrs. Grace was a vital spirit in our association, and she and I resolved to commission Borglum to make the bust. My correspondence with him began in the summer of 1927, a year when he was in an emotional turmoil over his treatment at the hands of the Stone Mountain Association. It was an interesting experience for me to see through his letters the reaction of a creative artist to the destruction of his work, his suffering over loss of the memorial and his outrage over the bungling pieces which were replacing it.

Contemplating Borglum's distress over the ruin and his large-hearted grief that the monument was lost to posterity, I could see that a lesser man might have worked with the Association, a man willing to share in their schemes, bow to their control, and acquiesce in their waste and delay.

I am convinced that the rift was due not only to commercial interests and misunderstandings but also to refusal of Association leaders to treat Borglum as an artist, to see that his certainty of power and imperious insistence on his concepts were but an expression of his artistry and integrity. They treated him like an ordinary man, and expected him to behave like a craftsman or business man, and a pliable one at that. Such a man could never have executed the vast monument he conceived.

In all matters as to creation of the Lanier bust, we in Macon found Borglum cooperative and sympathetic. When he was positive and insistent, I knew that the value of his ideas outweighed all else. It was a joy to read in his letters of his enthusiasm for Lanier, whom he regarded as one of the greatest

Americans. It was equally agreeable to find that he sympathized with our desire to have the bust portray the young Lanier, whose strong and spiritual face expressed the promise of his genius and the triumph of his art over suffering.

In 1927 I wrote to Borglum of my hopes for the Lanier bust, and arranged for him to have pictures of the poet and to meet the Charles Day Laniers at Greenwich, Connecticut, for further intimate Lanierana.

In the course of our correspondence I learned first hand of Borglum's bitterness over Stone Mountain, though he wrote, "I wish the subject could be taboo." Still, as the unhappy events of the windup of the Mountain affair made the headlines, he did discuss it. I believe that my indignation and sympathy created a bond between us, so that he wrote to me quite freely, as if to relieve his feelings.

In May his letter called destruction of his Lee head "a mortal sin against the memory of Lee." Yet, he declared that "if the Association were purged of those who have destroyed it, I would gather up my machinery they have worn out . . . and which they have used to wreck what I built; I would reassemble it and I would draw the confidence of the nation again out of the wreck they have made; and I have faith enough in America to believe that it is possible."

This letter, with others evincing how hard his hopes for realization of the memorial died, came from South Dakota where he was working on the Mount Rushmore Memorial.

After I had written Mr. Randolph asking him to defer destruction of the wonderful Lee head, and announcement came that the head was blasted from the mountain, I received an understandably sad and angry letter from Borglum.

"It is a dreadful, dreadful thing," he lamented, "to think that in our time the hand of the law has no courage, that it will not arrest such vandalism." He wrote to me of the executive committee's attempts to bribe Tucker and Villar, another assistant, for testimony against him, and added: "Tucker is working for me in the Black Hills. Villar has stayed with me when I had scarcely enough money to pay his board bill."

I was sympathetic and amused to read his account of an incognito trip to Atlanta where he viewed the destruction of his Lee and Jackson heads, and the beginnings of a new memorial.

"The head of whomsoever it was meant to be looks like an under-risen biscuit and is about half the size of my head, not more than that; looks flattened and chalked over. I understand they have washed it with cement to give it a luminous appearance; that it is in such low relief it cannot show. The horse that is under this figure is so out of proportion to the man that he looks like a figure with a hunchback, shortened rather, between the shoulders and the waist.... The horse is so out of proportion to himself that the rider could reach back, without tipping his body, and get the horse by the root of the tail, so shortly coupled is it. And all of this is just painted on the mountain with the exception of the head and shoulders."

Borglum explained that he had slipped into Atlanta to confer with State Senator Kelly and others who wanted to know if he would help in a new memorial plan. He asked me to say to Mrs. Grace that he would "aid them in every way I can, provided they will adhere to an all-Confederate design and that the U.D.C. will be in charge, with a safe, reliable majority of control, and that I shall have an absolutely free hand in the work of re-financing and carrying out the plans."

But it did not work out.

Meantime, Borglum went on with the marble bust of Lanier and wrote me most gratifyingly of his understanding and appreciation of our poet. So strong was his admiration for the subject that he gave us the marble pedestal for the bust, material, work, and design, since our fund of $3,000 was insufficient to cover the cost of a pedestal. I have been told since that Borglum might have charged us $5,000 for the bust alone and still be within reasonable limits for such a piece of sculpture.

In 1928 the sculptor collected all possible photographs of

Lanier, and I sent him sketches by the Macon artist, Edward Shorter, now of Columbus, Georgia. The sculptor complimented the sketches warmly for their "charm and spirituality."

Soon he sent us the plaster model of the bust for inspection and approval. We put it on view for several days in the library, and invited interested Maconites to come and appraise it.

Among the most eager and happy visitors to this showing were my mother and Virginia Conner Hopson, Lanier contemporaries and admirers who remembered him. Both, in fact, had known the poet well. Mrs. Hopson's husband, W. A. Hopson, had been an intimate friend of Lanier and cherished many letters from him. These two beautiful old ladies with scallops of white hair showing beneath their coronet bonnets with draped black veils sat long and quietly before the image of their friend Sidney Lanier. Mrs. Hopson recalled that her brother had gone with the boy Lanier to buy his first flute, a small wooden one that cost $1.50, when Sidney was about twelve years old.

My mother said: "It is an excellent likeness. The general expression of the face is so like the man that it gave me an uncanny feeling when I entered the room."

Other citizens came to view the model and left their written impressions of it in a nearby receptacle provided for their appraisals. Approval was practically unanimous, and very enthusiastic.

We set the unveiling of the marble bust for February 3, 1929, Lanier's birthday. I had planned to have Borglum come to Macon and speak to the Memorial Association and our guests on the great occasion. However, he wrote reminding me of the old indictment against him which forbade appearance in Georgia. Arrest, he said, was one last insult "I will not submit to."

I was determined that we should have our artist on hand for the ceremonies, and that something of the injustice should be removed, or compensated for, by his coming to Macon and being honored. I enlisted the aid of John T. Boifeuillet, for many years clerk of the Georgia House of Representatives, whose political writings in the *Atlanta Journal* and long service in the Capitol had accrued for him considerable influence in the state.

Mr. Boifeuillet secured from the Governor assurance that Borglum might come with impunity, that the indictment would be lifted temporarily so he might enter the state without fear of arrest.

I wired Borglum of the arrangements, and his reply, though laconic, was eloquent: "Coming. Borglum."

After the program, Mr. Lamar and I entertained in honor of Mr. Borglum, Sterling Lanier, the poet's grandson, and Dr. Edwin Mims, Lanier biographer. It was a happy occasion for all of us, and the sculptor was particularly intrigued by the remark of Mrs. Lucille Flanders Selden. When she was introduced to him, she said, "I met you, Mr. Borglum, a number of years before the Mutilation Association destroyed the fine piece of work you were doing on Stone Mountain."

"The Mutilation Association!" he repeated delightedly. "What a fine name for that bunch. That's a good one!"

And, as Reporter Willie Snow Ethridge wrote in the *Macon Telegraph,* "As he was leaving, I heard him saying under his famous breath, 'That's a good one, Mutilation Association!' "

SIDNEY LANIER
ADVANCEMENT

SIDNEY LANIER, A SLENDER, MERRY, MUSICAL BOY, WAS A close companion of my Uncle Charlie Wiley and a favorite with the belles of Macon when my father was courting my mother in 1860. My mother remembered Lanier's youthful grace, his music and gaiety, the sweetness of his personality, and his keen sense of humor. She rejoiced in his valor in the War Between the States and the characteristic unselfishness which kept him beside his young brother, Clifford, refusing promotions that they might not be separated. She knew at first hand of his postwar illness, his courtship, marriage, and early family life, and she watched the long struggle for fulfillment of his art against great odds.

My mother used to tell a story about Lanier's wedding. Came the point in the ceremony when the young poet and author of the novel, *Tiger Lilies,* known to be as poor as the next Southerner in those days, and with less prospects than most, must repeat the words, "With all my worldly goods I thee endow."

"There goes *Tiger Lilies!*" whispered one of the guests. The young lady's stage whisper, louder than she intended, carried over the congregation and rang for decades in the amused memory of Lanier's contemporaries.

In school and at home we recited Lanier with the poems of English immortals, knowing that he articulated the best aspirations of our people and our way of thinking. So it often surprised and grieved me as the years passed to find that Lanier was not only half forgotten and neglected by the country at large, but by our people at home.

On the anniversary of Lanier's birth, February 3, 1921, I presented a program and spoke on "Lanier, the Musician," in the Wesleyan Conservatory Chapel. My talk recalled some early and generally forgotten Lanierana which seemed fresh and personal, and traced his passionate devotion to music, which so beautifully affected his writing. The boy, the man, and the mature poet seemed to come alive to us that night.

The Lanier recollections I presented interested so many people that I had my talk printed, and dedicated the booklet to the Saturday Morning Music Club.

Lanier's widow, Mary Day Lanier, wrote from Greenwich, Connecticut: "How shall I find words to thank you halfworthily for the bright surprises of your friendly greeting, your 'Sidney Lanier' . . . Your work, I know, has taken its place too clearly to need anything more, save my happiness in it . . . It will be one of the dear family possessions."

This graceful bouquet from a revered source recalled a pilgrimage which my husband and I had made in the spring of 1913 to the Greenwich home of Charles Day Lanier, son of the Sidney Laniers, to meet the widow of Macon's genius.

We drove to Rock Ridge, Greenwich, Connecticut, and were charmingly welcomed by the exquisite woman, known so affectionately through many of her husband-poet's lines. Frail, but alert and appealing, she entertained us and drew us out. She asked about many of Macon's old families, expressed affection for them, and in parting looked straight into my eyes and said, "Let me look at you, for you are a part of Macon I shall always love."

She showed us a collection of Lanier's letters and also a collection of Lanier's poems, especially adapted for use in high schools by herself and her son Charles, editor of the *Review of Reviews* at that time.

Mrs. Lanier also reassured us as to her husband's birthplace, since so many people questioned whether Lanier was actually born in the gabled cottage on High Street in Macon. "He was indeed," she said, adding that she had answered many similar inquiries.

The publication of my talk on Lanier brought me a letter also from Henry Van Dyke, who wrote me: "You are right, and I think you prove it, in regard to the part which music played in the life of this poet. But there was no dividing line between the two arts in his mind. They were like twin peaks of the same mountain range."

The Sidney Lanier Chapter U.D.C. in Macon and other Lanier enthusiasts up to this time had read and talked and promoted our poet as a Confederate hero. However, our enjoyment of Lanier hardly amounted to a campaign for his revival. The success of the 1921 Wesleyan chapel observance marked the beginning of such a crusade, for it launched my public activity on the poet's behalf and brought on the foremost labor of my life, the advancement of Sidney Lanier for the Hall of Fame of New York University.

In 1930 the U.D.C. created a committee to advance the name of Lanier for the Hall of Fame, and appointed me chairman. Chief among my committee was Mrs. Frank F. Jones (Mary Callaway) of Macon, the scholarly daughter of a distinguished Confederate family, who followed in her father's footsteps as a careful and devoted writer on Southern history. Miss Margaret Rouquie of Georgetown, South Carolina, a poet herself and another loyal partner in the campaign, assumed chairmanship of the committee in the years when I served as President-General. The late Mrs. T. L. Caudle of North Carolina also headed the committee for a while, making heroic effort to have a Lanier postage stamp issued, but without success.

With the help of the faithful and dedicated few on the committee, we made the years from 1931 to 1946 an era of vigorous renaissance for Lanier. Before election time every five years we bombarded the 105 electors of the Hall of Fame with appeals and persuasive presentations, accompanied by endorsements of our candidate from prominent figures. We importuned writers all over the country for Lanier endorsements and received valuable estimates of our poet with which to convince the electors. Whenever we found a contemporary who did not know Lanier's poetry, we promptly enlightened him.

As early as 1932 I began to assemble testimonials to Lanier, among the most effective statements of which was biographer Gamaliel Bradford's letter: "Lanier is just the sort of influence that I think our young people most need at present. He was spiritually progressive; no one could be more so; yet he had the delicate sense of how deeply the present and future are rooted in the past, and how difficult and dangerous it is to break altogether and roughly with the traditions which through a long succession of centuries have made us what we are."

In 1932 the Georgia biographer, John Donald Wade, then a Vanderbilt professor, stated: "I think Sidney Lanier belongs in the Hall of Fame so unquestionably that it is hard to tell precisely why. He was in the first place a very noble man. He was among the ten or twelve most notable literary persons who have lived in America, and among the four or five most notable in America outside New England."

George Herbert Clarke of Queen's University in Kingston, Canada, wrote he had not "the slightest doubt that Lanier should be in the Hall of Fame." H. Douglas Wild of Rutgers was most helpful with advice and high praise. He urged the honor for Lanier "for his intrinsic worth as a poet and personality . . . and for America's need of the quality of life that he stood for . . . and for that rare kind of rhythmically sensuous, impassioned beauty which will live as one of the most noble and precious attributes of American manhood."

Many such endorsements I solicited with letters, enclosing Lanier pamphlets or booklets of my own. I also had printed, from quinquennial to quinquennial, a folder containing quotations on Lanier from celebrated contemporaries, called "A Brief for Sidney Lanier," which I sent to electors to acquaint them with authoritative opinion on our candidate. I distributed in addition another small brochure called "Things to Know about Sidney Lanier," including a brief sketch of his life, career, writings, and appraisals of his music and poetry.

One of the most valuable pieces of promotion I was able to arrange, in the summer of 1935 close to election time, was in the *Saturday Review of Literature.* I wrote to Editor Henry Seidel Canby asking for some space in the *Review.* Dr. Canby asked me to write a Lanier article, which, on publication, was quite important in making friends for Lanier.

In these years we received considerable support from pulpits in the South and other sections of the country. In 1935 I arranged for all Macon ministers to speak on the Sunday nearest Lanier's birthday, February 3, about the poet, whose writings so readily enrich religious discourse.

A fervent and helpful Lanier admirer was Dr. Maurice Trimmer of the First Baptist Church in Macon, who frequently used Lanier lines in his sermons and presented Lanier's life as an example of Christian principles and fortitude.

Dr. Albert Grady Harris, pastor of the First Presbyterian Church, of which Lanier was a member, helped us in the early years and throughout our advancement of Lanier. His sermon on February 1, 1942, was on "The Spiritual Legacies of Lanier," connoting the centennial of Lanier's birth.

In 1935, when the New Deal was at the height of its concern with "The Forgotten Man," and its efforts for the common people were pumping new blood into our sick economy (and before its trend to centralization and invasion of states' rights), I found that Lanier in his day had called for "A New Deal," in phrases less political and more profound and poetic.

When I went to New York that year for an **NBC Lanier**

program, I spoke of him as a "Prophet of the New Deal." I quoted his recurring apostrophes against Trade, as opposed to the development of the human spirit.

"In his poem, 'The Symphony,'" I said, "Lanier inveighs against the cruelties of Trade. He speaks of the awakening of Industrialism, and discusses the brotherhood of man. Can anyone doubt that he foresaw the New Deal?" I found next day that this discovery, which I had simply wished to share, was ringing through many a headline over the country as a newsworthy comment.

Highlight of our 1935 effort was a broadcast over a national NBC hookup from Radio City in New York, where I read "The Symphony," accompanied by a thirty-five-piece orchestra, conducted by Joseph Honti.

In preparation for this 25-minute program I conferred with Mr. Honti, who selected excerpts from Grieg, MacDowell, Chopin, Tschaikowsky, Rachmaninoff, and Wagner to accompany the poem—flute, clarinet,, and violin calls illustrating the wood-sounds Lanier so loved, and rich, full orchestral passages to sound the laments and the triumphs of the poem.

The broadcast was one of the happiest experiences of my Lanier work—indeed, of my life. I am convinced that for thrills incomparable, one must talk on one's favorite theme from the top of the world!

I had ample assurances that Lanier spoke beautifully and thrillingly for himself in the broadcast, and immense personal gratification that I had served as an effective instrument to bring his message. After the broadcast, in addition to wires and letters from friends and family, I heard from strangers far and near.

I was especially pleased by a spontaneous note from a distinguished New Yorker, a man of musical taste and accomplishment in addition to his political gifts. He wrote:

WHEN ALL IS SAID AND DONE

November 26, 1934

Dear Mrs. LaMar:

Permit me to congratulate you on the beautiful reading of a beautiful poem. Your rendition was the most perfect I have ever heard over the air. The Lanier poem ought to be repeated real often, particularly in these days.

Sincerely yours,
F. LaGuardia, Mayor.

We revived a vogue for Lanier among U.D.C., and their cooperation bore fruit in many Southern states in the form of memorials, tablets, markers, and busts to commemorate our poet. Those states which had no spot to mark where Lanier lived, worked, or paused awhile in his quest for health honored him none the less with programs of music, readings, and sales of Lanier brochures. I visited many states to give Lanier readings to music and make radio talks.

After long preparation and work with the Lanier family, I was able to give aid to the Centennial Definitive Edition of Lanier, edited by Charles R. Anderson and published by the Johns Hopkins University Press.

I was called on to aid many writers on Lanier, because of my study of his work and life and my connections with the Lanier family. I became friends with Aubrey Harrison Starke, with whom I enjoyed a lively correspondence and whom I aided considerably in his exhaustive Lanier biography and appraisal.

We started early in our preparation for the Hall of Fame's quinquennial election in 1935. We assembled testimony from the quick and the dead, from Walt Whitman to the liveliest of living poets at home and abroad. Many of these authorities were electors themselves. Others were simply friends of poetry, novelists, poets, publicists, politicians and diplomats, journalists, and people of taste and culture in positions of influence.

In 1932, Stephen Vincent Benét wrote me that "Lanier was a true poet in a difficult time, the most important poet produced by the South between Poe and the present time." Henry Seidel

Canby early espoused our cause, deeming Lanier "certainly one of the really important poets." Dr. T. L. Rush of Columbia University's Hall of Philosophy encouraged us with his enthusiasm for Lanier's work and character and his hope that "so gracious a figure would receive the honor."

In 1933 my fervor induced me to venture where angels should fear to tread. I wrote to Henry L. Mencken for his opinion of Lanier, hoping to glean a good word. I held my breath for a week, awaiting his reply, not knowing whether both my poet and I would be castigated with withering brilliance, or whether I would find a soft spot for Lanier in Mencken's heart.

On October 7, I received this reply: "Regarding Mr. Lanier's poetry, I am in sufficient doubt to avoid offering a categorical opinion. But I believe that his 'Science of English Verse' is one of the best works of criticism ever published in America, and it seems to me that it is alone sufficient to justify giving him a place in the Hall of Fame." Of course I was quite willing to swallow Mencken's doubts about Lanier's poetry in my joy at this superlative view of his prose. Later I received another cordial note from Mencken in which he deemed Lanier certainly the best Southern poet, and went even so far as to be "delighted" to assist us.

As election time approached in 1935, our list of literati and distinguished citizens espousing Lanier grew apace. Ellen Glasgow, an elector, promised to do "all in my power" for Lanier, though "in my heart I feel that he would be profoundly indifferent to any honor that depended on winning votes," because "the one and only way to honor a poet, in my opinion, is to read his poetry." I hailed her help just as joyfully, for all her misgivings about vote-getting, feeling that Lanier's place in the Hall of Fame would certainly bring him the true honor of more readers.

Dr. Douglas S. Freeman, biographer and Virginia newspaper editor, wired me that "the Daughters of the Confederacy are exemplifying their finest ideals when they urge the inclusion of Sideny Lanier in the New York Hall of Fame. He was a great poet, a great Southerner, and a great American."

Editor Albert Shaw of the *Review of Reviews* in 1935, who was an elector, wrote, "I agree with everything you write," and he also stated that he had no doubt of Lanier's deserts.

John Finley, an elector, and editor of the *New York Times,* sent me the most magnificent of all the letters I received that quinquennial. "If Lanier were only here with his flute," said he, "he would lead the entire electorate up the Hall of Fame and find himself a permanent resident of the Hall of Bronze Immortals."

Southern author DuBose Heyward at my request wrote to the Board of Electors at this time, urging Lanier for the Hall, not only as a great poet, but "as an innovator whose theories upon the relationship of music and poetry have exerted a definite influence upon the poetry of the United States." Archibald Rutledge called Lanier "one of the immortal princes of American song." Georgia's Senator Richard B. Russell also espoused him as "one of the great American poets."

That same year my friend and associate director of the Robert E. Lee Foundation at Stratford Hall, Mrs. Robert Worth Bingham, wife of the ambassador to England who was also owner and publisher of the *Louisville Courier-Journal and Times,* briskly bestirred herself from the Embassy in London, with a barrage of letters to important friends in politics, diplomatic circles, education, and letters. At this time, Miss Helen Knox, of the Chase National Bank, another Stratford director, made valuable connections for the committee.

We worked together and produced impressive endorsements for our candidate. They included further the writer and diplomat, Meredith Nicholson in South America, Ambassador William E. Dodd in Germany, Newton D. Baker, John A. Davis, Elihu Root, William E. Gonzales, editor of the noted *South Carolina State,* Chancellor Alfred Hume of the University of

Mississippi, Senator Joseph T. Robinson, William Marshall Bullitt of Louisville, Ambassador to France William C. Bullitt, Governor Albert Ritchie of Maryland, President Mary E. Wooley of Mount Holyoke College, President Hamilton Holt of Rollins College in Florida, Helen Keller, and the famous country editor William Allen White of the *Emporia Gazette* in Kansas.

President Francis P. Gaines of Washington and Lee wrote high praise of Lanier, and editor Clarence Poe of the *Progressive Farmer,* an elector, signified his intent to vote for Lanier, and we obtained the support of Charleston's author, Herbert Ravenel Sass.

We secured support from the Peabody Conservatory of Music in Baltimore, where Lanier was first flautist in the Peabody orchestra. Director Otto Ortmann endorsed our poet-musician because "combining the arts of poetry and music he made artistic and cultural contributions in no small measure . . . he himself is perhaps one of the very best known men whose achievements embrace work in these two fields."

The estimate of Lanier from the writings of the famous Dean Inge of London, is pertinent: "Another mystical poet who should be better known on this side of the Atlantic is Sidney Lanier, whose Shakespearean sonnets combine fine and delicate feeling with a perfection of technique comparable with Shakespeare's own."

After five years of effort and support of so many enthusiastic and distinguished advocates, our committee was rewarded by seeing in the spring of 1935 the name of Sidney Lanier among the nominees for the Hall of Fame. But when election results were announced in the summer, his name was not there. Elected to the Hall of Fame in 1935 were Simon Newcomb, scientist; Grover Cleveland, Democratic president; and William Penn, founder of Philadelphia—a worthy company, we had to concede, despite our disappointment.

After this failure, we girded ourselves afresh. Since electors are not properly approached until the spring of the quinquennial year, before the fall election, we did not begin our reminders again until March of 1940. But in the meantime, I wrote again to new and old friends of the Lanier cause. We also inspired and promoted many more observances and memorials. One of the most impressive in 1939 was a tablet the Daughters placed in the old French Protestant Huguenot Church at Charleston, the church where Lanier's Huguenot ancestors worshipped.

During the years between our 1935 failure and our 1940 effort, I was grieved and dismayed by the death of some friendly and powerful electors. Thirty of them were gone, including Miss Glasgow, who retired from the board long before her death. Most of the lost electors were Lanier devotees of long standing or converts to our cause. So I was obliged to begin on their successors. I compiled and had printed new brochures for this work.

The passing of Dr. Finley of the *Times* struck me with personal grief as well as distress at this weakening of our cause. His interest in Lanier, and incidentally, his memory and admiration of my father and of President Cleveland, had endorsed his taste and judgment to me. Dr. Finley had become President of the Electors, and it had been reassuring to have a Lanier friend in that post, although as President he was not free to speak his views.

Ranks of our supporters were also thinned by the demise of Arthur D. Little, Newton D. Baker, William E. Gonzales, Senators Joseph Robinson, Elihu Root, and others. Nevertheless we labored afresh on new electors, and as 1940 came, I found that we had a sufficient array of formidable friends to feel most sanguine about the results.

Struthers Burt wrote in February that he had already voted for Lanier. Judge Florence V. Allen of the United States Court of Appeals at Cleveland sent me a very useful letter, complimenting my brochure on Lanier and assuring me that she was a Lanier lover who knew "The Marshes of Glynn" by heart. I was delighted also with a cordial note from Dorothy Canfield Fisher, and gratified to find her of like mind with me, despite her resignation as an elector. "I've just read your booklet . . ." she wrote, "with the greatest enjoyment and appreciation. I think your quotations are wonderfully well chosen and the whole essay gives an impression of Sidney Lanier as that most remarkable human phenomenon, a lovable genius. I don't think anyone ever heard of a lovable genius before."

Historian James Truslow Adams, an elector, wrote that Lanier was one of his favorite poets as a boy, and "I still enjoy his work." Librarian John C. French of Johns Hopkins University, where Lanier had lectured, contributed an immense service to our advocacy for 1940 when he sent each elector a copy of the Johns Hopkins Lanier Centennial Celebration program planned for 1942 in Baltimore. Harrison Morris, a poet himself and an elector who had known Lanier personally, promised his vote. Professor John H. T. McPherson of the University of Georgia assured me that "you *know* you can count on me." As an elector, he said, he had been working for Lanier for thirty years, a record of active devotion exceeding my own! Dr. Edwin Mims, an elector, author and educator, whose writings include a biography of Sidney Lanier, wrote that he would certainly vote for "*our* poet to go into the Hall of Fame."

So went the work.

In 1938 six money awards were given to writers on Lanier. The *Southern Literary Messenger* presented three prizes of $125 for literature on Lanier. Virginia Division, U.D.C., gave a $50 prize for the finest poem on Lanier. One donor gave $50 for a 4,000-word Lanier interpretation, and five Lanier kinswomen gave a $26 prize for a sonnet.

We enjoyed the impetus this year of the support of a Northern group of literati headed by Dr. T. C. Mabbott, author and critic, and poet-publisher Loker Raley, whose Poe literary society petitioned the Hall of Fame for Lanier's election. In Georgia, the Habersham Chapter, U.D.C., sponsored the dedication of the Sidney Lanier Bridge over the Chattahoochee River.

In 1939, radio storyteller and commentator Ted Malone wrote to Mrs. John L. Woodbury, President-General of the United Daughters of the Confederacy, for advice about including Sidney Lanier in his projected "Pilgrimage of Poetry," a series of programs he proposed to broadcast in 1940 from homes and shrines of American poets. Mrs. Woodbury referred the letter to me, and I soon settled Mr. Malone's doubts as to where to locate his Lanier program. Incidentally, I was happy to learn that a vote of college presidents had selected Lanier among Emerson, Lowell, Longfellow, Whitman, Poe, Joel Chandler Harris and Amy Lowell to be so honored on the air.

In June I wrote Mr. Malone of my pleasure in his plans, sent him my brochure on Lanier, reminding him that Macon was the birthplace of the poet and the scene of his marriage, and that the parlors of the house in which I now live are where Lanier often played his flute. The Billington Sanders Walkers, who then lived at Lanier Cottage, were agreeable to use of their home for the broadcast, and Mr. Malone decided to include Macon instead of Baltimore on his Pilgrimage itinerary.

Arriving on Saturday, February 10, for his Macon broadcast from the poet's birthplace, Mr. Malone came to my home. I approved his proposed broadcast and presented him next day to the Sunday radio audience, in company with Lanier's first cousins in Macon, R. L. Anderson and Mrs. John McKay.

Malone began his story, "Here in this House," with Lanier's birth, went with the boy-poet and his flute to war, recounted his struggle with ill health and poverty as a race with death to write and make music before death came, and called this race "brief and furious." He interpreted the effect of hardship and suffering on the artist—"A reed cannot speak until a sharp blade has notched it, and a flute cannot sing until the metal has been melted." He emphasized Lanier's sense of values thus: "Only a poet dares to believe that there is something more nourishing than food, something more secure than security. Sidney Lanier was a poet, and he found the Holy Grail."

In the spring of 1940 Sidney Lanier was among the forty or more American greats named by the public, and sent to the College of Electors in March. All through the summer, as Lanier was slowly advanced to what seemed the necessary number of electoral votes, our hopes were high.

But in October, announcement was made that the popular ballad-singer, Stephen Foster, was the only one chosen for the Hall of Fame. The news came hard.

The Lanier committee and U.D.C. over the country were resolved to try again. They sponsored a reprint of my "Sidney Lanier, the Musician," which received wide circulation from such Lanier friends as Dr. Charles W. Dabney of Winter Park, Florida, an elector who ordered copies for his friends.

In 1942 the National Park Service Committee on Geographical Names, furnished with Lanierana by Daughters, approved the plan to name a Great Smoky Mountain peak for Lanier. On recommendation of Secretary Harold L. Ickes, a Hannah Mountain peak 3,145 feet high, in the Tennessee area of Great Smoky Mountain National Park near Montvale Springs, where was laid much of the scene of his novel, *Tiger Lilies,* was named Mount Lanier.

The Department of the Interior announcement of Mount Lanier further aided our cause with this appraisal: ". . . during his life's brief span, the social order in which he was born and reared was overturned, and his personal fortunes ruined. Yet his record for nationalism and his influence in the New South were so well recognized that in 1876 he was chosen to write the words that inaugurated Philadelphia's Centennial Exhibition, marking the 100th anniversary of American Independence."

WHEN ALL IS SAID AND DONE

In 1942 the Centennial of the birth of Lanier gave keen impetus to our advancement campaign. Our promotions bloomed that year with programs of Lanier poetry, music, talks, and memorials over the South and in Eastern cities. So vigilant and thorough had been our U.D.C. committee promotions that Lanier was remembered in programs, radio celebrations, newspaper stories and pictures throughout the land. The greatest Centennial celebrations were in Macon and Baltimore, where formal observances attracted national attention.

Baltimore, the city of his adoption, presented a program and unveiled on the Johns Hopkins campus a bronze memorial, a huge plaque with a life-size Lanier figure in relief. By sculptor Hans Schuler, it depicts the bearded and fragile Lanier seated with his books, while figures of Poetry and Music hover nearby.

The Baltimore ceremonies delighted us who were at the poet's birthplace. Many Lanier admirers were torn between the two cities, his birthplace and his adopted home, for a choice of celebrations to attend.

I was in Macon, of course, having arranged in cooperation with Mayor Charles Bowden and a Lanier committee a daylong celebration. A goodly company of Lanier relatives were with us that day, while many others went to the Baltimore Centenary. We were eager for the honor of entertaining Miss Eleanor Turnbull, the revered friend of the Laniers throughout their Baltimore stay and in whose family lot Lanier lies buried. She with her brother had helped arrange the poet's fruitful connection with Johns Hopkins University. But we had to agree with her that her place was in Baltimore, where her sympathy and friendship had contributed so much to Lanier's realization of his genius.

The Johns Hopkins-Peabody Institute commemoration was highlighted by the opening of a Lanier Memorial Room at the University, furnished with his desk and other pieces, his pictures, and a large part of his correspondence and original manuscripts.

SIDNEY LANIER ADVANCEMENT

Dr. Bowman, Maryland's Governor Herbert O'Connor, and Dr. William Lyon Phelps eulogized Lanier at the afternoon program of which Dr. John C. French, the Hopkins librarian and Lanier scholar, was chairman. Lanier poetry was read and there was music by the Peabody orchestra.

We in Macon held our program and rejoiced in the tributes at Baltimore, exchanging greetings during the day with Dr. Isaiah Bowman, Johns Hopkins president.

Macon's Centennial celebration drew distinguished visitors from other sections, including a number of Lanier's relatives. The day began with a visit of guests to Lanier Cottage. At noon I presented to Lanier High School for Boys the Lanier family coat of arms, on behalf of the Sidney Lanier Chapter, U.D.C. Special guests were Lanier relatives and Mrs. R. D. Wright of Newberry, South Carolina, U.D.C. President-General. Visiting Laniers were the John Shipley Tilleys of Montgomery (Mrs. Tilley, Wilsie Lanier, daughter of Clifford, being my cousin with whom I worked later in collecting family material for a definitive edition), Mrs. B. B. Comer of Columbus (daughter of Lanier's only sister, Gertrude Lanier Gibson), and a Lanier great-niece, Gertrude Gibson.

Mr. Tilley addressed the large company at luncheon at the Lanier Hotel, where were entertained many out-of-town guests including Judge and Mrs. Gordon Saussy and Miss Caroline Meldrim of Savannah, Mrs. Theron Lamar Caudle and Mrs. C. A. Yarborough of North Carolina, U.D.C. Lanier committee members.

The Lanier chapter unveiled a tablet marking Lanier's brief service at the bar, 1868-72, in the Second Street office where he worked with his father and brother, Clifford, before yielding to the irresistible urge to make his way in letters and music. The tablet itself was unveiled by young cousins of the poet, Clifford McKay III, Robert Lanier Anderson III, Helen Barnes Anderson, and Sally McKay.

The daylong program was climaxed with a dinner sponsored

by Mercer University and promoted by Mercer President Spright Dowell. Speaker at this affair was Dr. Edwin Mims. I introduced him, and this longtime friend of Lanier advancement addressed several hundred educators, civic leaders, and Lanier lovers to conclude a full and remarkable day of homage.

Centennial celebrations did not cease with February 3 programs. They continued through 1942 with various observances over the South and other sections.

On May 12, I appeared on Ted Malone's "Between the Bookends," and again enjoyed bringing Lanier's message to thousands from "the top of the world," as Radio City always seems to me. I was accorded the deep satisfaction of reading "The Marshes of Glynn." Again, letters and messages from many places told me that the beauty and religious truth of the poetry had reached sympathetic ears.

On we moved toward the 1945 election, gathering new advocates as we advanced. There came a brief but heartening note in 1945 from Steepletop, the Austerlitz home of Edna St. Vincent Millay. Her husband, Eugene Boissevain, assured me that "Miss Millay will vote for him for a place in the Hall of Fame as she has done in the past." President Rufus C. Harris of Tulane University also promised his vote for Lanier in 1945.

After the disappointment of 1940, my discouragement was actually much greater than I cared to let anyone know. I reviewed the effort I had expended to revive and interpret Lanier, feeling that if, after all this, the goal was still not reached, I was not inclined to push him again. My reverence for Lanier and my love for his art precluded any thought of further importuning judges who seemed for the most part turned against him, or unable to appreciate his worth. I felt as strongly as ever our poet's right to be in the Hall of Fame, but I was too proud for our genius to send him begging. We proceeded with our

SIDNEY LANIER ADVANCEMENT

Lanier observances and publicity, apparently with the same ardor as in previous years, though my hopes were low.

In 1943, I took heart, and as chairman again of the U.D.C. Lanier Committee, reported on the previous year's Centennial work, and outlined plans to spread anew the Lanier gospel, with more emphasis on disseminating Lanier's message than on obtaining a place for him in the Hall of Fame.

On October 31, 1945, I was thinking sadly of our fifteen-year labor for Lanier which had come to naught, it seemed. I reflected that, though Lanier would not attain the Hall of Fame, at least we had done a great deal to bring the poet to appreciation in our time.

About mid-morning the telephone rang, and I was called to receive a Western Union message. "Athens, Georgia, October 31, 1945," the voice came to me. "Congratulations. Sidney Lanier in the Hall of Fame at last. Signed, John T. McPherson."

My surprise and the elation I felt really showed me how keen the frequent disappointments had been. I had managed with resolution—and consoling gratitude for our success in spreading the Lanier gospel—perhaps to hide even from myself the weight of disappointment. And when this burden of failure was suddenly lifted, my happiness showed me in joyful contrast just how downcast I had been beneath my seeming courage and hope.

In my pleasure also was a sense of grief that my mother, who had early led me to a love of Lanier, and my husband, who had supported so loyally and proudly all my work, were not with me in the flesh to enjoy this happy end to my years of hard work.

Scores of my friends called, phoned, wired, and wrote to me to increase my happiness in the victory. My niece, Eugenia Blount Anderson, and her husband, Charles, who was at work on the definitive Lanier, wired this brief and singing congratulation: "The game is done, you've won, you've won!"

Next day we read in the newspapers that Negro educator

WHEN ALL IS SAID AND DONE

Booker T. Washington, Revolutionary philosopher Tom Paine, scientist Walter Reed, and poet and musician Sidney Lanier were elected to the Hall of Fame for Great Americans at New York University. Our Sidney Lanier became the 77th genius to be voted into the Hall.

Of all the messages I received, a few might be mentioned to show how much this labor of love meant to so many people.

May Lanier (Mrs. Charles Day Lanier) wrote her love and congratulations over this honor to her husband's father. Also greetings came from Dr. Mims. Next day the William Alexander Chapter U.D.C. of Greenwich, Connecticut, Mrs. Lanier's chapter, sent me a wire announcing they were claiming the distinction of making the first contribution to the bust of Lanier for the Hall, with a gift of a $100 war bond.

From Winship Grammar School in Macon came a note: "Dear Mrs. Lamar, We wish to express our deep appreciation for your success in getting Sidney Lanier's name included in the Hall of Fame. Thank you for everything you have done. Sincerely, Seventh Grade."

When the news of Lanier's election was announced in the local papers on page one with a picture of me and an account of my fifteen-year work for the poet, there arose a spontaneous movement among my fellow citizens to have part in establishing Lanier's bust in the Hall of Fame. Between the time of Lanier's election and the unveiling of the bust in New York, Macon gave $3000 to the fund.

Our joy over the triumph of Lanier continued until the unveiling of the bronze bust in the fall, and I was kept busy with details until the day of the dedication, October 3.

Shortly after notification of the Lanier success, and following the newspaper accounts of the election, I was dismayed to receive from director James R. Angell of the Hall of Fame an announcement that "proponents were privileged to pay $5,000 for the creation and establishment" of the Lanier bust, and that the sculptor would proceed only when this sum was in hand.

Expense of the bronzes, bust and pedestal, was of course to be borne by U.D.C. This was so understood throughout. But, since Lanier's election came as a surprise to us, the whole sum was not in hand. Although there was already $2,000 subscribed at the Houston Convention when I announced Lanier's election in 1945, the Daughters would not meet in general convention until November of 1946, and it was impossible to collect the additional amount before the time set for the unveiling.

Dr. Angell's requirements, nonetheless, were unequivocal and inflexible. Even though I reminded him of an instance where the sponsoring organization had not advanced the cash so far ahead, this precedent did not seem to affect our situation. So in order not to delay the great hour, and confident of course in the integrity of the Daughters, I advanced $5,000 without interest to the Hall of Fame so that the sculptor might begin his work.

I was anxious to have a replica of the youthful Lanier by Gutzon Borglum. But this choice, too, it seemed was not for us. Dr. Angell selected Hans Schuler of Baltimore to do the bust. I had hoped to have the work of art depict the young Lanier with the strong, yet spiritual and delicate beardless face, which seems to typify the undefeated soul of the genius we espoused more than does the grave, hollow-cheeked man of sorrows which has been so often portrayed. So I wrote the sculptor. Dr. Angell chose Schuler and the bearded period for the bust, and I yielded to his preference.

These matters having been settled in February, I suggested on behalf of U.D.C. that our distinguished friend and world-renowned Southern historian, Dr. Douglas S. Freeman, be invited for the main address. But Dr. Angell, I learned, had already selected Dr. Isaiah Bowman, president of Johns Hopkins University. Dr. Bowman, educator, literary man, Hall of

Fame elector, and Lanier lover, was of course acceptable to us.

Our next problem was the inscription for the marker. I had hoped to see "Thyself, Thy Monument" inscribed on the pedestal. But the Hall of Fame had other plans.

Dr. Angell suggested: "His song was only living aloud, His work, a singing with his hands."

This seemed to be good enough Lanier, but wholly inadequate, lacking as it does his spiritual depth. Later Dr. Angell offered another Lanier quotation, "Weakness in freedom grows stronger than strength with a chain." And the "weakness and chains" quotation was used. The significance of Dr. Angell's insistence on this line seemed clearer when I found that Lanier was placed in close proximity to Abolitionist Harriet Beecher Stowe in the rotunda!

As I reported to the U.D.C. General Convention in November, it should be known that when one plans placement of a candidate in the Hall of Fame and enters upon preparation for consummation of the effort, one leaves choice of all this or that behind. I was asked with great formality whom I should like to have for a speaker, only to find that the University had invited one. I was asked for inscription suggestions, but mine were rejected and the University selection used. Prepared to suggest a sculptor, I was told that this was the right of the Electors' committee.

There were many times during the months preceding the presentation of the bust when I had to remind myself to be quiet and happy in the one privilege which was accorded the Daughters of the Confederacy without reservation, namely the honor of subscribing the $5,000 for the work, and that right quickly!

Dr. Bowman and I exchanged a series of letters, in which he was kind enough to welcome and adopt my suggestions for Lanierana we hoped to see incorporated in his speech, and graciously put himself in accord with our hopes and plans for the dedication.

SIDNEY LANIER ADVANCEMENT

I advised Dr. Angell of Lanier descendants, and that the poet's grandson, Sidney Lanier, was the Lanier to unveil the bust. I referred him to young Lanier's mother, Mrs. Charles D. Lanier, who assembled thirty relatives for the ceremony.

My last few letters from Dr. Angell were cordial and grateful, and it was with satisfaction that I realized I had weathered some serious shocks and disappointments, in addition to a heavy burden of work and travel, without betraying overt resentment or hard feeling.

The unveiling of the Lanier bronze on October 3, 1946, was marked by dignity, beauty, and consecration which fitly climaxed our years of work to honor Sidney Lanier, and compensated for all the years of work and disappointment, and fulfilled the proud expectations of his native city.

The great day came. The University authorities sent seven-passenger limousines to the Waldorf for U.D.C. guests. We were accompanied by General Blanton Winship of Macon; Dr. Robert McElroy, historian and Hall of Fame elector; Miss Margaret Rouquie and Mrs. Tommye Finney, my personal guests. Of course the faithful on the Lanier committee, Mrs. Frank F. Jones of Macon, then U.D.C. Historian-General, Mrs. T. L. Caudle of North Carolina, and Mrs. Edwin W. Cook of Clemson, South Carolina, were in our party. Lanier's daughter-in-law, Mrs. Charles Day Lanier, attended as a family member and as President of the Robert E. Lee Foundation at Stratford, with four Stratford directors. A delegation of ex-Presidents-General of U.D.C. led a large representation of Daughters.

The official party, University and Hall of Fame officials, U.D.C. officers, members of the Lanier family, and other guests, entered the Hall. Organ music hailed our arrival at the auditorium platform, where the assembled audience was greeted by New York University's Vice Chancellor Harold O. Voorhees. Then Dr. Angell took over.

The veiled Lanier bust, on a dais in the center of the stage, was presented to the Hall of Fame by Mrs. John M. Wilcox, for

U.D.C. Young Sidney Lanier stepped forward and lifted the veil, revealing a beautiful bronze which depicted the noble Lanier head, slightly bowed, as if in deep thought.

Wreaths of greenery culled from three states closely associated with Lanier's life were laid at the foot of the pedestal. The Macon and Habersham wreaths were made of foliage from Lanier locales woven into tributes by a Macon florist. Mr. Anderson, Lanier's cousin, placed the wreath from Macon; it contained ivy and magnolia leaves from the High Street birthplace. Three great-grandchildren of the poet, Mary Day Lanier, Sandra Lanier McKean, and Michael Lanier Trimpi, placed wreaths that were gifts from the Maryland U.D.C. and from Baltimore. There were also wreaths from North Carolina U.D.C., from the U.D.C. from coast to coast, from Habersham Daughters, and from the White House.

Organ music accompanied these presentations and flute solos were played by John Wummer, first flautist of the New York Philharmonic Symphony Orchestra. Miss Jean Dickenson, radio lyric soprano, sang songs beloved of Lanier including his own "May and Maiden," set to music by Carpenter, and Lanier's own music to "Love That Hath Us in the Net."

I felt that the Hall of Fame had wrought a beautiful tribute to Lanier in the music, including his favorite flute numbers, and the one available piece of music written by Lanier. This was not easily achieved, as much of the music was out of print and could only be obtained with the help of music scholars at New York University, the New York Public Library, and Johns Hopkins University.

Dr. Bowman satisfied us thoroughly with his Lanier tribute, recalling our poet's art and courage. He sounded a triumphant note, an understanding of Lanier's spiritual achievement, explaining that the poet overcame all difficulties with the "impulse of the artist" and that he "surmounted obstacles which a character less strong could not have faced."

I had expected to feel some trepidation when the time came

SIDNEY LANIER ADVANCEMENT

for my address, since it seemed to me the most important speech of my life, to be delivered to a distinguished company on an occasion crowning my greatest effort. However, when I arose, I found that a calm happiness and confidence had banished all nervousness and uncertainty. I spoke with as much ease and pleasure as I could wish, telling from my heart what I knew of the beauties and values of Lanier's life and art, as follows:

What come we out for to see?—
A poet who wrote some verses?
A piper who made some tunes?
A student who reveled in dusty tomes and the science of sound? Aye! All these and more! We are come out to look upon and to honor a poet who told in perfect rhythm of God and man and nature, and who interwove these three with faultless minstrelsy. W behold also a student whose guiding star was conscience; an idealist who believed that mental beauty and spiritual beauty must go hand in hand; one who said that the beauty of holiness and the holiness of beauty mean one thing—burn as one fire—shine as one light. And we see a genius "whose song was only living aloud, his work a singing with his hand."

The life of Sidney Lanier began in a little gabled cottage in Macon, Georgia. His earthly life ended in the autumn-clad hills of North Carolina. 'Neath a coverlet of ivy in Baltimore, the city of his adoption, he sleeps his last sleep, the place marked by a granite boulder on which is inscribed a line from his poem, "Sunrise,"

"I am lit with the Sun."

Within the brief span of life allotted him on this sphere, Lanier left a deathless message which breathes love of truth, of God and of his fellowman.

There is an instrument known to science that exaggerates the faintest sound to the ear as does the microscope a mere speck to the eye. Such an instrument shall be these tributes to Lanier, Musician and Poet, echoing to the world gratitude for the life he lived, the song he sang and the love he taught. Come also rhapsodies from the throats of the winged songsters that he loved, the mocking bird, "upon a plumed spray that high above the general leafage grew," the lark, the robin, the plaint of lonesome doves, the deep tones of the wise old owl and "all the feathered things my father God hath made."

Sure of his calling, Lanier wrote: "I am conscious of a certain sense of exaltation. I suppose every man of letters comes soon to feel a sense of consecration and priesthood, 'as one who hath mightily won God out of knowledge and good out of infinite pain, sight out of blindness and purity out of a stain.'"

O that America might turn from those who pervert their talent by pandering to low standards; who stress the seamy side of life and belittle the good; and who, by encouraging the works of modernistic ideology and joining the struggle for exploitation of sadism and pornography do choke the flowers of Truth and Decency.

If the youth of our land will study Lanier's life, his prose and his poetry, an impelling inspiration will be felt, a strong realization will come that purity is power, that holiness is beauty, that the award of courage is not alone to the soldier in battle, but to whosoever faces life's problems with a clear conscience and a righteous antagonism toward greed, selfishness, and idleness.

Despite the "slings and arrows of outrageous fortune," Lanier fought with increasing fervor for the opportunity to devote his life to Music and Poetry. With a song on his lips and a prayer in his heart he drank the toast: "Time, let not a drop be spilt. Hand me the cup whene'er thou wilt, 'tis thy rich stirrup cup to me; I'll drink it down right smilingly." Such was the philosophy of one who believed "Howe'er thou turn'st, wrong earth, still love's in sight and we are taller than the breadth of night."

In the presentation of the Lanier bronzes to the Hall of Fame, the Daughters of the Confederacy fulfil one of the cardinal principles of the Society, namely education of mind and soul in the fundamentals that made America great. Thus do they strive to stem the tide of Commercialism run rampant, of Atheism that seeks to corral a bewildered generation. So inspired, they have spread the knowledge of Lanier in the belief that with such knowledge will come nation-wide recognition of his genius, that the steady light from his own five-point star radiating Hope, Faith, Love, Loyalty, and Courage may yet show a piteous world out of the morass of muck and misery that has trapped humanity.

With reverence and affection we dedicate this portrait in bronze of Sidney Lanier, a worthy companion to the noblest of these who have found place in this corridor and in so doing, we give into the goodly company a poet made up of joy and sorrow, of love and laughter, of sympathies large and discerning, of every day thoughts in magic garb, one who glorified our country's past and prophesied her future. Because all these and more are in him blended we would that all who know him should rejoice in this noble figure and that those who do not know him may learn of him and be guided to his poetry.

SIDNEY LANIER ADVANCEMENT

We salute a Poet whose diamond-tipped pen raced with death and won out for all time, a musician whose genius matched his superb soul, a Christian gentleman in word and deed, a soldier "sans peur et sans reproche,"
Sidney Lanier
"Thyself, Thy monument."

The attention given my speech and the momentary quiet at its close, with the long applause which followed, told me of the warm and loving thanks of Lanier lovers, of the Daughters, and of the Lanier kin for my work to place our genius in the Hall of Fame.

We left the auditorium and marched across the campus up the slight rise of ground to the beautiful bronze and marble rotunda, the Hall of Fame itself. It was a happy and satisfying conclusion, to see Lanier's place in the Hall of Fame, between marble columns open to the sun and sky and trees he loved.

Several days later Mayor Bowden notified me that the citizens of Macon wanted to give an appreciation dinner for me, and asked me to set the date. Of course I was very proud and happy over such an expression of love from home.

Indeed, this October of 1946, when I was in my eightieth year, seemed to be a charmed time for me, and the days at home before November 15, the time set for the appreciation dinner, I recall as flower-decked and singing with messages from friends and colleagues far and near. Indeed, bouquets, baskets of flowers, and orchids filled my home, and my mail was heavy with words of affection and pleasure in the tribute my townsfolk planned for me.

Mayor Bowden and his committee sent invitations to several hundred U.D.C. associates, electors in the Hall of Fame, New York University officials, Stratford directors, and other friends gleaned in the long years of the Lanier advocacy. There were of course many regrets from far places, but most of them were accompanied by such warm greetings that I was almost as gratified as I would have been had all my friends and Lanier lovers been able to come. Mr. W. C. Turpin, Jr., presided eloquently.

One of the pleasant features of the occasion was the artistic programs, designed and assembled by Warren Roberts, including a sketch of my life by Mary Callaway Jones, a copy of my address at the Lanier unveiling, the Hall of Fame program, a poem of mine written in 1927, "The Flute to His Master," a current picture of me and one captioned, "Dolly Blount, age two." The folder was handsomely done on glossy paper, tied with a silken cord, and highlighted by this tribute from Dr. Freeman:

> The whole of the South stands around the table at which tonight you honor Mrs. Walter Lamar. No woman of our region more perfectly understands the spirit of the Confederacy and none has a higher conception of what the old Southern traditions are to be hereafter. Her diligence is monumental, but her catholicity in all that concerns the Confederate cause is no less amazing. She knows its literature as well as its heroes and though too young herself to have been a direct participant, she is in spirit a sharer. I love to think of her not only as a supreme daughter of the Confederacy, but a supreme daughter of America. Congratulate her, please, in my name and that of other Southern writers and permit me to be among those who do homage to her.

My nephew, the Reverend Walter Douglas Roberts, who sat on my left, opened the program with an invocation. Then came General Walter Harris's address, containing praise which made me wonder "who can this woman be?" My head quite spun with endearments, from "Macon's sweetheart," "Macon's first lady," to "Our very own Dolly," and "Dear, Darling Dolly," used by various speakers.

I was greatly moved by General Harris's résumé of my public life, and the emphasis he put on my work for my home, my state, and my region:

> Endowed by nature with an intellect far beyond that of most women and of most men—highly educated, reared among statesmen and diplomats, at ease in the company of the great ones of the earth, as regal as royalty itself, brilliant in conversation, fluent and eloquent, with a

BIRTHPLACE OF SIDNEY LANIER

determination that bent others to her will, with feminine charm that made them glad to do her bidding, ambitious as Caesar, she might have been a political leader holding high office in the nation. And she has remained here hard by the place she was born, and all her mighty works have been wrought for the people of her own city and of her own section of the country.

Complete as is her character, versatile as is her genius, varied as are her activities, many as are her accomplishments, one singly holy motive runs through all. She is a seer. Where others' eyes were blinded by the light of visible things, she caught the glory of the invisible. Where others sought the false wealth of earth, she found the true wealth of the spirit.

She set herself to show her own people how God had manifested himself in the history and traditions of the South.

I have called her Macon's greatest citizen. To be great one must have a great objective and press on toward it. The measure of greatness is the height of the obstacles surmounted. Thus defined and thus measured, her greatness so appears that I am justified in calling her America's greatest woman.

R. L. Anderson's speech, thanking me on behalf of the Lanier family for the poet's advancement, recalled my early interest in his life and work and the struggles of the Lanier advocacy, "but more than all else" he saluted "her indomitable spirit which triumphs over difficulties and transforms defeat into victory...."

A surprise pleasure of the evening was the presentation by Dr. Albert Grady Harris, pastor of my church, of a magnificent token, a silver platter inscribed:

Eugenia Dorothy Blount Lamar, gifted with charm of personality, brilliance and courage, her spirited leadership has contributed in a distinguished way to the cultural, patriotic and spiritual life of the South. Presented by the citizens of Macon, Georgia, at a public dinner in her honor November 15, 1946.

And then it became my sweet privilege to thank my assembled friends for the tribute they had carried out in my honor. The dinner was so profoundly gratifying to me that I was forced to invoke humor in order not to embarrass myself and all my friends with tears of joy.

WHEN ALL IS SAID AND DONE

When I first arose, I could only say, "All this and heaven, too?" which was a propitious beginning, I suppose, because it brought some laughter to help me over the danger of being overcome by too much happiness. Then I told an amusing story on myself, from the 1912 Confederate Veterans' Reunion, on which I had worked with General Harris.

This had the hoped-for result of easing with more laughter my tightening throat and the fears of the assembly that I might break down. I then expressed my pleasure over the honor my good friends did me, and closed with a brief quotation from my tribute to Lanier at the Hall of Fame. Through it all a sense of humility came upon me, and thoughts of loved ones no longer in life were with me the whole evening, so that my heart was full.

All of this loving and extravagant praise from my friends might have induced delusions of grandeur, but for the protestations of another friend who is frequently at hand to prick any possible ballooning of my self-esteem. Next day, in a happy post-mortem of the grand affair she adroitly managed to jerk my head from the clouds of praise and plant my feet firmly on the ground.

It was lovely, she said, and they were all so happy at the success of the dinner. I had been charming and clever and my gown was stunning, and everything went off beautifully. But, Dolly, it *was* going a bit too far for Walter to say you were "America's greatest woman." That was *too* extravagant, really, in fact, absurd. Didn't I agree? Everything was grand, but Walter laid it on so *thick*."

And this, despite the fact that General Harris had by a graceful adjusting of events and with a lawyer's clever powers of ratiocination led up to this superlative tribute!

Thus chastened, I was put back in my place amongst ordinary mortals, with my head out of the clouds and my feet on the ground.

MIRACLE
OF THE DEPRESSION

LOOKING THROUGH THE PAPERS OF HER FATHER-IN-LAW, in 1928 Mrs. Charles Day Lanier found a long lost address by the poet delivered in Macon before a reunion of Confederate Veterans. The speech was dated October 13, 1870. It was in the ornate style of the day, touched with Lanier's grace and sincerity, and closing with the following resolution:

> That we invite our countrymen to unite in some enduring testimonial to the stainless life and glorious services of our departed general and that in the judgment of this meeting such monument would assume its best propriety in the form of a great hall of fame to be built by such voluntary contributions as shall be within the compass of the humblest citizen who loved him and who desires the grateful privilege of laying some tribute on his tomb.

Almost coincident with her discovery news came to Mrs. Lanier that Stratford, Westmoreland County, Virginia, birthplace of Robert E. Lee and home of generations of the Lee family, might be purchased.

Realizing that the place could become the "enduring testimonial" envisioned by Sidney Lanier, Mrs. Charles Day Lanier assumed the leadership. She first interested the William Alexander Chapter, U.D.C., at her home in Greenwich, Connecticut, in the tremendous project to purchase, restore, and enshrine the historic home of the Virginia Lees, "Stratford Hall."

Bravely and enthusiastically the Chapter entered into the

fulfilment of the poet's exhortation. With $9.33 in its treasury, and a loan of $5,000 from Mrs. Alexander Field (mother of Mrs. Charles Lanier) and believing that the United Daughters of the Confederacy would take over the purchase, they signed the contract. Confidently and blithely, May Field Lanier took a $5,000 option on the place owned by Charles E. Stewart.

She was greatly shocked in November, 1928, though not permanently dismayed, upon learning at the U.D.C. convention that the organization could not finance so great an undertaking, in addition to their many historical and educational projects. However, the Daughters voted later the sum of $10,000 for repairs and refurnishing of the room in which General Lee was born, and still later they gave $50,000 as the final payment on the property.

Undaunted, with driving vision and a lofty disdain for such obstacles as money, Mrs. Lanier set about raising $240,000 to purchase Stratford Hall. Though somewhat in disrepair, the great house was still a sturdy and imposing edifice, massive and austere, potentially one of the worthiest shrines in our nation—the house of the Lees built by Thomas Lee in 1729.

How May Lanier raised the funds to purchase this shrine has been called the "Miracle of the Depression." Her zeal, her devotion, her extraordinary way with financiers and with the board of state directors implemented her vision.

I received my invitation to become a member of the Robert E. Lee Foundation through a telegram from Mrs. Lanier while I was on a house party in South Georgia. Much worn with the preceding year's effort to enlist public interest and contributions for placing a marble bust of Sidney Lanier at the Washington Memorial Library in Macon, I very nearly refused this new call to duty. But my good angel, my mother, urged me to accept and through the remaining years of her life she continued her interest in the purchase and restoration of Stratford. Several times when she was quite ill and I was planning to give up an official trip to Stratford, she would insist on my going.

MIRACLE OF THE DEPRESSION

On January 19, 1929, the formation of the Robert E. Lee Foundation, Inc., was announced at a Lee Birthday Party held in the Hotel Astor, New York, at which time payment of $10,000 was given by Sons and Daughters of the Confederacy. Resultant publicity began in the *New York Times* and spread over the country.

Our Certificate of Corporation was signed ceremoniously March 25, 1929, by Mrs. Lanier and Mr. Stuart, witnessed by Mrs. Alice H. Richards, Regent of the Mount Vernon Ladies Association, after whose foundation our organization was modeled. Following this pattern the directors, who make up a self-perpetuating board, elected Mrs. Charles Lanier, founder and temporary chairman, to the presidency of the Foundation.

Men and women from every section of the country responded eagerly to the call for help in restoring the property which had not yet been purchased—and this in the first calamitous year of the Depression! Nationally distinguished men were honored to serve on our advisory committee, and exciting reports began to come in from various states.

State directors met six times that year in Richmond, Washington, and New York, beginning a busy and friendly association of women which has changed little in more than twenty years.

The "Miracle of the Depression" showed its first astonishing flower on July 13, 1929, when we made a down payment of $50,000 to Mr. Stuart, with a mortgage of $190,000 due in 1932. Thus began our amazing and exciting success. On the occasion of our first meeting at our own Stratford in October, Mrs. Fairfax Harrison of Virginia announced as the contribution of the Garden Clubs of Virginia their plan to restore the Stratford gardens in the grand manner of the 18th century, which restoration continues to delight visitors and to rejoice the hearts of the directors.

In the early days, Stratford directors, repairing thither for semi-annual council meetings, were hard put for housing near

WHEN ALL IS SAID AND DONE

the Lee place. We tried at first, commuting from Fredericksburg forty-five miles away, and later lodged at private homes in Montross six miles away. All plans were unsatisfactory; so we built, at individual expense, log cabins appropriately placed in the woods and well out of sight of the Mansion itself.

Cabin life at Stratford proves to be one of the most delightful and rewarding aspects of our Stratford work. Each structure is named for a species of trees in the Stratford woods. These cabins are temporary homes and social retreats where we enjoy fast friendships, and do much serious work for Stratford. With good beds, hot water in plenty, and electric lights, we rough it *de luxe*.

Our life there together indicates the peculiarly happy selection of directors. In the twenty-two years of our service, we have grown in attachment to and enjoyment of one another. Directors are all women of gracious background, of culture, and of special talents devoted to the work. Our congeniality is perhaps unique in the annals of such organizations.

I think of Mrs. Granville Valentine of Richmond, representing on our board the Lee Family Society; Mrs. Peter W. Arrington, Director of North Carolina, Chairman of Fine Arts—she personally restored to its early splendor the Great Hall; May Lanier, our first and longtime president, who dreamed her dream and summoned to her aid women from all corners of the country. She is so merry, so sweet and approachable, so scornful of money and yet so effective in collecting it for Stratford that we all found ourselves happily working for the Foundation, giving to its maintenance and furnishings; Mrs. Harry B. Hawes of Missouri, who ably assumed the duties of President following Mrs. Lanier, and who was later succeeded by Mrs. A. C. Ford of Clifton Forge, Virginia.

At "The Cedars," the cabin of directors for Virginia, South Carolina, Tennessee, and Georgia, we have dwelt together since the movement crystallized, and later we furnished our commodious cabin. The four are Mrs. Horace Van Deventer from

Tennessee, a pioneer who helped in the organic structures of our Foundation; Mrs. A. J. Geer of South Carolina, our Chairman of Gardens and Grounds; Mrs. A. C. Ford of Virginia; and myself.

Some of the other directors are Mrs. Breckenbridge Long of Maryland, wife of a former Ambassador to Italy and our erudite expert on antiques; Helen Knox, our treasurer, ex-president of the Women's National Banking Association and head of the women's department of the Chase National Bank until her retirement in 1944; Mrs. Harold Berry of Maine, author and humanitarian; Mrs. Edmund Ball of Indiana, who is also on the Kenmore Board; Mrs. S. J. Campbell, chairman of finance—a difficult job which she does well; Mrs. Walter C. White of South Carolina and Ohio; Mrs. Rufus Garrett of Arkansas, a wizard in financial matters; Mrs. Alfred I. Du Pont, a fervent worker in Delaware and Florida; and Mrs. Robert Worth Bingham of Kentucky, widow of the former Ambassador to the Court of St. James.

Eager for Georgia to do her part toward enshrining the Lee home, I, like other directors, set about raising funds to that end. Many were the projects and generous was the help received in these efforts.

One of the projects was a Water Carnival I staged to raise Georgia's part of the necessary funds, to which interested parties came from far and near. It was a gay and spectacular success, and a delightful collusion of fervor for the Stratford cause with our best town talent—musical, histrionic, and terpsichorean.

Having enjoyed at Mobile a Stratford benefit through the staging of the "Show Boat" in the harbor, I returned home with the determination to copy it as nearly as possible for a Georgia benefit.

I had no waterfront and no showboat, but I borrowed a nearby lake, transformed the diving heights into the "Robert E. Lee" and staged an excellent performance on its decks. I overcame the town's rather lazy reluctance to do the impossible and soon enlisted carpenters, painters, performers, and costumes with cooperation from officials, dignitaries, and artists in every line.

Mr. Lamar provided the lumber and graciously averred that the dismantled planks were just what he needed for repair at his peach farm and accordingly bought the lumber at a fancy price.

I commandeered the park's supply of rowboats for a parade of scenes from song and story. Our tableaux ranged from a Carmen setting for one boat, from which Eunice Harper (a former diva turned teacher in Macon) sang arias, to Tennyson's Barge of the Dead where slept Elaine, the lily maid of Astolat.

How to move this lavish procession of mimes and music was a problem we solved with the help of Bruce Carr Jones, a local attorney. Mr. Jones is a stately, smiling symbol of impervious dignity hereabouts, well-endowed with Confederate ancestors of the finest local tradition. He was wont, however, on past occasions to stoop to folly with his hobby of motorboating on the river. Such was his ardor, it is told, that one Memorial Day his roaring, chugging progress up and down the red waters of the Ocmulgee drowned out Memorial Day Services in Rose Hill Cemetery, where sleep Confederate war dead on the river bank. Later, he expressed deep regret for his forgetfulness of the ceremonies in progress.

Obviously, Bruce was the man to move our water parade with his motor launch. He consented gladly.

The Water Carnival evening came clear and warm, with a fine sunset preceding a bright moon. Lakeside was thronged with people. I had rented concessions for refreshments, and these decorated added to other festive trappings. The crowd was pleased with the salty waterfront look of old Lakeside, and delighted (in the local spirit with which Macon enjoys its own talent above all imported art) with the show, and the audience was dazzled by the richness of the floats.

MIRACLE OF THE DEPRESSION

Suddenly, the water parade of tableaux stopped! Spectators on the banks could see Mr. Jones examining his motor—but without the fretful concern of a lesser man in such a crisis. His smiling dignity was undisturbed. Rising in his launch, he stripped off his coat, plunged into the lake, and with the help of lifeguards, towed the procession to a triumphant finish.

It was a memorable performance for Macon and for Stratford, unexcelled in the annals of the town as far as I know.

Husbands of many of the directors caught the enthusiasm for Stratford and contributed to various phases of the restoration, some of these gifts running into the thousands. All directors rally to the aid of chairmen of special objectives eager to help the work forward and to secure its future through endowment. "Ole Man Maintenance" is always in need and always gets help, particularly from the "Friends of Stratford" fund, which each director collects in her own state. The working staff is deeply interested and adds greatly to the success of the enterprise.

The new dining room built by contributions from directors (to replace the one destroyed by fire) is a great asset for our public as well as for members of the Corporation.

The Council Chamber is a gem of Colonial architecture given to the Robert E. Lee Foundation, Inc., in honor of the Founder, May Field Lanier, by Jessie Ball DuPont (Mrs. A. I.).

In a gratifying compliment to me my husband presented four showcases for display of historic relics pertaining to the Lee family. Up to the acquisition of the cases such relics were kept at the Chase National Bank at considerable expense. The cases were selected by the Relics Committee, and are now in the Mansion where their contents add great interest to the Shrine and are displayed in the Treasure Room.

Our first superintendent, General B. F. Cheatham, co-ordinated in masterly fashion the industries of a Colonial plantation, and the charm of the Great House. At General Cheatham's death the directors chose as his successor, Colonel Cooper

Winn, whose fine war record is a source of pride to all who know him and whose success in the business world of New York City commends him for the place. Colonel Winn and his wife have proved more than worthy of this great trust with its manifold duties. They not only administer in wisdom and perfection the duties of the position, but contribute from their fine social qualities to the happiness of the directors as well as that of visitors.

The Foundation honors the numerous men and women of the Stratford Lees. We glory in the émigré, Richard Lee, I; in the honorable services of Thomas Lee to the Crown and to the Colonies; in the patriotic contributions of the six Lee brothers (sons of Hannah and Thomas Lee—two of whom were signers of the Declaration of Independence); in the fine qualities of statesmanship and military ability of Henry Lee, Washington's favorite general. We note also the wise marriages that contributed through generations to their sense of honor, their lofty patriotism, and their assumption of civic responsibility.

But Stratford in its entirety is now the fulfilment of Sidney Lanier's resolution of 1870 that we establish "a testimonial of just propriety to the memory of Robert E. Lee," and on that basis the Foundation points with pride to Stratford.

Robert E. Lee sprang full panoplied at the start for life's battles, adding glory to a great name, and standing ever as a symbol of purity, courage and selfless public service—a standard-bearer of high and noble purpose. He was, as Douglas Freeman says, "The full flowering of men and women who made no mésalliances; he came into the world genetically prepared for the great things life might present."

Accordingly, whatever his hand found to do, he did it with all the strength of his superb mind, body, and soul, whether in the conduct of battles, or acceptance of the arbitrament of war, whether the immediate hour called for affectionate care of his family or the training of the youth of his stricken land for support of a reunited nation. Faith in his God and his fellowman

MIRACLE OF THE DEPRESSION

colored his every act and made him the one figure in all history whose name there has been no effort to besmirch.

Behold a man who early found the Holy Grail and never lost the vision!

RELUCTANT POLITICIAN

AROUND 1919 THE MILITANT MOVEMENT FOR WOMAN SUFfrage, which was already victorious in Scandinavian countries, in England, and other parts of Europe, was in full cry in the United States, and began to move South gathering converts to the Susan B. Anthony amendment.

The Southern fight against suffrage was as furious as that in other sections of the country; perhaps more so, since the Federal amendment granting equal suffrage carried threats to our delicately balanced race relations, our white primary, and our strongly entrenched ideas of the traditional protected position of Southern women.

The Southern struggle, however, did not seem to be distinguished by the insults and even violence that Northern suffragettes brought on themselves from their masculine opponents. This may have been due to the fact that advocates in the far South were less aggressive and more dignified in their technique. Few mounted soapboxes to speak on street corners for their cause, and few opened themselves to attacks from foes who hurled tomatoes along with derision and insults.

The debate was carried on, not of course without great heat, frequent high feeling, and even personal attacks, but at orderly meetings, through newspaper forums and reasonable and dignified avenues of discussion.

With most of my friends and associates, I was staunchly antisuffrage. This view was inherent in the tradition to which I was born and reared, and in the convictions which had governed my life up to that time. The Federal amendment, dictating to the states how their franchise should be used, was an invasion of state sovereignty.

A hidden threat to Southern customs was of course in the amendment's grant of equal suffrage to *all* women, thus upsetting the restrictions of the white primary, which since Reconstruction days had left Southern political affairs in the hands of white voters. Obviously this encroachment on our system would lead to universal suffrage and serious political unbalance over the South.

I believed, too, that women wielded much greater and more effective power as women and as home makers. The few scattered states which had granted suffrage had won no great benefits from women at the polls. So I was convinced that the body politic would gain no good from votes for women, but would lose immeasurably by diverting and scattering women's interests and energies.

In 1911 I entered with zest and conviction the work of the local and state branches of the National Association Opposed to Woman Suffrage, and in the course of the next few years found that my interest and my service had carried me to the vice presidency of the National Association, and into many a local, state, and regional debate and struggle.

Our Georgia war on suffrage was distinguished by furious upheaval in the Georgia Federation of Women's Clubs, by ringing oratory pro and con in the state legislature, by rifts between women friends, and by the surprising championship of the movement on the part of several Georgia women who defied their class, their background, and their family traditions to espouse the cause.

It is still interesting today, after thirty years of women's voting, to look back on the high hopes of the reformers and suffragettes who thought their vote would bring the millenium to American politics and society. Even during the days of the suffrage fight, it was apparent that the suffrage states had gained little in these reforms. Judge Ben Lindsey himself, male champion of the suffragettes, had in 1912 rebuked the women of Colorado who failed to support government reforms. He said then, "We are twenty years behind Massachusetts, in spite of suffrage," and that "Colorado has made a science of corrupting her public men."

I could not but agree, and with the pressure of our local problems vivid before us in the South, I warned: "Look out for the scalawag in our midst, and the influx of carpetbaggers from the would-be controllers of the Negro vote. Theirs would be a solid Republican asset. . . . When some man wants office so badly that he, a renegade, will appeal to the government to enforce the law, perhaps the Southern Suffs will wake up."

I stressed that there "is not nor will there ever be any doubt as to the maintenance of white supremacy in the South, but it has taken us forty years in the South to counteract the evils of the Fifteenth Amendment, and here are our Southern suffragists lending their time and talents to letting loose upon us the evils of unrestricted suffrage!"

The chief inspirer of our anti-suffrage activities in Georgia was Columnist James Callaway of the *Macon Telegraph*. His logic, his sincerity, and his hard-hitting defense of the Constitutional rights of the states made of him a powerful ally from the earliest days of our fight. Another champion was Miss Mildred Rutherford, a brilliant and effective orator who fought valiantly for our viewpoint. They are well-remembered leaders of the large number of people in Georgia who influenced the legislature to defeat the Federal amendment in our state four times.

In 1915 Miss Caroline Patterson, president of the Georgia Association Opposed to Woman Suffrage, appointed me as head of a delegation to address the Georgia legislature. I spoke for forty-five minutes before the House Committee considering the Suffrage Bill, the Committee on Amendments to the Constitution of Georgia, marshalling all the anti-suffrage arguments at my command. To this day, Georgia has not ratified the 19th Amendment, though it was presented to the legislature four times.

At another time I addressed a North Carolina legislative committee which had the Suffrage Amendment under study. I went to Raleigh with a group who sought to dissuade North Carolina from ratifying the amendment, at a time which would have provided the suffragists with their "Perfect 36"—the last, or 36th, state necessary for a majority to pass the amendment. North Carolinians also voted against it.

One of my most interesting trips in this cause was to Dayton, Ohio, to call on Governor Cox, the Democratic presidential nominee in 1920, who was advancing suffrage with Tennessee state representatives then considering the amendment. A Nashville meeting of the executive committee of the Southern Women's League for Rejection of the Susan B. Anthony Amendment decided to send a committee to Candidate Cox to ask him to desist, in the name of democracy, from advocating endorsement of the amendment in Tennessee, which was now the much-needed "36th."

Mrs. S. J. Pinchard of Alabama, president of the Southern Women's League, appointed for this mission Mrs. George Washington of Nashville, Mrs. W. S. Pleasants, wife of the Governor of Louisiana, Mrs. W. E. P. Wyse of Maryland, Miss Kilbreath of New York, and myself.

We reached the Governor's office at Dayton at the appointed hour of 5 p. m. His suave young buffer, named Morris, met us and explained that the Governor had gone home sick and left no word about our appointment. In learning that we represented seven states, he got Governor Cox's wife on the telephone and informed us that the Governor would arise from his sick bed and see us at home.

The Governor sent his car for us and we met with him at "Trail's End," his home, for an interview which we found to be a masterpiece of evasion on his part.

WHEN ALL IS SAID AND DONE

Mrs. Washington asked the following question: "Governor Cox, are you going to intimidate the legislature of Tennessee by endeavoring as Democratic Presidential nominee to make the members endorse this Federal suffrage amendment?" The Governor replied, "Well, no—not intimidate." When she told him of reports that he had emissaries over the state striving to persuade Tennesseeans to surrender their rights to handle their own affairs, he answered, "There are a great many reports about me."

Mrs. Pleasants talked very frankly about Cox's prospects to become President if he should sign the "force bill," and about the reaction of Southern Democrats. To this he answered that he would sign no "force bill." She also told him of strong opposition to his reported policy and his candidacy on account thereof among Louisiana Democrats.

Mrs. Wyse reminded Cox of Maryland's rejection of the amendment, of resentment over efforts to force female suffrage on the state, and of an inclination of many Democrats there to vote Republican if suffrage should be forced by Democrats.

I told the Governor that Georgia was the first state to reject the amendment, and that men who advocate suffrage as a reward to women who worked faithfully in wartime insult those women who worked from patriotism and without thought of reward. "Democratic candidates," I said, "seem to take stock and with nonchalance toss in a corner the Solid South vote bundled and labeled, 'to be called for.'

"My section has problems that demand state control, and if the Democratic party abandons the only basic principle upon which the two great parties differ, then there may be a mighty shuffling of votes in the hitherto Solid South.

"This struggle, Governor, is not a Ladies' Battle; it is the call of the blood of our fathers against irreparable federalization.

"Mr. Cox, you say you are obliged to advocate this amendment because the Democratic platform does so; I would cite the independence of platform Mr. Wilson demonstrated when he yielded to pressure and advocated this thing despite the declaration of the Democratic Party to the contrary. Why did he do this?"

"Well," said Governor Cox, "why did he also disregard the party platform declaration for one term only?"

Thus the governor parried our questions, sometimes avoiding the discussion with friendly and irrelevant questions about our families, our friends, and our state activities.

When Miss Kilbreath reminded him of the Pressure System of the Suffrage Party, as evidenced by the card index method, which through systematic blackmail coerced men to their views in the twinkling of an eye, our host rose nervously, gave a hollow laugh, and said:

"Nobody believes that. I promised to let you ladies know when it is time to catch your train. The time is at hand and my car awaits you. My secretary will accompany you to the train."

Despite the Governor's haste that we make the train, we waited twenty-five minutes at the station, thinking with sorrow that the Democratic Candidate for President was irredeemably joined to the idol of Federal Control of State Affairs.

However, Woman Suffrage became law in 1920. Georgia, which had never ratified the amendment, was nonetheless forced under the Federal law into giving votes to women.

So ended the "Battle of the Ladies." The prediction of Mrs. C. C. Harrold of Macon that "men and women of the South will regret that they didn't help in the great outcome" is realized in reverse, for adoption of the Amendment precipitated great derangement of life in our section, has helped to break down the Bill of Rights, and has bred discontent and dishonesty in the voting public.

Quod erat!

The feminist and Federal victory, with the adoption of Woman Suffrage, posed a question for public spirited women who had opposed the vote. I felt immediately that it was the duty of all citizens to vote. Woman Suffrage was the law of the land, and women's participation in elections was henceforth an obligation. Therefore, I have voted in every election, local and national, since 1920, when the Amendment became effective in August in time for fall elections.

Because of my father's twenty-year service in Congress, the lively interest of my mother in politics, and my own close attention to elections since my Washington days, I was thoroughly *en rapport* with the political scene. And, with the ballot and the part which intelligent women must now take in political affairs, I soon found myself somewhat active in politics. I never wanted a political office, but often through the years have participated to the extent of making public my attitude on measures and candidates and speaking and writing for what I believed right.

Like all good Democrats, I was elated in 1932 when Franklin Delano Roosevelt was elected to the presidency and began his vigorous administration after so many years of Republican misrule which had accompanied the nation's descent into the disaster of the depression.

Georgia, as did all states of the Union, quickened, stirred, and began to recover from the paralysis of the depression when the New Deal initiated its series of transfusions in the way of Federal money into the sluggish economic veins of localities. After the Federal Emergency Relief Administration, which was a program of direct relief for the hungry and helpless in each state, the Administration planned a series of work programs to help the needy without the stigma of the dole, and at the same time to benefit the states and localities.

One of these programs was the Civil Works Administration, governed under Washington by a state board, half of whose members were appointed in Georgia and half in Washington. On the Georgia CWA board I had my first experience in public office. I was appointed from Washington as a CWA commissioner to the Georgia board, and approved by Governor Eugene Talmadge. Appointed directly by the Governor and approved by the CWA administrator Harry Hopkins were Ronald Ransom, an Atlanta banker; and Steve Nance, a labor leader. Later the Governor added to the board John Rourke of Savannah and C. E. Vandiver of Lavonia.

When the CWA program was in full swing, by appointment I visited Warm Springs to confer with Mrs. Roosevelt and receive her advice about possible work programs for women in our state, I being the only woman on the board of the CWA.

I have enjoyed several meetings with Mrs. Roosevelt, meetings the more intriguing because of profound political differences between us. However, for all my espousal of state sovereignty and attachment to the *status quo* in Southern race relations, I have never happened to cross swords with her.

When I wrote Mrs. Roosevelt for a Little White House appointment, I received a cordial reply and a date was set for my visit. Mrs. Roosevelt, indeed, seemed delighted at the opportunity of having the pleasure of telling me what to do—which seems to be one of her strong points.

On the appointed day, Mr. Lamar and I set out by car for Warm Springs, taking with us Willie Snow Ethridge, at that time a newspaper reporter turned gossip columnist after her marriage to a newspaperman, Mark Ethridge, and Mrs. Leon Dure, the wife of another journalist. The two girls went along for the ride, Mrs. Ethridge hoping to pick up some uncommon tidbits for her *Macon Telegraph* Sunday column, "Gossip."

At Warm Springs I left the girls and Walter in the car while I was ushered into the guest house, a cottage just across the road from the Little White House. Very quickly Mrs. Roosevelt appeared. She had been riding and wore a broad blue ribbon in her hair. Knitting all the while, she proceeded right away to talk about projects she had in mind for the Georgia CWA program. I took notes and several times rose to leave, thinking I might be staying too long. But each time, immediately the First Lady would say "and" or "also," and thus continue our conference. Her talk was leisurely and helpful. Her whole presence was most pleasing and she was both cordial and charming. When I looked directly at her while she was talking she seemed quite pretty. The upper part of her face is lovely, and her eyes are very blue.

Finally, when I thought I must go, I remarked that Mr. Lamar was sitting in the car and would like so much to see Mrs. Roosevelt.

"Oh, where is he?" she asked. With no formal ado, she rose, stepped out on the porch, and called, "Mr. Lamar, oh, Mr. Lamar!"

Walter, delighted, came to meet her and presented her a silver-covered box full of cracklings, which, he explained, he thought Mr. Roosevelt might find palatable.

I interpolated that they should be prepared by a Southern cook, explaining the Georgia niceties of cooking this strictly Dixie delicacy. The First Lady rejoined that their cook was from Atlanta and would certainly prepare Mr. Lamar's cracklings to perfection.

Mrs. Roosevelt and Mr. Lamar became so pleased with each other that he ventured to ask if he might take pictures of her. Indeed, he might. So, they had quite a session of movie-making on the porch and grounds of the guest house. Then, I must take the camera, to catch the First Lady and Mr. Lamar shaking hands. This they did quite happily and repeatedly until they were sure we had some worthy views.

At that time we were quite pleased with Franklin D. Roosevelt and his lady, as were most jubilant Democrats, especially Georgians, with their adopted son ensconced at Warm Springs. Later, however, with the clash of my conservative convictions with the Roosevelt New Deal, our feeling toward the Roosevelts changed considerably. Our opinions became more and more divergent, and Mrs. Roosevelt shared fully in the ignominy of my disapproval; but neither of them seemed at all distressed by such frowns from Georgia!

Things went well for a while with the CWA board and

RELUCTANT POLITICIAN

Georgia's works program in general admirably directed by Miss Gay B. Shepperson, a Virginia-born, nationally-known social worker who had pioneered in depression relief in Georgia.

But in the winter of 1934 trouble broke out on the Commission, emanating from the Governor's office. The board appointed a number of purchasing agents and employed a woman's work agent to set up and supervise projects in various localities. This agent was selected and appointed by Miss Shepperson, with my endorsement. Talmadge appointees on the board opposed the appointment, as well as the hiring of purchasing agents, and they were vetoed by the Governor.

The controversy took on a wider interest because of Mrs. Roosevelt's espousal of the women's programs, which were now to be nullified by the Talmadge board maneuvers. In a Thanksgiving speech at Warm Springs, the First Lady called on women of the state to support these projects, and aroused much enthusiasm for them. Interest and activity also were increased by a state-wide meeting which I called at the Biltmore Hotel in Atlanta, pursuant to executing my role in CWA. I addressed community leaders among women from over the state and rallied their support, laying before them Mrs. Roosevelt's suggestions.

The controversy with Talmadge boiled to a crisis later in the winter, until the rebellion in Atlanta called for a Washington ruling.

Every move of the Commission had been supervised by and adapted to the wishes of Mr. Talmadge. On one occasion my inexperience as a politician and Mr. Talmadge's maneuverings trapped me into innocently acceding to his wishes.

Having finished the current work of the Commission after several days in Atlanta, I had one foot on the running board of my car to depart for home, when a hotel messenger called me back to the telephone. Talmadge, from his office, asked me to drop by the Capitol on the way out of Atlanta to talk with him.

WHEN ALL IS SAID AND DONE

At his office, I found him most gracious and jovial. He said a recent order from Washington authorized appointment of fourteen salaried representatives over the state, and that he would like for me to name the one for the Macon territory. Without hesitation, I suggested the name of Eddie Jacobs.

"Now, Mrs. Lamar," said he, "take the Governor's chair and call Mr. Jacobs."

Amused at the unusual position in which I found myself, not questioning the Governor's authority, I telephoned Mr. Jacobs, told him of the appointment and that he would receive official notice later. Because of this action, by which Talmadge assumed an appointment which was the privilege of the Board, Washington authorities promptly dismissed the Commission and directed Miss Shepperson to take over CWA work with all its ramifications, under Washington direction.

Our dispute was further complicated by a State Constitutional provision which forbade borrowing. This obstructed Georgia's efforts to match WPA funds for additional jobs, under CWA, for Georgia unemployed. The state already had used up its quota of 80,000 CWA jobs, and sought 140,000 more which were available under WPA. At this point, Representative Carl Vinson and others of the Georgia delegation in Washington were conferring with CWA Administrator Hopkins to iron out this crimp.

Governor Talmadge refused to approve or permit appointments of the purchasing agents and the women's work agent, essential personnel in the program mapped by Miss Shepperson and the CWA board members.

Meantime, Washington was not idle. The provision of the Federal relief act to lift the CWA program from its Atlanta complications and obstructions and return it to Washington administration reads as follows: "The Federal administrator [at that time, Hopkins] may assume control of the administration in any state where more effective and efficient cooperation between state and Federal authorities may thereby be secured."

The first news the public had of the disagreement was a story from Washington that the Georgia CWA board had been dissolved, and its authority vested in the state director, Miss Shepperson. No statement came from the Governor's office, from board members, or from Washington, except to cite the provision which enabled the Federal authorities to take over in order to continue the work in Georgia.

I was importuned by local reporters and other newspaper people for an explanation. I felt that Georgia had been cheated of its just due of relief in a time of crisis and great human need, and that some explanation was due. So, I made an announcement to the *Macon Telegraph* which was relayed over the state by the Associated Press.

I described the board situation as one of "open rebellion against a certain ruling of the Federal administrator involving appointments," and stated that a condition requiring the Federal administrator's assumption of control had arisen. I expressed the view of minority board members thus:

"Our view was based on the belief that the President of the United States through the Federal relief administration had launched this great humanitarian enterprise, that the Federal government was financing it, and that therefore the Federal government had a right to say how and by whom it should be run."

I outlined the history of the board, with the Washington-approved, Talmadge-appointed Ransom and Nance, and myself, and the later addition of other members not approved in Washington. I related that the early appointees had after the initial meeting in the Governor's office, gone to a conference in Washington with the Federal Relief Administrator and representatives of forty-eight states and governors of many states.

At this Washington meeting we heard an address by Harry Hopkins, who was just winning his spurs in the Administration. Later, we filed through the President's office for a handshake and greeting. Our exchanges were brief, and I remember only his cordial smile and warm reply when I told him I was from his "other state, Georgia."

My statement to the paper concluded:

"For six weeks, averaging two days per week, through the heat of summer, at great sacrifice of time and energy, the board members contributed without compensation of whatever ability each possessed, all the while being subjected to a fusillade of harsh criticism and a modicum of faint praise. Each of us answered in between times heavy mail from over the state, received delegations from various counties at our homes between meetings and answered as best we could long distance telephone calls for information on the program. Yet each member of the commission doubtless feels, as I do, a sense of gratitude for the opportunity of having a part in promoting the National Recovery Program and a yet greater sense of relief that our arduous services are no longer needed.

"Georgia is fortunate in having the work of the Commission carried forward by the best equipped social worker in the country, and as a former co-worker and ardent supporter of Miss Shepperson, I wish to commend her to the people of Georgia, and the people of Georgia to her."

My experience has shown that whatever resolve a Southern woman of the old school may have about not taking part in politics, if she has any concern for the welfare of her locality or state, there are times when it seems imperative for her to raise her voice in politics.

NOTABLES:
LITERARY AND OTHERWISE

PAPA'S RIGID SUPERVISION OF MY READING AND MAMA'S loving tutelage produced in me a taste for and an enjoyment of good literature. From the solid disciplines of English historians, the stately blandishments of Victorian novelists, and the varying influences of a wide variety of poets, I branched out to wider reading, including French works which I read in English and in French.

After my debut, I was invited to join the Athenaeum, a band of literature fanciers, poetasters, and musicians. After a few years the group languished and expired, and Macon society and intellectual circles seemed to me and some of my friends the more arid for lack of it. So I called a select group of professors, book-lovers, artists, and prominent intelligentsia to my drawing room on Georgia Avenue for a reorganization of the group.

Among those in the revived Athenaeum around 1910 were Colonel Pendleton, editor of the *Macon Telegraph,* Professor J. R. Moseley, then at Mercer University and later hailed for his profound books on religion and mystical experience, Rabbi Weiss, and Judge W. H. Felton. The revival of our group however, lasted but a short time because of business engagements in and out of town for many of our members. Already the pressures of twentieth century life were making inroads on the leisurely and contemplative pleasures of former days!

WHEN ALL IS SAID AND DONE

The same hunger in the community for intellectual stimulation is nowadays met in the monthly sessions of the Palaver Club, composed only of men, who contribute printed theses, have a good supper, and mull over various papers presented.

My reading and writing more often than not have been incidental to my study of matters Confederate, and my work with the U.D.C. But whether it was a book for its own sake, or a biography whose author came to me for help in facts and ideas, my ventures into letters have been lively and have brought me into famous company for longtime friendships.

In 1929, when Mama was approaching her ninetieth birthday, she read with great zest and approval Claude Bowers' *The Tragic Era*. It was a non-partisan view of the fraud and corruption of Reconstruction which had devastated the defeated South, an outsider's passionate and indignant exposé of proceedings my mother remembered but which had so far been neglected in all but Southern accounts.

I, too, read the book with approval and excitement. We both wrote to Mr. Bowers, praising his scholarship and his absorbing presentation of long-neglected truths. The historian replied, and there began a cordial Bowers-Blount-Lamar correspondence in which Bowers told my mother that his greatest satisfaction in the book was the reaction from many Northerners. Former Union veterans wrote him that they had never before realized what had happened to the South after the war, and that his revelations had served to bring them understanding and friendly feeling for an afflicted people.

In January of 1930 when I was in New York en route to Europe, remembering Mr. Bowers' hope that we might someday meet and talk of subjects Southern, I telephoned him and he asked if he might call on me.

How to find each other was a problem. So, in a spirit of frivolity I gaily told Mr. Bowers he would know me by a corsage of pink rosebuds I would wear over my heart.

At the appointed time, wearing pink rosebuds as I promised

NOTABLES: LITERARY AND OTHERWISE

and enjoying the fun of such identification, I descended from my hotel room to the lobby to look for the famed and distinguished Mr. Bowers. There was no one about who looked authoritative and impressive—only a bespectacled little man, several young people, and some obvious traveling salesmen. I sat down to wait, and the small man rose from his high bishop's chair in the lobby, with his brief case under his arm, and approached me and introduced himself. He was Mr. Bowers, who, eying my identifying corsage solemnly and with just a faint sparkle of amusement, recognized in me his friend from Georgia. We soon settled down for a duly serious and edifying talk, particularly about Jefferson Davis.

My admiration for Robert E. Lee seems to have won me the position, without portfolio, as local official reviewer of books about the great Southerner. I have a considerable collection of such books (and, incidentally, a collection of Lee photographs which is unique). In the course of reading and writing about Lee books I have become fast friends with the celebrated historian Dr. Douglas Southall Freeman of Richmond. It is a source of pride to me that I was able to correct him as to the date of Georgia's secession, when he was writing one of his books. The date I well knew to be January 19, because that was the date of my mother's birth.

I treasure a commendation of Dr. Freeman's thanking me for "your fine review of Volumes I and II of Lee" in which he says, "You have done a magnificent work in condensing so greatly the salient points of more than a thousand pages . . . I envy you that fine quality of condensation."

I made other literary friendships in the thirties, when as President-General of U.D.C. and earlier as Historian-General, I worked to promote a true evaluation of Jefferson Davis.

In this period there came from the University of North Carolina Allen Tate's study of Jefferson Davis as a crotchety statesman of impractical ideals and gifts for antagonizing the best talents of the Confederacy. I reviewed Mr. Tate's book and took him briskly to task for his harsh and unfair view of the Confederate hero. As U.D.C. Historian-General, I also wrote to Mr. Tate. We corresponded with considerable zest and cordiality, but each of us remained committed to his own view.

In my literary pursuits I have kept faith with my parents' views of morals and manners, as well as with Southern history and tradition. I read and enjoy modern fiction with the same pleasure and tolerance which I try to bring to my association with young people of different standards, manners, and viewpoints from my own. Just as I have enjoyed my friends among the flappers of the twenties, the jitterbugs and bobby-soxers of the thirties, and the decidedly emancipated young people of current days, I have enjoyed literature with ideas I cannot accept and subject matter I do not discuss. However, what tolerance I have achieved does not mean that my standards have changed.

I was enthralled by Margaret Mitchell's *Gone With the Wind,* with some reservations here and there. In hyperbole, I hailed its historical value, protested its coarseness in spots, and lamented mildly that the book didn't achieve a whole picture of the true Southern lady. In my report as U.D.C. Historian-General at the 1935 convention I called the book a tremendous contribution to English literature which corrected many false ideas about the South. My review of the book so pleased Miss Mitchell that she wrote me that it gratified her more than any other because of its high estimate of her historical accuracy and value in enlightening the world about the South.

Peggy Mitchell and I met often, notably at Atlanta's premiere of the movie, "Gone With the Wind," where, as U.D.C. President-General, I was guest of Mr. David Selznick, the producer. I became "Miss Dolly" to Peggy and her husband, John Marsh, and was welcome in their Atlanta apartment, where they lived quietly withdrawn from the public clamor that dogged their days.

She was a delightful personality, quiet and retiring to those

NOTABLES: LITERARY AND OTHERWISE

she did not know well, but sparkling and animated to intimates. It was interesting to see her relax and to watch her talking gaily with a small group in her home. When she entered the conversation, the warmth, humor, and sparkle of her share in the talk would command the delighted attention of everyone. I recall with most pleasure her ready response with laughter when she was amused. She radiated fun, and I can see her now on her sofa laughing, so amused that she would double over like a doll and as quickly spring back.

Another famous author dear to my heart before he ever took pen in hand was Colonel Robert L. Scott, hero of the Flying Tigers in China, whose triumphant homecoming to Macon I arranged. It is hard to separate his books from the young man himself. His style is vivid, breezy, and exciting, and I was amazed that this high-strung, courageous young man of action should write so thrillingly.

In 1942 I was thrilled to see in *Life* magazine the Macon hero of the China front featured in an illustrated article on General Claire Chennault's Flying Tigers of the China-Burma front. The article called him the "D'Artagnan of the Flying Tigers," and reported that he had shot down twenty-two Jap planes and was called by his fellow fliers a "one-man air force." I did not know him, though I had already read in the war news of his exploits.

I was concerned that he had received no recognition from his home town, which should acclaim a native son like Robert L. Scott with great pride. Why didn't we do something about Scott, I wondered. That question was the seed from which grew two of the most spectacular celebrations in Macon's civic history, social and patriotic high spots in our memory.

I called on Scott's wife and his parents, Mr. and Mrs. Robert L. Scott, Sr., and secured their cooperation for a street dance in his honor. Mayor Charles Bowden and the Junior Chamber of Commerce backed the plan enthusiastically. We roped off a downtown street, built a platform for speakers and decked it with a giant picture of our hero, and had our dance for him *in absentia* on October 2, 1942. Townspeople, the family, and military notables attended.

After the tributes to young Scott, in faraway China, the imported band struck up a merry two-step. Junior League girls, grouped at the corner of Cherry and Third streets, started the dancing, to make sure the party did not lag. The music was fine, the crowd was proud and happy, and the dancing lasted until one A.M. It was a delightful community party, doing honor to one of our bravest sons, and an uncommonly gala treat for the townsfolk, who had been rigorously busy with war work.

In March of 1943, Colonel Scott came home, after the Flying Tigers had become the China Task Force in the United States Army, with the Colonel in command of its American Army Air Force Fighter Pilots.

He arrived in Macon amid great rejoicing and welcoming. I could not see him for nearly a week, being ill, but the rest of Macon found him an obliging, modest, and energetic conquering hero. The town buzzed with stories about his boyhood and early flying career—that he had been an Eagle Scout with a record number of fifty-four merit badges, that he had wonderful energy and determination always, that he courted his Fort Valley girl from a Texas flying field, that he persevered to get into war flying after he was "over age."

From my sick bed I helped to arrange the welcome for him, a mass meeting at the city auditorium. I was bitterly disappointed to be abed with laryngitis. When my old friend and family doctor, the late J. P. Holmes, saw my disappointment, he relented and offered to take me. So, we drove to the auditorium and slipped backstage. Just as I walked on the stage I heard the master of ceremonies, General Walter Harris, expressing regret at my illness and wishing me a speedy recovery. Of course my surprise appearance at that moment caused laughter and applause, as I saw my friend, Colonel Scott, for the first

NOTABLES: LITERARY AND OTHERWISE

time. He walked across the stage to greet me, and though I had no voice to speak with, I bowed and smiled with pleasure.

Colonel Scott's speech delighted his fellow townsmen with its modesty, commonsense, and patriotism. He denied that he was a "one-man air force" and said the war must be won by the teamwork of 130,000,000 Americans supporting the fighters.

Later that year, Scott planned to come home again, but on his tour of the home front for the War Department, he was called to New York to put his experiences in a book, *God Is My Co-Pilot*. Then he became a literary lion as well as a war hero.

In 1944 Warner Brothers bought his first book for a movie, and he and his wife Catherine went to Hollywood, where he worked as a technical director.

I determined that Macon should have the première of the big show. Mayor Bowden and civic leaders agreed, and we invited Warner Brothers to bring their opening to us.

When the Scotts, the stars, and the movie arrived in Macon in February of 1945, all of Georgia was excited over the event. The town outdid itself for two days of patriotic and social celebration. All our full-dress, lavish celebration was in a good cause, in addition to hailing our hero. The première raised $15,000 for the Red Cross, and our Hollywood visitors raised more thousands in brief Red Cross appeals between visits to hospitalized service men. The brilliant Robert Scott Ball of the Junior League also enriched the coffers of the Red Cross.

Colonel Scott in 1947 was presented the Cross of Military Service, to add to his half a dozen or so American and foreign decorations for valor. U.D.C. members, with other Americans, were thrilled at one of his exploits performed as a salute to his home in the South. He recounted in a "Memorandum for United Daughters of the Confederacy" how in May of 1945 he circled the globe with Tokyo as his goal, flying the Confederate flag, "with landings ranging from darkest Africa to the white snows of the Himalayas." His memorandum recalls that "The flag of the Confederacy was raised over the soil of Japan immediately after the landing on the night of August 25," and describes puzzled Japanese who "never did understand who this new nation was that represented the flag with the Red, White and Blue and thirteen white stars."

A propos of my interest in new writing and trends in literature I recall the furore aroused by Laurence Stallings' *What Price Glory* in the early twenties. Laurence was a Georgia boy and his mother lived in Macon for many years; so it was with pride that Maconites read or saw his play on Broadway, produced out of his World War I experience. It was a pioneer in the realism and shocking sordidness which brought American letters down to earth at that time. Too far down to earth, and well into the mire, in the opinion of many—including myself.

On publication of Stephen Vincent Benét's wonderful *John Brown's Body*, I wrote him of my joy in his work for its human and historical truths portraying both sides of the war, and for the delight of its poetry. I also took occasion to inform Mr. Benét of his errors in appraising Confederate President Jefferson Davis, citing chapter and verse from my reading and study as evidence. This provoked another memorable exchange of letters, but Mr. Benét, alas, was immovable in his unfavorable view of Davis.

One of the cherished friends of my life since our gay girlhood Washington days has been Annie Wheeler, the daughter of the famed and beloved "Little Joe" Wheeler.

After our Washington period, the Wheelers returned to their old home place in Alabama, where Annie devoted her life to her father, but still found time for a spectacular career of service. My husband and I visited her there in later years, and she, with her sisters, were my guests on one auspicious occasion in Macon, to honor the memory of General Wheeler.

Whether at the Court of St. James in regal attire, or as joint hostess with mother and sisters during her father's long service in Congress, whether serving as a nurse in the Cuban War and

NOTABLES: LITERARY AND OTHERWISE

the First World War (in both of which she was a ministering angel to wounded soldiers), Annie Wheeler was the same. Circumstances of pomp and glory, of hardship and danger in no way affected her courage, her poise, her sweetness.

The great force in Annie's life was devotion to her father. She was intensely proud of his brilliant services to the Confederacy, and of his valiant soldiering with the United States Army in 1898. As the daughter of a Confederate hero, she was of course often asked about her famous father, and always emphasized with pride his loyalty to his re-united country.

Her colorful and valorous parent, whom I knew in Washington, has ever been a hero to me. It seemed incredible that so much force, spirit, courage, and intelligence could have been contained in this fiery little figure, scarcely over five feet tall.

From early in 1862 throughout the War Between the States he was almost continuously in battle. He was wounded three times. In one engagement thirty-six staff officers fell by his side. During the war sixteen horses were shot down under him. Among his more notable exploits was saving the Confederate Army at Shiloh by the capture of a Federal general and two thousand prisoners. The second day of Shiloh he held the rear steady in the retreat. Wheeler's assaults on the rear and flanks of Bragg's Army resulted in the destruction of millions of dollars worth of Army stores and the capture of many thousands of prisoners. And it was Wheeler who hung onto Sherman's rear and flanks and confined that desolating march through Georgia to a narrow path.

While Wheeler was in Congress, the Cuban War broke out. Immediately upon declaration of war, "Little Joe" was discovered sitting upon the White House steps in the wee, small hours waiting to offer his services. The President invited him in to breakfast, and soon he was commissioned. He rendered valorous and efficient service in the war.

All her life, Annie Wheeler has been as game as Little Joe was. In her late years she suffered illness and operations, including removal of cataracts from both eyes and enough distress to fell a dozen younger women. However, she stood these ordeals with courage, and never seemed to lose her spirit or her charm.

The Wheeler place in the country has become a shrine to Southerners who come from far and near to call on Annie and see the old home. She receives everyone graciously and with the interest which illumines her personality. She is alive and keen and talks eloquently, quoting poetry glibly and history accurately. She looks like a sweet and retiring old lady, but is much more than that.

The old house with its tremendous high-ceilinged rooms is beautifully run by its mistress, and is a lived-in museum, with a wealth of antique furnishings, relics, and mementoes of the Confederacy and General Wheeler. The walls are almost covered with pictures of the General, and Annie has great tomes of clippings and photographs, recording the various phases of her father's career as well as that of her brother. A glass cabinet in the hallway contains, in eloquent contrast, the gray uniform he wore during Confederate days, and the uniform he donned later as a Union soldier. The cabinet also displays his uniform as a West Point cadet.

Early in World War I Camp Wheeler was built near Macon and named for General Joe Wheeler. As I knew the family well, I felt it would be proper for me to promote a tribute to General Wheeler's memory in the form of a military review at the camp. I suggested this to General John Hayden, commanding officer at Wheeler, who seemed pleased at the idea and told me how it might be done. Full of enthusiasm for the project, I went ahead with plans.

The review was set for October 8, 1918, and our party—Senator and Mrs. William A. Harris (the former Julia Wheeler) and their little daughter, Julia; Birdie Wheeler, the oldest Wheeler daughter; my especial friend, Annie Wheeler; Mrs. Gordon Buck (Caroline Wheeler); Mr. Lamar, and I—motored to Camp Wheeler in two cars, were duly established in places of honor in the reviewing stands, and enjoyed a splendid review of forces commanded by General Hayden on horseback.

Confederate flags flew for the first time since the sixties when carried through the streets of New York in the funeral procession of General Wheeler in 1906. This procession was conceded to be the largest and most impressive which had ever marched up Fifth Avenue, and marked the only occasion on which Confederate colors had participated in a public function above the Mason and Dixon line.

There was a rich array of political celebrities at the Southern Commercial Congress in Atlanta in 1911. Here were assembled leaders of the Southern States to review our section's recovery and to plan and publicize its potentialities in the Union—just fifty years after the War Between the States.

There was political drama and contrast in the ceremony which opened the Congress. With President William Howard Taft presiding, a procession of flag bearers from every Southern state advanced to the front of the auditorium, while a concealed band struck up the stirring strains of "Dixie." Slowly each escort, including famous Confederates and contemporary Southern leaders, advanced to the stage to place the flag of his state there, in the order of the Secession of 1861. Then, all the states symbolically restored to the Union, an American flag was unfurled from the rafters, forming a huge and spectacular backdrop, with the words *"E Pluribus Unum"* furled across it. It was a spectacle that provoked profound emotion. There were shouts and tears mingled with the applause, as the South offered its loyalty and its strength to the Nation.

Attending the Congress, I was impressed with a first-hand view of three United States presidents—the current head of the country, a former president, and the young Virginian who was to become president.

President Taft gave a scholarly and informing talk upon the

doings of the Congress. Unhappily, the chief executive was placed last upon the program of a long evening. After waiting patiently, the audience listened for a few minutes to the President's address; then, impelled either by fatigue or the necessity for catching suburban trains and outgoing cars, they began to leave. There was so much disturbance that the genial Mr. Taft paused a moment for the noisy recessional to end. Then, with good humor and gentlemanly style, he remarked: "Horace Greeley said he counted a lecture a success if more people stayed in than went out."

Perfectly dressed, suave in manner, forceful in words, and apparently good humored when his address came at 12:10, the President made new friends and strengthened old ones.

In addition to introducing Mr. Theodore Roosevelt, John Temple Graves, Sr., spoke on "The Press." Throughout his address there were innumerable witticisms and flights of impromptu wisdom that left his hearers uplifted and grateful. This celebrated Southerner was a bright star of the Congress.

When Mr. Roosevelt (Teddy), having just returned from an African big game hunt, spoke to the Congress, he stepped forward a bit, rose on his toes, his shirt front bulging, his trousers a little short, his coat scant of cloth for his bulk, and shouted, "Fellow Georgians!" His personality must have made his oft-repeated politics go over. Certainly the gleam of his teeth, the uplifted forefinger, the queer little quirk to his voice held one's attention. Yet his words left little food for afterthought. This was a great surprise and disappointment, for this man who had really done so much for the world and had written so strongly (though frequently with ill information) ought not only to electrify, but to affect permanently his hearers.

During his speech a fire alarm caused some noisy withdrawals. He paused a moment, glared, and said he could not talk above the counter-attraction. Then with characteristic impatience, he said, "When I lived on a ranch out west and our cattle stampeded, we just stood aside and waited until it was over." One could not but contrast this reaction of the rough-rider with the polished good humor with which President Taft commented on a similar disturbance.

In the person of the Governor of New Jersey, a future President of the United States, Woodrow Wilson, was introduced. Tall, dignified, and rather austere even in those younger days, he was yet gracious and compelling. He rose to the acclaim of the multitudes, gathered the reins over that vast audience, and with clarity of thought, inimitable diction, and courage of conviction drove home vital truths and made clear needful devotion to fundamentals.

TRAVEL MEMORIES

AT VARIOUS TIMES I HAVE TRAVELED THROUGHOUT THE United States and to many parts of the world. In this chapter I will only describe some of the places and experiences that stand out in my mind.

I did not travel abroad until I had viewed the wonders of my own country, its far reaches and lofty mountains, its waterways, its great cities and their treasures.

On a trip West, I went with Mother and Sister to visit Montana Glacier Park, an area of great beauty and grandeur.

During an excursion in the park, I had a great piece of good luck that few tourists enjoy. On a walking trip, the party sat down beneath frowning walls of granite, two mighty peaks towering high in the heavens that seemed to have been riven asunder in a convulsion of the earth and stood separated by a wide chasm. The distance between them seemed small to the humans below, though in reality it was a tremendous gap.

Presently the prize sight of the park was vouchsafed us. A huge, snow-white goat stepped with ease and grace among the jagged rocks and made his way to the edge of the chasm. There he stood for a brief moment; then with head high, with his shining, straight, long black horns piercing the blue of the cloudless sky, he leapt across and made his way along the other peak.

We had gone to this immediate vicinity hoping to see an original of the goat that advertises the Montana Glacier, but we did not know he would put on a special performance for our

TRAVEL MEMORIES

benefit. It was a rare thrill in action and beauty—a breathless moment.

Another stop was at St. Mary's by the lake. After supper in the community eating place, we were told that we could find our cabins by number up the side of the mountain. But before we began the climb, we witnessed a marvelous picture in the heavens.

Standing on a crag that overhangs a glacial lake, I looked in awed silence and listened to a mighty storm brewing in surrounding mountains. I saw the waters of the lake lashed to fury, the western sky a panorama of fearsome looking clouds—great splashes of deep purple, red and muddy yellow on a backdrop of black. From time to time the swiftly changing picture was shot through with angry, forked lightning followed by bellowing, reverberating thunder that was repeated from cliff to cliff. Terror struck me; I felt a sense of the infinitesimal that I was with a new realization of the might, majesty, and glory of God above.

Another vivid recollection is my visit in New York state to Saratoga, the Queen of Spas, which is still, even as on my first visit there in 1901, preeminently a summer girl who flirts with Fortune, flaunts fine clothes, then fades from the ken of men until the next season. She brings men and horses, women and their dogs to worship at her shrine and invoke her ruling deity, Chance. She boasts of innumerable health-giving springs, most notable being Vichy, Congress, and Hawthorn Waters.

The glory of Saratoga lies in her natural advantages—her fine climate, beautiful scenery, and salubrious waters. There is no desirable ruling social leadership; and the kinds of people, the style of dress (undirected and unintegrated by the taste and standards of social leadership) are many and varied. One may see (or we did, in 1901) women gowned in creamy lace over silks and satin before eight in the morning. To the race track came showy gowns of *point de Venise* or filmy folds of chiffon in pink and blue, while, to make Saratoga style consistently inconsistent, one sees shirtwaists and skirts among many gorgeous costumes in the ballroom at night.

The motley daylong fashion parade was a rich and colorful one at the turn of the century, the heyday of the high-coifed, slim-waisted, flare-skirted Gibson girl. Whatever the surprises for us in the lavishness of morning attire and at sporting events, or the inept severity of coat-suited women at night, the procession of fashion plates was a gay one.

At Saratoga where I found many hotels and people by the thousands, all interest centered on the race track. As early as noon people began to secure conveyances to the track. There was a whirring of vehicles—carriages, surreys, buggies—up and down Broadway, programmes circulated, and the wiseacres began to show off their knowledge of horseflesh.

Because of my acquaintance in Washington with Mr. W. C. Whitney, President of the Racing Association, I enjoyed some special privileges. He particularly stressed to me his friendship and admiration for my father. He did a graceful thing for our party from Georgia. He sent his courier to our box to tell us he had played "King Bramble to win" for the four Georgia ladies and having won a good round sum in their name sent it with his compliments and best wishes. We accepted the fruits of this graceful attention by a merry note expressing the hope that he would be the next President of the U.S.A., but he assured us he was quite out of politics. One of the advantages we enjoyed through Mr. Whitney was a tour of Horse Haven, where more than 1,400 beautiful horses were housed, fed, and carefully curried for the day of trial.

I had all the fun I wanted picking a horse I would like to win. One day, out of the eleven horses in the race, I chose the one which came in three lengths behind the rest. Indeed he may be coming yet.

Steeplechasing is the prettiest but the most dangerous of the races. A jockey's life is most uncertain and is full of falls as his poor frame is of broken bones. One of them said, in answer to

TRAVEL MEMORIES

my inquiry as to whether he had ever been hurt, "Why, ma'am, I haven't a whole bone in me today, 'ceptin me neck!"

My stay at Saratoga included a visit to the American Monte Carlo. Our party crossed the threshold, trod the red velvet carpet, mounted the gorgeous stairway, glanced around the cafe—a symphony in green, pink, and white—and stepped on to the flower-decked balconies overlooking the gaming outfit. Faro and the roulette tables lined each side of the long, red-carpeted room. Lights gleamed as men played the games of chance. No sound betrayed the loser's misery or gave key to the winner's gains. Only the whir of the wheel and the click of the chips sounded the note of the gambler's greed. With quickened heartbeats we peeped into the beautiful little garden where fountains played and crickets chirped. Here doubtless the winner counts over his gains, the loser regains his composure, and each smokes the soothing weed for further pursuit of the Goddess of Chance. There was a whispered story that here, too, came heavy losers to end it all in this garden when life seemed too dark to go on.

AND SO TO EUROPE

In 1922 I began a tour of foreign countries. My first stop was England. Through the English-Speaking Union at London, I was put happily on my way to visit Sulgrave Manor, the ancestral home of the Washington family. It was bought in 1914 by the British Peace Centenary Committee, the property vested in the Regents of Mount Vernon, the British Ambassador to the United States, and the American Ambassador to Great Britain. It is maintained on income from an endowment fund raised by the National Society of Colonial Dames of America.

From London by rail I went to Northampton where I was met by a most acceptable guide and chauffeur, as planned by the Union. Our first stop was at Little Brington Church, beneath which Lawrence Washington (who bought the church from the Crown in March of 1539), lies buried. Here, and in the rectory garden, my admiration of the flower beds inspired the rector to give me introduction to a Mrs. Grant at the next town. She was most cordial and told me that her daughter wanted to open a tearoom hard by Sulgrave because the name of Grant would be of great interest to people of the United States! Without disturbing her complacence over that thought, my mental reservation was very strong that American interest in the name of Grant would depend on the section from which that American might come. She invited me for lunch and showed me all over her lovely gardens, and then sent me on my journey with an introduction to Lady Spencer.

At Lady Spencer's estate I was delighted with the ancient beauty of the place with its storied walls, its Queen Anne gardens, its up-to-date grounds, its tapestries, armor, and other things of historic value and great beauty.

From there I made my way to Sulgrave. When the caretaker read my identity in the visitors' book, "Mrs. Walter D. Lamar, member of the National Society of Colonial Dames of America," he announced to the other tourists with a low bow from the waist, "The manor and grounds are maintained by the Colonial Dames of America, one of whom we have the honor to have with us today—ladies and gentlemen, Mrs. Lamar of America!"

Here in this ancient garden there comes faintly, as a perfume, the sense of peace and continuity of generation unto generation. Here are old flowers of sweet association, carnation, lavender, mint, savory marjoram and the marigold that goes to bed with the sun—daffodils, violets, pale primroses, bold oxlips and the crown imperial, liles of all kinds.

I left with a bit of rosemary which the caretaker surreptitiously plucked. "Just for you," he said, with great unction.

So closed a joyous experience, to be one of my cherished travel memories, redolent of the old garden surrounding Sulgrave Manor.

I traveled from London to Wales via the old walled city of

Chester, and thence to the Welsh town of Llandudno, where innumerable cabbies met my train. I chose one. To my dismay, he asked where I wanted to go. Ahem! I had forgotten; so I said quickly, the Prince Edward. "Which one?" asked he. "Oh, the one nearest the station," I replied.

Though I was not expected at this small caravanserai they received me cordially and helped me plan what I should see. Later, in passing, I recognized the Prince Edward, the hotel where I held reservation, but I turned the other way. I trust they are not still holding that reservation for Mrs. Lamar of the States!

The steep mountainsides of slate looking out to sea are depressing, but the extensive rock gardens are luxurious in their brilliant beauty and make the heart to sing.

The Druidical remains speak in solemn tones of that ancient sect as well as provide a meeting place for the Eisteddfodd, the annual singing contest of the provinces where all the people, high and low, rich and poor, assemble on equal footing.

The castles in Wales are largely in disrepair. Carnarvon, the largest and most interesting, has a well-preserved exterior, but is in ruins within. All these sights interested me greatly, as I was instructed in the history of Wales by a well equipped chauffeur and guide who finally delivered me to my friends en route for Scotland.

There the beauties of the Lake Country unfolded as I remembered Sir Walter Scott's *Lady of the Lake*. In the vicinity of Edinburgh we found the delights of Abbotsford, home of Scott. At Holyrood Castle, ghosts of Rizzio and Queen Mary greeted us with eerie tales, while the University of Edinburgh lured us to its cultural heights.

From Edinburgh we went on to Leith where we launched out on the Firth of Forth for the North Cape, traveling through the dark, forbidding waters of fiords, where one could sometimes reach out and almost touch the towering sides of rock walls.

WHEN ALL IS SAID AND DONE

The Norwegian city of Bergen afforded first-hand views of Thorwaldsen's majestic Christ at the entrance to the great Cathedral. Beautiful memorials to Ole Bull and Grieg were here, and I felt awed by the grandeur of the scene.

At the North Cape, the Midnight Sun, a great, luminous ball of orange fire, seemed to descend within a few feet of the horizon and then change its mind and rise upward. It was a strange feeling to go to bed at an appointed time while the sun was high and the natural world about us was wide awake.

I enjoyed several interesting stops, including one at Molde where are the famous paintings of Axel Endel, whose "Resurrection Morn," an altar piece, is perhaps best known.

After a visit to the Cathedral at Peterborough and its ghostly reminders of Bloody Mary, I took boat for a rough channel trip from Harwich to the Hook of Holland, and thence to the main object of my solo journeyings, namely, visiting the old towns of Belgium.

Greater satisfaction hath no traveler than I had in the treasures of ancient Bruges, Ghent, and Antwerp. Brussels is a gem, a small Paris; its palaces, museums, works of art, guild halls, and its proximity to Waterloo make strong appeal. But the works of art in old Bruges, and the town itself, much like Venice with its waterways and the arch of its bridges, charmed me most. From the tower of the Great Carillon one has a clear view of the famed port of Zebrugge, and the many out-of-door shrines in corners of buildings, all prepare one for the beauty of the golden shrine of St. Ursula in l'Hopitale de Saint Jean. I beheld in a small chapel at Cologne the bones of the 11,000 massacred virgins of her train. This lovely miniature temple by Memling containing the arm of St. Ursula is a treasured memory of faultless beauty. Here in Bruges one may study the beginnings of art and its progress through the ages.

At Ghent is a beautiful out-of-door memorial to the Van Eyck brothers carved in stone. Seated on a pedestal, the great painters are approached by two converging lines of men, women, and children bearing a delicately carved garland of flowers as they march up a stone stairway to honor the artist brothers. Their most famous painting, "The Adoration of the Lamb," a triptych altar piece in the Cathedral, is now completely restored after being rudely dismembered by various conquerors.

Antwerp still holds many of the works of her famous son, Rubens. All of Belgium is unique in architecture and rich in art treasures.

In the vicinity of Berlin at Potsdam is the interesting palace Sans Souci of the Emperor Frederick the Great with its special burying grounds for his grey hounds and the room weirdly decorated with monkeys and reptiles which he contrived for his off-and-on friend, Voltaire. Berlin itself in 1930 presented a grey stone city without beauty, vast and frowning, typically Teutonic.

The Passion Play at Oberammergau was perfect in construction, in costuming, in Anton Lang as the Christus, who was well supported by all the actors in the tragic events, beginning with the Saviour's triumphant entry into Jerusalem, preceded by the multitude rejoicing in their king. The production was climaxed by the gloom and tragedy of the Crucifixion. Yet this awesome scene was followed by the glory of the Ascension and gratitude in the message left the world, "And I, if I be lifted up, will draw all men unto me."

The call of color has ever been strong and stirring with me, and I was charmed and thrilled by the gorgeous hues of waterproof velvet and satin apparel of the forty-five singers whose voices opened the play. Every actor was clad in colors his character might indicate, and thus the psychic power of color was used magnificently in the Passion Play.

"Chillon's dungeons—deep and old" for years meant to me the Prisoner in that forbidding place as described by Lord

Byron, because I recited it as a small girl at Miss Clifford Cotton's preparatory school in Macon. Memories of Switzerland's beauteous lakes and snowcapped peaks, its crisp, invigorating air, with its pastoral scenes and friendly inhabitants, awaken a love for this land of the free which remains impervious to entangling alliances.

Prague, old in story and ancient in structure, is the home of much cruelty perpetrated through the centuries. Among its interesting sights are traces of constructions and burial places, unearthed in latter day excavations. Walls and gates of the twelfth century, sumptuous chambers of the time of King Rudolph II (1615), the Church of St. Vitus, the Presbytery of St. Wencelaus, scenes of the grim, tragic trial and execution of John Huss, are a few highlights of this now afflicted land.

Its people have produced the most artistic glass known to us, have valiantly survived many terrors, and certainly deserve a better fate than their present torn and devastated land affords. The little street of the goldsmiths' tiny houses gives one the feeling of walking in the fairyland of Hansel and Gretel.

"Oh, Paris is a woman's town with flowers in her hair," and here in the Louvre I was baptized into the glories of the Greeks. Though I enjoyed the excellence and beauty of other *objets d'art* none ever stirred me as did the Winged Victory of Samothrace at first sight.

Père la Chaise holds the remains of men and women who have marked their names indelibly on life's calendar. Here lie the earthly remains of the famous lovers, Héloise and Abelard, of Chopin, Rossini, Sarah Bernhardt, Fontaine. Of especial interest to a Daughter of the Confederacy was the tomb of Judah P. Benjamin, Attorney General of the Confederate Government and later Secretary of the Treasury.

The Sorbonne brought to mind a long list of distinguished students, brilliant writers and scientists, especially recalling to

TRAVEL MEMORIES

me the fervor and delayed triumphs of Mme. Curie and of Pasteur. Notre Dame, the Arc de Triomphe, sweet pastoral scenes, parades of fashionables along the Bois de Boulogne, the atmosphere of ancient history at Carnavelet and the Luxembourg, together with night spots of the Left Bank, afforded varied enjoyments.

One of my most amusing travel memories is a trip, in 1922, to a Paris salon. Immediately upon entering the salon, a fashion plate of a woman asked with solicitude, "Madame, have you a *vendeuse?*" If it is one's first visit to this particular source of modes and one admits that she has not such a friend at court, a charming young saleswoman is immediately introduced to the newcomer. She sits beside her customer answering questions as to possible variations in an admired costume, whether in color, material, or ornamentation, and makes intriguing suggestions, which will make the visitor think, "Well, maybe that will do for me." She carefully avoids vulgar mention of price. That comes later.

A dainty booklet carrying the fanciful name of each model gown, and its number, together with an artistic wisp of a pencil, is given Madame. Then begin the entries.

A tall blonde floats in, apparelled in pale green georgette and flesh stockings for evening, slippers and costume jewelry to match. She is Number 60 and is named "Sea-Foam." She undulates about the room, pauses in a dreamy way in front of someone who has expressed interest in her garb, and, with apparent indifference to all save her own charm, is lost to sight.

Then comes a black-eyed houri in a shiny armor of jet like a sheath about her dainty form. As she makes her way about the salon, she gleams and glows with hidden glints of color, and soon Number 110, "Mirage," disappears.

Next a model enters wearing a white georgette draped very low at the back though high in front, and edged about twenty-four inches up from the bottom of the skirt with picot-finished half ovals of the same material, applied close together; she carries a fan of georgette made in the same ovals. Fan and skirt flutter with inconceivable grace and lightness as the young woman moves swiftly about, and soon "Poesie" has vanished.

A charming vision named "Citronelle" next appears in lovely lemon colored georgette with many panelings, overlapping like the petals of an inverted rose. With this the fair model wears a teardrop necklace and bracelet in lemon and crystal. "Prelude" wears white and black with pleatings and intricate double-face use of black satin that reminds one of flats and sharps on the piano keyboard.

There are shown sport suits in checks with little capes, sometimes three models appearing simultaneously in different colors of the same name. A nifty equipment for the equestrienne is called "Galpade."

Patou was showing a charming model in cream lace of small flouncings converging upward to center front, each flounce edged with tiniest pipings of cream satin, and on the left side front an exquisite fantaisie of pink satin calla lilies, the confection being called "Joli Coeur." Lucien Lelong's very best, designed for a young matron for afternoon wear, showed a short wrap with pendant fur overjacket, high fur collar, deep fur cuffs, and the popular irregular hemline, all in soft beige, the ensemble being called "Fin de Journée."

One of the loveliest of the evening gowns, by much adapting on the part of the coutouriere, the vendeuse, and the client, became the property of the writer, a lady twice the size of the slender model. "Distinction," from Drecoll-Beer, where I bought several creations after adjustments were made, is a long-lined, light blue moire with a swirl of rhinestone embroidery on the right side just below the natural waistline, and with gleaming straps across each shoulder.

Black and gray flowered georgette with infinitesimal tuckings and edged with spider-web-sheer lace cheered through and through by its deep peach-colored lining had the lovely name of "Meditation."

TRAVEL MEMORIES

Among fanciful names which play a large part in the witchery of the salon are Astrale, Aventeureuse, Caprice, Causerie, Chimère Fidèle, Evocation, Inclination.

The evening and afternoon dresses were all sweeping the floor on sides and front, though oftentimes much shorter in the back. No dress was shown shorter than ten inches from the floor. There was much grace and sweetness in plaits and godets, and the awkwardness and narrowness of yesteryear were gone!

Fashion displays in leading houses in Paris are really art feasts in color, form, and method of display. One can buy exquisite things, however, from less expensive places if one has a professional shopper at hand. One of the most exquisite gowns I purchased owes its perfection to beauty and line of material and the use of dainty shirrings in which the French excel.

The show goes on morning and afternoon, and not the least interesting phase of the exhibitions to me was the audience. Seated around the room on gracious comfortable chairs and inviting fauteuils were women fashionably attired, some holding in laps or by a leash the latest fad in canines, some accompanied by fidgety husbands who soon lost their restlessness when the alluring models paraded.

There was quite a flutter among ladies with poodles, dachshunds, and other small dogs when a lady appeared at the doorway with a huge Dane, large as a grown calf and powerful as a bull. The little dogs began to sniff, the ladies began to flutter with anxious airs over their pets, until the owner of the giant brute took counsel with the manager and did her viewing from a distance, safe in the adjoining room.

There was an exquisite Spanish woman present, accompanied by two very handsome young Dons, to whom the show was a great delight.

And now just a peep into a Paris milliner's shop. The best are up several stories reached by flights of stairs, or by means of an electric elevator which one must manipulate oneself.

WHEN ALL IS SAID AND DONE

We arrive at the door of Camille Roger. We are introduced by a card from our vendeuse at Beer, and after a brief interval one of the dozen young girls conveys to Mme. Prescia that she is needed for Madame.

She arrives with the air of an empress, welcomes us, listens with intense interest to our needs, causes the greatest excitement among her aides by calling for this and that. She holds out one hand to the assistant—*"Elise, une épingle!"*—and adjusts on our head with the other hand the possible shape we have dreamed of but knew not how to describe. As she jams the chapeau down, she stands off and exclaims, *"Charmante, madame!"* and we feel and know that we are ravishing.

"How would you like, madame, *cette petite fantaisie, à ce cote?* It is so *chic!* These little piqué flowers, madame, are the very newest things and you should have one or more on thees hat."

With the Paris modiste nothing in hats or dresses as to color or line is impossible. "Yes, the color, a little more deep, or a bit more light. For you, madame, we turn the hat on thees side and add thees velvet ribbon.

"*Oui,* madame, thees straw is not the very color we want for you, but it shall be dyed the right shade for you."

The unparalleled beauty of Vienna is stamped on my memory—its surrounding castles, its palaces, historic St. Stephen's Cathedral, the wonderful art of the Lipizzan horses, white and gaily caparisoned, still prancing through my mind, although they no longer perform for emperors and courtiers. Near Vienna I was delighted to see the statue depicting that avenging hero, the Pied Piper of Hamelin.

Naples, Capri, and Sicily offered inspiring beauties of nature and of art, while the devastations of Vesuvius and Aetna in this part of the world appall. Genoa and its associations with maritime industries brought memories of Columbus. Pisa, almost synonymous with the Leaning Tower, is the repository of valuable and beloved work of great artists which were all too quickly reviewed. Here Byron wrote his "Don Juan" and Shelley composed his "Adonais."

Florence is full of wondrous works recalling descriptions of its glories from George Eliot's *Romola*. There are amazing gifts and memorials here of the princes of the House of Medici, but above all stands forth the beauty of Michelangelo's "David." The delight of the Della Robbias, the Raphaels, and the Fra Angelicos painted on the walls of the monastery in well-preserved contrast with the ill-fated fresco of the Last Supper, and the splendid bronze doors of the Baptistry, all crowd with joys the grateful traveler. From Casa Guidi's windows looks the piquant face of the English poetess, Elizabeth Barrett Browning, long a resident of Florence.

At nearby Fiesole in the chapel of the monastery is the exquisite marble balustrade carved by Donatello, its intricate pattern of leaves, flowers, grapes, and tendrils carved as gracefully as one might drape fine lace.

Rome, sacked and burned and left in ruins by so many conquerors through the centuries, presents an interesting composite of ancient days and new structures achieved under Mussolini. Here in Rome lie buried Shelley and Keats, the English poets, twin spirits and devoted friends.

Other interesting features of Rome are so many, so varied, so well known that I need not recount their wonders, only to say that here is so much that is superb in architecture, painting, *objets d'art* that I could hardly enjoy the experience for regretting that there was so little time to look and learn and rejoice in all these things I had read about and loved from my youth up.

On leaving Naples, we took a stand on a windy deck to view the wonder of Stromboli. Miles before reaching it, we saw a wide slanting gash, red and gleaming, tumbling down the steep rock to the sea. From time to time there were upward spurts of flame, and a red glow round about. Later from my cabin window I saw a farewell upshoot of the fire fountain, and Stromboli vanished. In a few hours we passed through the Strait of Messina, and safely experienced Scylla and Charybdis.

Debarking at the port of Piraeus for the famed glories of Athens, we were soon ascending to the Acropolis. Some of the great pillars of the Parthenon lie prone, some utterly shattered and some still standing in their pristine beauty of shaded pinkish yellow. Through the marble forest gleamed a blue, blue sky. The Theatre of Dionysius, the cell of Socrates, Mars Hill where Paul stood for his mighty speech to "Ye men of Athens," all gave me a sense of far-reaching immortality through aeons of time. The Museum of Athens holds treasures of Phidias and Praxiteles, some of them taken only a few years ago from the bay, numerous and varied Etruscan treasures dazzling in their beauty and intricacy of design.

Among unforgettable things seen in Turkey were the ancient palaces of the sultans, recently opened to visitors, where were collections of richest jewels, china, glass, and apparel of the sultans. Among the most notable was the peacock throne of gold studded with 50,000 pearls "of purest ray serene," and also the largest emerald in the world, used in the decoration of the headgear of the sultans. Innumerable beautiful mosques, which we entered with guides after slipping straw sandals over our unholy feet, the Dardanelles, and Leander's Tower, and the intense blue of the waters of the Golden Horn are but further glances into the land of Scheherezade and the Thousand and One Nights.

Despite the strict regimen of our typical Scotch Presbyterian Sunday afternoons in our childhood, its influence was not lost on our natures. Love and reverence for God, the Father, and belief in Jesus Christ, His only Son, and the resurrection of the dead, grew with our growth and strengthened with our strength. There are lines from the Bible which could never be effaced from our consciousness. We each encountered rough going at times, but always felt the comforting messages, "Let not your heart be troubled," "He is not dead, but sleepeth," and "If I be lifted up, I will draw all men unto me."

Pilate's question of the Saviour, "What is truth?", resounds down the ages. Cults and creeds have essayed answers, yet within the human soul whether in the jungles, or among the Yogis, or from any one of the Ten Great Religions, there shines forth but one answer, "He that believeth on me shall never die."

When I visited the Holy Land, I carried clear within my brain and deep in my heart these lessons of my childhood.

As I journeyed in an American automobile from Haifa toward Nazareth, we passed from time to time a turbaned and white-robed man walking beside a donkey, on whose back was seated a wide-eyed woman in black. For a moment, as we passed one such group, I thought, "Why, there are Mary and Joseph on the way to Bethlehem to be taxed!" Or, perhaps some women and children by the spring in Nazareth might even be Mary and others of her time. And I went on, past the scene of the raising of the widow's son from the dead, the place of the wedding of Cana at Galilee, the Mount of the Transfiguration, looking away at Mount Gilboa where Saul was slain and where Rizpah mourned her seven sons, glancing from time to time across the country to the great Highway which leads from Egypt into Palestine and across Jordan—and by and by with eager thoughts forerunning we came to a great sea of blue, bursting brilliantly into view. "Galilee, sweet Galilee, thy waves bring back His voice to me." From Carpernaum and Tiberias on toward Jerusalem and Bethlehem and Jericho and Bethany and Gethsemane we journeyed.

Two things I had vowed to do. First, (it was the latter part of February) I wanted to go out on the hills of Judea, and watch with the shepherds over their flocks by night, hoping for some heavenly vision. The time and conditions, alas, interfered. The night was black and rainy, the ground stony and the sheep safely herded away from the cruel, searching winds. So, feeling that wisdom was the better part of valor, I took heed of my sore throat's warnings and my husband's concern, and thus lost the coveted experience.

The other thing I had devoutly anticipated was that I should walk to Emmaus. That story to me has ever been the most human, and at once the most thrillingly supernatural of all the accounts of Christ after His resurrection from the dead. The picture is still vivid and life-like, as the two disciples walked and talked together when a third one, a stranger, joined them. How naturally and how sorrowfully, and how without hope did they go their way, did they tell the stranger of the happenings of the past three days! Not until they stopped for refreshments at Emmaus, where their guest blessed and broke the bread, were their eyes opened and they said to one another, "Did not our hearts burn within us?"

I was fixed on walking that storied way, of sharing their grief, their surprise, and their mystification as He vanished from their sight! This too was denied me, there being now no road to Emmaus and no path through the boulders and brambles. However, as in the case of many disputed scenes of miracles and happenings in the life of our Lord, the actual spot mattered little, for the whole land was consecrated. Whether the manger was here or there, whether the body of our Saviour was buried in Jerusalem or outside the walls mattered not, for "He walked with me and He talked with me."

The Garden of Gethsemane seemed more actual to me than any other spot in Christ's historical setting. There, I re-lived the betrayal scene, the arrest of the Saviour, and then when the others of our party had gone a few paces, my husband and I paused, and looking across the Brook Kedron toward the cruel city, I repeated Lanier's poem, "A Ballad of Trees and the Master," softly for him and me.

TRAVEL MEMORIES

Were the world at peace and things as they were in piping times, I would like best to re-visit the Holy Land. I would turn my face to Palestine and the Land of the Pharaohs.

The Holy Land is the visible heart of the Christian Faith. In 1930 it still held a peculiar people, all types of the Hebrew race, of Arabs high and low. A garrison of British soldiers kept down any insurrection in the environs of Holy Places.

Mr. Vestre, the son of a missionary, told me of an interesting happening when General Allenby took over Palestine from the Turks. General Allenby asked Mr. Vestre as a long-time resident of Jerusalem to name any specific article which he should require of the departing Turks. Immediately Mr. Vestre said there were two definitely valuable things, sacred and historical as well as authentic, which must be acquired lest the Turks carry them off, namely, a stone taken from the ancient temple on which is inscribed in Hebrew: "Let no Gentile enter here on pain of death." This is believed to be the only writing extant on which the eyes of the Saviour looked during His brief life on earth.

The other was a stone taken from the arched roof of a conduit hastily hewn by order of King Hezekiah for the purpose of diverting the waters of the pool Gihon which supplied the valley where Sennacherib and his army of Assyrians were at opposite ends of the proposed conduit. Where the two sets of workmen met in the rough hewn archway they carved a stone thus: "Here the workmen of King Hezekiah met and finished the conduit ordered by the King."

Alas! in the confusion of incoming troops and outgoing Turks these suggestions were forgotten by General Allenby. En route to Palestine we visited the Museum at Constantinople and I saw each of these stones, read them with interest, and heard of them with regret from Mr. Vestre, who, as a boy while wading knee-deep through the waters, had seen the stone in the arch from which it was taken.

Beneath the dome of the Mosque of Omar we stood beside

the great rock of Mt. Moriah on the threshing floor of Araunah, on which Abraham made ready to sacrifice his only son, Isaac. We were soon encompassed by tourists of all nations, among them many Arabs, who are most devout.

Driving up through the wilderness from Jericho toward Jerusalem, we saw a strange freak of nature. The moon shone brightly while a gentle shower descended on the scene of weird shaped rocks and mysterious caves, for the wilderness is not a tangled wild wood or morass, but a harsh, forbidding abode of thieves and cut-throats, a fit setting for the story of the Good Samaritan.

Another exhibit of nature which interested me greatly was seen as we traveled from Jerusalem to the Suez on a train which was known as the "Milk and Honey Special." Riding along through the desert sands we saw in the distance the tossing waves of the Red Sea on one side and a rainstorm over the desert on the other. At the Suez Canal we boarded a dirty, greasy little tug for passage over the short water crossing and soon were on our train to Cairo.

Into the land of Egypt we entered, I, for one, awed and inspired to reverent and thoughtful consideration of all that I saw. Cairo! with its muezzin call from many mosques, its medley of treasures and catch pennies in the shops of the mousky, its long lines of women in black robes peering through veiled eyes, eager for the sights, some of them nursing infants, some feeding larger children with confections as they followed a draped, uncoffined corpse. Best of all were the museums containing treasures thousands of years old. Taken from the tombs of kings were things of exquisite beauty and refined uses, beds, chairs, treasure chests, alabaster jars, finely wrought ornaments of gold and silver thickly bejeweled. There were eggs, potatoes, bread, all petrified but perfect in appearance.

The city of Cairo and vicinity are in the Libyan Desert, beyond which over the mountains lies the great Sahara. Of the ancient city of Memphis, the fallen statue of Rameses II and the Alabaster Sphinx are all that are left worthy of note in this, the once proud capital city of Egypt which stretches for miles in every direction.

Near Mena House amid peals of laughter and screams of alarm over many upsets we were mounted upon camels, well trained to kneel for the mounting and to unfold their long legs for the uprising. Finally we were off to the Great Pyramid, the wonder of the ages, built with no evidence of antique machinery to hoist the mighty stones. None of us wished to make the difficult climb up the immense stones because of the awkward method of ascent. When a visitor makes the ascent he is pushed at the seat of his breeches by one attendant and pulled by another. A native offered to climb to the top in a given time for a given sum, and we gladly paid him to show us how the feat could be accomplished without assistance. We watched with interest the white-robed Arab as he went to the top and back in an incredibly short time. After riding a short distance, we stood in awe before the Sphinx, the recently uncovered forepaws reaching far beyond the figure, bathed in that great silence which hears everything and tells nothing.

Overnight in a de luxe Pullman, we arrived for breakfast at the sumptuous Luxor Hotel and from its balcony looked down on wondrously colorful gardens, past the thoroughfare along which were seen tall men in flowing white robes and gorgeous head-gear, loaded donkeys and camels, vendors of beads and shawls. When one of the men tried later to sell me a "scarab of great antiquity," I protested that it was not genuine, but merely a copy. Whereupon he smiled sweetly and with dancing eyes replied, "Yes, yes, genuine antique—made last night!"

Crossing the Nile we were on our way to the tombs of the kings. Steps of carved stone led down into the halls and chambers, special treasure rooms, their sides and many columns carved and painted in colors still clear and beautiful as if freshly done. Each holding a candle, we often had to bend almost double to enter the low winding passages. Lest thieves break through and steal treasures from the tombs of dead kings, there was always a false entrance with a mummy nearby, to throw marauders off the track. Our first invasion of this sleeping place of the dead was into the tomb of Queen Hopetan of some 4,000 years ago, and among the younger kings was Tutankhamen whose tomb was much rifled by French, British, and American archaeologists until the Egyptian government realized its great importance and claimed jurisdiction.

Four days up the Nile on a houseboat gave us many sights and scenes in the land of the Pharaohs, including a visit to the temple of Dendera, part of which is decorated with pictures of Cleopatra and Caesar and their son.

Lotus columns, carved walls, mammoth statues surrounded by great limestone mountains are a part of my Egyptian memories. Drifting along the lazy waters I wrote letters to my mother telling her of the various stops, the sleeping places of kings and queens, of the six-mile ride on a donkey's back to visit the oldest of all the temples dedicated to Osiris and with extensive sections erected by Seti I and his son Rameses II, who was the Pharaoh of the oppression.

The marvels of ancient Egyptian building are crowned in the temple of Osiris, the achievement in which the sun's rays, through exact calculations of centuries ago, reach through the blackness of the inner night to light the altar deep within.

The spell of Egypt even now is upon me and I find it difficult to close this picture of the land. On completing our journey up the Nile we visited with intense interest the ruins of Karnak and soon thereafter entrained for Alexandria whence we embarked on a three-day voyage to Brindisi. We encountered rough weather off the island of Crete which, I take it, must be the hiding place of Euroclydon, the fierce storm encountered by St. Paul on his way "unto Italy."

With farewells to the scenes of the sacred story of our Saviour and His followers, together with a guilty feeling of one who had invaded the burial place of kings and queens of ancient

TRAVEL MEMORIES

Egypt, I arrived at Brindisi on the coast of Italy for further sightseeing on the European continent.

I think travel is the most lasting, the most accurate, and the most enjoyable form of education. Worthy things, of whatever nature, when seen with one's own eyes never cease to bring satisfaction, certainty, and a degree of ease under all circumstances not obtainable otherwise. I am grateful for whatever of travel I have enjoyed and I am always ready to go on another trip, far or near.

XVII

AND THEN SOME

A MEASURE OF SUCCESS, WEALTH, AND PROMINENCE IS NOT an unmixed blessing. I recall, ruefully and with amusement, some drawbacks of the advantages and responsibilities which have been mine.

I have, for instance, a fairly faithful letter writer, anonymous, who is impelled to berate me whenever my favorite picture appears in the local papers. This picture is, I fancy, an agreeable cut of me pompadoured, black-gowned, and embellished with two ropes of pearls, and I am pleased to consider it a good flattering likeness.

However, on a recent appearance of this picture, my correspondent wrote me: "The Macon people are tired of seeing your ugly mug in the paper." And, adds this final thrust, ". . . as for that old drunk, Sidney Lanier, he once wrote a poem to my grandmother."

In my young days I suffered some shock and grief from such attacks, but nowadays I take them calmly and often with amusement.

It is more perplexing to ponder frequent appeals for money from acquaintances and even strangers whose families are bitterly hard up, whose children are hungry, or whose rent is overdue. "Send $10 or $15 for groceries," they plead, or much more for heavier expenses. Puzzled, and often dubious, I frequently do send money, but I suffer much dismay over the bottomless pit of need in the world.

There are also many blithe appeals for money from loving

AND THEN SOME

kin. A relative with a decided taste for the better things of life hoped I could give her $37,500 for a really nice house she had selected. Her background, her position, her tastes required it, as she felt I would appreciate. I did appreciate her need for such niceties, but not to the tune of nearly $40,000.

Another young relative wanted $2,000 for a trip abroad. Still another called on me for $5,000 for a prize bull with which she and her husband hoped to breed livestock for a profitable beef cattle farm. I believe in good breeding as much as anyone, but could not finance the purchase of so august a beast as that.

THE LITTLE THEATER

My husband and I have always tried to give our support to projects devoted to the improvement of our beloved Macon.

When the Little Theater became a new movement in the fast-growing cultural life of our community during the early thirties, all of Macon enthusiastically supported it. It was not without several false starts, however, that the Little Theater was achieved in 1934. I recall a much earlier movement which collapsed with a disconcerting crash.

There came to Macon a former actress who impressed the townsfolk no little by wearing dashing picture hats and promenading with a La Tosca cane. The lady interested some of us in forming a Little Theater, whose productions she would supervise. We came by a young man of indefinite origins and dazzling aspect—wavy hair, snow-white teeth, and a beguiling smile—who would serve as treasurer and grace many a drama.

We selected a play, something funny, and then cast about for a theater. For days and weeks we toured the alleys, inspecting old stables and deserted carriage houses for a home for our theater which would be properly outré. Meantime, we enlisted patrons, at $100 each, and other supporters for our artistic endeavor and turned the contributions over to our handsome young man.

Shortly, alas, our treasurer decamped with some of our funds, and to this day has been unheard from. We were quite stricken for a while, but we rallied with the help and sympathy of our kind patrons. They generously and cheerfully accepted 50 per cent of their subscriptions back, since that was all we had left to give them—and laughed it off, as if the joke were well worth the money!

On January 14, 1934, the new Little Theater was organized with a board of directors with whom we were thoroughly acquainted—lawyers, a musician, businessmen, a newspaperman, and Mayor Herbert Smart. Our 47 charter members were compelled to move over and make room for 153 more, because of the demand for ground-floor association with the movement. Regents and patrons were secured, and Walter and I joined as regents.

Watching with interest the fervor with which Maconites went about organizing their Little Theater we naturally wanted to contribute to the enterprise. It occurred to us that an abandoned laundry plant we owned on Ocmulgee Street, in disuse for 12 years, might serve as a theater. We offered to lend it to the newly-organized board for their use.

They accepted our loan with great enthusiasm, and immediately recruited interested Maconites in the big job of decoration and repairs. The old plant, at that time several blocks from the business district of town (but since then somewhat surrounded by the spread of downtown toward a new river section), was in good repair, but needed complete transformation within.

We could scarcely recognize the old plant on the great First Night of March 14. When the audience assembled in evening dress for that first performance, *Hay Fever* by Noel Coward, and the curtain rose, excitement and satisfaction were enormous. The play was a great success; it could scarcely seem otherwise to such happy devotees. But it was actually extremely well done, and set the standard for 17 seasons of excellence which has

AND THEN SOME

been a spirited contribution to life in Macon. The Theater group seemed so happy with their cleverly decorated and well adapted home that in 1936 Walter and I decided to give the building to the Theater.

The Theater has flourished, from its first-season membership of 225 to a current enrollment of some 1,400. It has maintained and improved a tradition of professional skill and talented performance, including such serious drama as Ibsen's *Doll House,* Maxwell Anderson's *Winterset,* Philip Barry's *Hotel Universe,* and some highly sophisticated comedies.

One of the most valuable and warming aspects of the Little Theater's spirit is the completely democratic policy with which it operates. While it is a social as well as a theatrical center for our city, and opening nights are occasions for the happiest between-act socializing, it is the one social institution in Macon in which service and talent are the only entrée to participation. Some of our finest performances have been given by people hitherto unknown to the community, and some of the staunchest pillars of behind-the-scenes work are from many walks of life in our town.

MUSIC

My mother felt that every girl born in the South should be musical; so I was early put to music lessons from a private teacher in Macon. Being a pay pupil, I was expected to be very diligent; instead I sometimes played hooky because the lessons were so painful to me. And when I practiced at home, I paid more attention to the clock than to the piano. My perversity taught the home and school authorities nothing, for my music was continued through Wesleyan and on to Wellesley on the theory that in the cultured vicinity of Boston a supposed latent talent would be aroused. There I studied both instrumental and vocal music. Mama was bitterly disappointed at the outcome of this long subjection to music. Papa was not so unhappy because he knew no more about music than I did.

In spite of all, my early sufferings over music have been

rewarded. I confess that many times I have exposed myself to good music without really understanding it, or enjoying it to the full. Some of this I attribute to the early rigors of my music training, but as the protest and distaste of my long enforced studies faded away I gradually found much pleasure in the muse. I have not, like Lanier, claimed music as "the chief mistress of my soul," but as the years passed, fine music began to charm me in such a way that I realized my youthful training was at last yielding understanding and appreciation I had never hoped for.

Early in my married life I found that my husband was a great lover of music, for he had inherited his mother's talent therefor. Because of the popular and foolish prejudice against boys becoming performers in any of the arts, he had not pursued musical studies. That fact probably accounts for the patronage on our part of everything concerning good music in our community and the state in that Walter, deprived of his own self-expression, chose to support music made by others and found great satisfaction in doing so.

Walter and I supported Macon's Symphony Orchestra through many years of changing personnel and setup and the Community Concert Association which brings great artists to our town for the winter season.

On February 28, 1948, I presented to the First Presbyterian Church at Macon a three-manual organ equipped with ample sets of stops, pipes and chimes, adequate for the full expression of great musical compositions, past and present, in the sacred ministry of music. The organ is dedicated to the glory of God in memory of my husband, Walter D. Lamar. The instrument affords constant satisfaction to the donor and is gratifying to all the worshipers as it dispenses a great part of the solemnity and beauty of the services, illustrating Sidney Lanier's words, "Music is love in search of a word."

Among the musical feasts of my life I count the strange and simple singing of Negro servants in Jones County. At Hale

AND THEN SOME

Nui we often gave delightful picnics, and a treat of the occasion was the singing of spirituals by the two Negro women who lived in separate cabins just below the Big House and acted as caretakers. Sis Ella sang soprano and Sis Rosa sang a bass of great range and sweetness. Oftentimes they interpolated strange words of which we had to make out the meaning. A song in which is described the Crucifixion they always sang with the wondering comment, "an' he never said a mumblin' word." Of "The Great Day Comin'," they sang "when he make up his jewelry." Sis Ella carried the air and Sis Rosa gave the notes of her deep mellow bass to the background.

No such music could be heard on a metropolitan stage because the situation would bring a sophistication, or a sense of showing off and doing as others do. And yet, out under the trees of our country place, or seated at the foot of the steps, they sang with abandon and gave great joy to our guests from Macon and friends from afar.

One of the great treats in Georgia both musically and socially has been for years the spring season of the Metropolitan Grand Opera Company, when it comes to Atlanta. I recall now the brilliance of the season early in the 1900's, when the golden-throated Caruso first came to the South. It was a rare privilege to hear him and other outstanding artists in all their glory on the operatic stage, and it was a delight to know them socially.

Grand opera was truly grand in those days. There were dinners, suppers, breakfasts, lawn parties, teas, and balls. The social program was so intensive that John Temple Graves, Sr., said in one of his brilliant after-dinner speeches: "Ah, it is a great thing to be in Atlanta for Grand Opera Week, but it is a far greater thing to have lived through it."

I particularly recall a delightful garden party given by Mrs. Lawson Peel, whose husband, William Lawson Peel, was president of the Atlanta Grand Opera Association. Mrs. Peel, the daughter of General Phil Cook, was noted for her services to U.D.C. and D.A.R.

WHEN ALL IS SAID AND DONE

Among the many operatic stars present at her party was the great soprano Gadski. In conversation with her I said, laughingly, "Ah, Madame, how I enjoyed your music! But you should hear me sing a favorite ditty of mine."

"Why not?" rejoined Gadski.

At the command of the diva I opened my mouth and behaved like a real singer, rendering for the great lady the choice "Song of the Old Family Toothbrush":

> The old family toothbrush!
> The old family toothbrush!
> First it was father's,
> Then it was mother's,
> Next it was brother's,
> And now it is mine!
> The old family toothbrush
> That hangs by the sink.

I became at its beginning an associate member of the Saturday Morning Music Club in Macon, now known as the Morning Music Club. An associate membership was as far as I would go, having long since accepted my limitations as a performer and contented myself with an appreciative capacity. This club has always held its standards high, has brought many noted artists to Macon, has provided bi-monthly programs of vocal and instrumental music, has sponsored Christmas carol singing, and is generally a leading force in elevating the public taste in music. However, Macon husbands, despite the zeal of the club members, are still in a minority at community concerts.

ALMA MATER

Since my first enrollment at Wesleyan, this oldest woman's college in America and cultural center in our state has seemed an integral part of my background. The red brick, tall-spired spread of mellowed buildings with their Victorian facades which comprises the old school on College Street, now the Conservatory, has long been the hub of artistic and intellectual life in Macon, and of much of our town's social activity. The halls, parlors, and galleries of old buildings in town are closely associated in my mind and heart with the Wesleyan which nurtured me and in whose service I have labored for years. This span covers seventy years of a lifetime happily and fruitfully highlighted with Wesleyan friendships, society, civic effort, and religious inspiration.

The facade additions (porches and trimming) to the College Street buildings are the fruits of a donation to Wesleyan of $50,000 from George I. Seney of New York when I was a student. He made his contribution in 1881 to "aid the work of female education." The news was hailed with joy by the Methodist Board of Trustees, by the faculty, and by the students. The gift was not an unmixed blessing, for it provided funds for the alteration of Wesleyan's beautiful columned front with its lovely feel of ancient architecture.

In the early twenties I was a busy alumna and secretary of the Class of '83. I was also a devoted member of the old Adelphean Society, even after sororities were banned at Wesleyan.

When Southern Methodists sought to expand Wesleyan and launched their Greater Wesleyan Campaign for a $2,000,000 endowment, I was appointed alumnae drive chairman for Macon to lead the funds-raising among former Wesleyan girls.

In 1922 I was nominated alumnae trustee of Wesleyan, and elected to the board. Later I was elected a full trustee for a three-year term. In July of 1926, Wesleyan was well enough along in the Greater Wesleyan campaign to break ground at Rivoli for the new plant. We spaded up the fresh earth very ceremoniously indeed before a throng of some hundreds who came to see the happy beginning. That July I conducted another ceremony at Old Wesleyan, presenting the college a marble bench on behalf of my sorority, Alpha Delta Pi. We celebrated Wesleyan's 75th anniversary with this gift.

The campaign for funds reached its climax in 1928 and 1929 when the institution reported a $2,000,000 endowment fund from a bond issue. And, like other ambitious and expanding institutions in that inflated period, Wesleyan fell into dire difficulties with the depression. However, before 1950, with the help and support of alumnae, Methodists, and other friends, the institution recovered and paid off its obligations—with the new Rivoli plant achieved and paid for. A bond-burning ceremony at the college emphasized the accomplishment.

In 1930 Walter purchased in Florence, Italy, an excellent copy of Murillo's famed "Madonna and Child" to present to Wesleyan in my honor. He shipped the canvas to Macon, with a letter to Dr. William F. Quillian, the president, saying in part: ". . . it gives me great joy to establish such testimony in honor of my wife, a Wesleyan graduate and the first woman in Macon to be made a trustee of the college. May the beauty in color, the spirituality of the message which this picture portrays be to the young womanhood of Wesleyan an inspiration along artistic, intellectual, and religious lines." This presentation is one of the happiest of my Wesleyan associations, for the tribute to me from my husband, for the permanent gift of beauty to the college, and for Walter's articulation of what Wesleyan has meant to me.

In 1936 Wesleyan celebrated her centennial lavishly, and all daughters of the institution in Macon and many from afar streamed to the Rivoli campus and to Conservatory programs in town.

Highlight of the observances was a stirring and colorful pageant, attended by thousands, which depicted the history of our venerable and progressive institution. The pageant unrolled quite splendidly, its action carried through loudspeakers to an audience that reached beyond the campus and far out on the Forsyth Road. Wearing a silver robe and a blue and silver overdress, which I had bought in Cairo, with a court train of silver and gold and a headdress of silver and purple velvet, I narrated the events as they were enacted.

In 1938 my associates gave to Wesleyan the Dorothy Blount Lamar Scholarship, a year's tuition in honor of my election as

AND THEN SOME

President-General of U.D.C. It was awarded to the winner of an essay contest on Confederate history.

During World War II Wesleyan, and, indeed, all of Macon, were stirred from their preoccupation with war work by the visit of the celebrated Madame Chiang Kai Shek. Wife of China's generalissimo, the "missimo" was well known and beloved in Macon as the delightful and irrepressible Mei-Ling Soong, brilliant daughter of China's great Methodist convert and liberal leader, Dr. Sun Yat Sen. She had attended Wesleyan as a young girl, and all of Georgia had watched her rise in recent years of China's turbulent history to her place beside the powerful Chiang.

The "missimo" was in America on a mission for more aid to China from the United States, and accepted an invitation to return to Macon for a stop at Wesleyan and a reunion with old friends and townsfolks who wanted to honor her.

I headed a delegation to greet our distinguished alumna when her special train arrived at the Rivoli station in the morning. I carried a bouquet of flowers and went to the platform, only to be informed by an official in the party that Madame Chiang could not be disturbed. So I tossed the bouquet to the gentleman, with our greetings, and returned to my duties as hostess to the assembled guests at a luncheon I was giving. This was in a period when the First Lady of China was extremely busy working under tension and the burden of illness. We learned that she was attended by a doctor and a nurse, and was under orders to rest.

Later, her appearances were amply satisfying. In her main speech at the Conservatory chapel she spoke fondly and humorously of her Wesleyan days and of Macon as her home. At the reception afterwards in the parlors, strikingly gowned in a Chinese robe most becoming to her svelte figure and Eastern coloring, she delighted us with her astonishing recollection of old friends. Graying women in their late forties and fifties, whom she had last seen as college girls in the middy blouse era, she recognized, embraced, called by name, and regaled with girlish stories of school escapades.

On one occasion with a group of these old friends she repaired down the street from the Conservatory to "The Pharm," a drugstore which for several generations has been a meeting place for Wesleyan girls. At the counter, she ordered a sundae piled high with whipped cream and strawberry syrup, violating her strict diet for old time's sake.

Wesleyan was gratified in the winter of 1941 when the Central of Georgia Railway named a new Pullman car "Wesleyan." Called on to christen the new car, I pointed out the coincidence of Wesleyan beginnings and the establishment of the Central of Georgia in 1836. In that year Macon citizens asked the city council for a grant of land for the Macon Female College, and received five acres on old Encampment Hill, the College Street elevation where the Conservatory now stands.

Also in 1836, Augusta, Savannah, and Macon were trying to secure for their communities headquarters for the Savannah and Macon Road. We find Jere Cowles, an early Wesleyan trustee, leading interested Maconites in financing the railroad, known then as the Monroe Railroad, and bringing its headquarters here. Cowles, "Father of Railroads," that year rode on horseback to a seven-state convention of delegates to pick a route for the line from Cincinnati to a Southern port, and pressed Macon's claims at the time.

Thus were established the college, heart of Macon's cultural development, and the railroad headquarters which through the years transformed a little village into a thriving city. With due deference to the size and financial aspects of both institutions, I stressed above all the devotion of their founders whose spirit of service lives on in the greatness of both school and railroad.

In the fall of 1944 I was happy to add a cherished bit of Lanierana to Wesleyan's collection of momentoes of the poet, who lived and worked for a time at the College and was married to a Wesleyan girl in the Conservatory chapel.

AND THEN SOME

The gift was the old flute on which Sidney Lanier learned to play, with several sheets of music which he used. It was given to me by a Lanier devotee, W. P. Fleming of Macon. He expressed his confidence that I would place it eventually in some honored place for safekeeping. Mr. Fleming got the flute from John R. Voorhees of Wilburn, New Jersey, who had the instrument originally from his Uncle Charles Campbell, early instructor and fellow flautist of Lanier.

I presented the flute with a Lanier program of poems and excerpts, and it is now in the Georgia Room of Wesleyan's library, with Lanier's old desk and other articles.

Another happy Wesleyan memory which I cherish is the Founder's Day tea in my honor in May of 1947. This lovely party celebrated my work as U.D.C. President-General, Historian-General, Stratford Director for Georgia, Wesleyan Trustee, Queen of the Kappa Alpha fraternity's Old South Ball here, and as an early member of the Adelpheans, the first secret society for college girls in the world, founded in 1851.

Such is my lifelong association with Wesleyan College, the religious, cultural, and intellectual dynamo of Macon's spirit. The college, from the days it was a stern and old-fashioned school for refined and circumscribed young ladies of Georgia to its present function as a flourishing center of learning for modern girls with their unlimited interests and unprecedented freedom, has been a vital part of my life, comparable in influence, pleasure, and inspiration to my home and my church.

SCHOOLS

For some years I have been an interested member of the Board of Trustees of Rabun Gap-Nacoochee School. This board is made up of business men, ministers, and a few women, with representatives from the community school at Rabun Gap.

Near the turn of the century the school was founded by Andrew Ritchie and his wife. From the furthermost mountain coves, from the last cabin on the creek, they brought children whom they trained half the day in books and the other half in trades and industrial arts. Keen interest and devotion, with financial help from friends in the South and the North, enable the Ritchies to make the school a success. There was instituted the novel plan of establishing in cottages whole families for a number of years, where the men learned scientific and practical ways of farming and the women were instructed in home chores and in the proper care of their children. This system of teaching farm families has enriched the lot of countless North Georgia families.

On the fly leaf of my valued copy of Andrew Ritchie's book on Rabun County history is inscribed: "With the compliments of the author of this book and with my gratitude for your constant and generous help in founding of the school."

In 1911 the Georgia Daughters of the Confederacy bought 100 acres of fertile land in the Rabun Gap area and built thereon several cottages for the school families as a monument to Francis S. Bartow, the young Savannah hero of the Confederacy. I remember with pride that as President of the Georgia Daughters I signed the check which purchased the land for this project.

The present Rabun Gap plant is under the guidance of the Presbyterian Synod of Georgia.

I have also had a share in another splendid educational enterprise for Georgia mountain children, the Tallulah Falls School, founded, owned, and operated by the Georgia Federation of Women's Clubs, and known as "The Light in the Mountains."

For many years I was first vice president of the Tallulah Falls School Board, and I resigned only when I was elected to the all-engrossing office of President-General of U.D.C., feeling that two such active jobs could not be efficiently carried on by one woman.

In Macon since May, 1927, a sign of Spring (as sure as jonquils, wistaria, and violets) is the appearance of Macon girls on downtown street corners selling the colorful Tallulah Falls

AND THEN SOME

tags for the benefit of this mountain work. I inaugurated, and for many years engineered, this pretty invasion, enlisting high school girls to work in relays vending our tags, and awarding prizes to those who sold the most. Our receipts were amazing, and Macon's Tag Day for Tallulah Falls School has become an annual event.

MACON CELEBRATIONS

I have helped to celebrate several centennial dates in Macon's history. Among them, already mentioned, were the centenary of Wesleyan College in 1936 and the 100th anniversary of Sidney Lanier's birth celebrated in 1942.

The Centenary of Macon, in 1923, was a three-day affair with Indians and early settlers, with grande dames and dignitaries, magnificent floats, and gala parades. For this, I designed a pantomime portraying *Aeneas Africanus*, a phenomenally popular short story by Harry Stillwell Edwards. Also I directed a playlet based on Sidney Lanier's poem, "The Tournament." I appeared as Peace driving Hate from the scene and later knighting a soldier of World War I. Third, I presented the story of one of Jefferson Davis' five visits to Macon, the various characters being well portrayed by leading citizens—both ladies and gentlemen. These scenes all took place in the open air at Central City Park.

On December 26, 1926, the Synod of Georgia met in Macon for the purpose of celebrating the centennial of the First Presbyterian Church. I gave greetings for the Woman's Auxiliary, and the Reverend William R. Mackay delivered the address.

In 1951 Alpha Delta Pi, a national sorority, celebrated its centenary in Macon. The members came from North and South, East and West, and although Wesleyan College no longer permits sororities in its program the authorities were most generous in allowing the visitors lodging and services of the college at Rivoli as well as at the Conservatory, where the societies were first established though later abolished. My invocation at the opening session embodied the petition that "God would put it into the hearts and minds of the authorities to invite sororities back to old Wesleyan." The reception at my home for 800 visitors was a festive occasion which I enjoyed as much as did my guests.

WAR YEARS

I have lived through three wars of our country, two of them world wars. I have known first hand and through my best loved friends of the fear, heartache, and felling grief of separation and war casualties. I have felt the pride, protest, despair, frustration, and sacrifice that war means to all of us. Thus I have partaken of the best and the worst of home front wartime experience.

I believe that Maconites brought their best to serve their community, their country, and the world in World Wars I and II. We not only worked, smiled, waited, and answered every call to duty, but also with heartfelt hospitality and friendship laughed, entertained, worked, and sacrificed to help fighting men who came our way. We did all we could, and we enjoyed and rewarded ourselves in the doing.

In World War I my first chore was the direction of a Red Cross Roll Call pageant to interpret war needs and to raise funds for the Red Cross drive. Our pageant was *The Roll Call Masque,* written by the poet and dramatist Percy Mackaye. It told the story of the Red Cross humanitarian service in wartime. I recruited the cast, technical workers, and promoters, and I directed the pageant itself with professional help from Camp Wheeler. The presentation was a thrilling success and we were called on for repeat performances, including a show at Camp Wheeler.

Our home front for World War II was formed in Macon long before Pearl Harbor, and it kept Macon civilians serving the war effort well through V-E Day and V-J Day. I was swept into heading the Women's Defense League of Macon, which eventually acquired a membership of 6,000 women engaged in active work of preparing themselves for emergency service. We served in cooperation with the Red Cross and under Army direction, giving assistance to many programs.

Groups were organized to help war programs in all capacities from cooks (who might relieve Army chefs in emergencies) to drivers. We regularly sent groups to hospital wards at nearby Army installations to cheer the sick soldiers with gifts, books, bedside ice cream parties, letter writing, and so on. I remember chatting several times, in 1942, at Camp Wheeler with a young Army private named Gordon Gray, who was recuperating from an operation. He soon recovered and was released from the hospital; so we lost track of him. In 1947 we had reason to remember our private at Camp Wheeler, when he became Assistant Secretary of the Army. Gray, interviewed in Washington, recalled his days at Camp Wheeler as "the most satisfying period in his life, certainly one of the most enjoyable" and Macon as "one of the friendliest places I have ever known."

Defense League work was not all visiting and hometown hospitality. A motor corps of thirty-five or forty young women were trained in driving and auto mechanics under a major at Camp Wheeler. We were instructed in handling cars during blackouts, in giving signals, and in preparedness for emergency convoys. I, who have never even familiarized myself with the steering wheel of a car, soon became privy to the innermost workings of a motor under the hood. For the duration, at least, I felt competent to cope with a few contingencies as a mechanic, but when peace came I promptly forgot my instruction and reverted to my former state of innocence about motor operations.

Defense League members were also trained in home nursing, with Red Cross cooperation, and in First Aid in order to arm the community against any surprise attack. No such attacks came, of course, but we lived under constant apprehension of them, blacked out by night, and always organized for the possible disaster. Members were well equipped for service in case of a raid, and the sense of preparedness relieved the general fear and anxiety and was well worth the hours of training and preparing.

It is with pride and satisfaction that I recall the contributions of young and old women in our community. Their efforts were not in vain, I am sure. If a new power for evil darkens our world today and threatens to undo our victory, that does not prove that our work was futile. It only shows that eternal vigilance is the price of liberty and that the struggle against wrong is never done.

MRS. LAMAR WITH 1934 GRADUATING CLASS AT THE TALLULAH FALLS SCHOOL

CONCLUSION

MINE HAS BEEN A GOOD LIFE, MOLDED, DISCIPLINED, AND illumined by the heritage of the Old South. Reviewing this life has been a considerable labor—looking back over more than eight decades, through four distinct eras, remembering the great events I saw and felt, the personal joys and griefs, the accomplishments and failures, the friends who loom tall and successful and the equally cherished ones who remained quiet and obscure. However, the labor of this work has been a happy and rewarding one, pursued with zest that overcame the tedium.

At the end of my written story, with this work and most of life's more tiring efforts behind me, it seems that the heritage of which I wrote in the beginning has carried me through as fruitfully and as happily as I could wish. The standard of genteel manners, the rigorous code of behavior, and the illumination and strength of orthodox Presbyterian faith are still, to me, the best arms with which to take up the battle of life.

I recall the long, persevering effort to reward our poet Sidney Lanier and to bring his message to my contemporaries. I recall the vigilant and often discouraging years of work to re-interpret Jefferson Davis, and I can see that my promotions have indeed contributed to U.D.C. success in making the world aware of the President of the Confederacy. Looking around me, at home or traveling, I see the South adorned with monuments and markers which tell the story of the Confederacy and hold before our young people the living ideals for which it stood. And I rejoice in my share in this work.

At home I recall exhausting effort to arrange some celebration, benefit, memorial, or cultural event for my townsfolk—services which have given me a richer sense of home and friendship with my neighbors. I remember the conflicts, the persuasions, and the writing and speaking I have done to support what I thought was right for our political life. Often I have been on the losing side, but I am not sorry to have spent myself working for what I thought to be right. In social, family, and friendship relations, too, I have often spent myself to the point of exhaustion and even illness. The love, the counsel, the time and understanding one gives to one's troubled friends, and the sorrow one bears with them, are often too intimate for recountal in a published record.

Thus one is "spent." However, I have learned that in the prime of youth and even in the ripeness of years this spending of oneself has surprising rewards in renewal of strength to keep on keeping on. Love, service opportunities, enjoyment, and even health are not given us to be conserved. Some of my busiest and most taxing years have been the most satisfying.

Although I enjoy extraordinary health, the time has now come when I must conserve. So conserve I do, since I am amiably instructed by my doctor to undertake no uncongenial chores and to do only what I enjoy. Thus I pass up the drudgery and tedium of some old work, but the more absorbing and less exacting civic duties I lightheartedly assume and relish. To be sure, I still carry on some quite taxing duties, such as the Stratford work and the needs and demands of friends and relatives, but I find I have more freedom and rest than ever before. I have leisure for music, reading, entertainment, travel, social life, and such civic and U.D.C. contributions as I can yet comfortably make.

I do not feel old, and am sometimes taken aback on party occasions when a kind and admiring young friend will rush up to me, regard me with wonder, and declare: "Mrs. Lamar, you are just *remarkable!*"

Ah, "remarkable," that wondering compliment of the young! They cannot imagine a lady of my years still in possession of her faculties, still able to enjoy a handsome hat, still with eyesight to read and sufficient *joie de vivre* to engage in party repartee. "Remarkable" that one still has one's own quite pre-

CONCLUSION

sentable teeth, a penchant for dress beyond black crepe with a lace collar, and an interest in everybody, old and young. Should one perhaps be consigned to a wheelchair and be trundled out for respectful greetings and soft compliments and the fond, condescending talk with which old folks are regaled?

Well, "remarkable" or no, it is a happy time of life for one who can and does participate in a daily round of pleasure and duties. I am grateful for my life's work done, and for so much of life's enjoyment still ahead of me.

INDEX

Able, J. H., 50
Acton, Lord, 139
Adams, James Trusloe, 181
Adams, John Quincy, 40-41
Aldelpheans, 74-75, 267
Aderhold, Henry, 50
Alexander, Elam, 26
Allen, Florence V., 180
Allenby, General, 251
Alpha Delta Pi, 263, 269
Anderson, Charles Roberts, 29, 176, 187
Anderson, Mrs. Charles Roberts (Eugenia Blount) 29, 33, 87, 98, 187
Anderson, Clifford, 4
Anderson, Helen Barnes, 185
Anderson, R. L., 182, 192, 197
Anderson, Robert Lanier, III, 185
Anderson & Simmons, 1, 3
Andersonville Prison, 117
Andrews, Matthew P., 116, 141-143
Angell, James R., 188-191
Anthony, Susan B., 208; Southern Women's League Rejection of Susan B. Anthony Amendment, 211
Appleton Church Home, 25
Arezzo, Joseph Paul, 133
Armstrong, J. R., 14
Arnold, Maria, 80
Arnold, Matthew, 80
Arrington, Mrs. Peter W., 202
Athenaeum, 88, 221
Atlanta Constitution, 108, 152
Atlanta Journal, 84, 169
Atlantic Monthly, 33

Bacon, A. O., 45
Bacon, Mrs. A. O., 4
Bacon, Mary Lou, 74
Baker, Mrs. George, 113, 114
Baker, Newton D., 178, 180
Ball, Mrs. Edmund, 203
Barfield, Mike, 15

Bartow, Francis S., 268
Bass, W. C., 30
Battle, A. J., 87
Battle, Cullen, 82
Baxter, John, 7, 82
Beauregard, P. G. T., 4
Beck, E. E., 47, 49
Belmont Farm, 7, 83
Benét, Stephen Vincent, 176, 228
Benjamin, Judah Philip, 242
Bennett, Claude N., 84
Bernhardt, Sarah, 87, 242
Berry, Mrs. Harold, 203
Bibb Manufacturing Company, 21
Bingham, Robert Worth, 178
Bingham, Mrs. Robert Worth, 203
Birch, Mrs. Margaret Snider, 37, 74
Blackburn, Joe, 55
Blaine, James G., 61, 99
Bland, Representative, 94
Blount, David, 3, 9, 13, 55
Blount, Dorothy (daughter of Joseph Blount), 29
Blount, Fanny, 28, 30, 55, 106, 234
Blount, James H., 1, 3, 5-6, 8-14, 16-19, 45-47, 54, 60, 75, 83-84, 92-94, 96-98
Blount, Mrs. James Henderson (Eugenia "Genie" Wiley), 2-10, 12-19, 54, 60, 222
Blount, Jim, 7, 24, 27-28, 32-34, 36, 53, 56, 58-59, 92, 98-99
Blount, Joseph, 16, 18, 20, 24, 27-30, 36, 53, 58, 82, 89, 92, 95, 101
Blount, Mary, 3, 8
Blount, Maude, 29
Blount, Thomas, 3, 13
Blount's Cavalry, 16
Boifeuillet, John T., 168-169
Bond family, 105
Bond, Mrs. Joseph, 35
Booth, Edwin, 29, 87

. 277 .

INDEX

Borglum, Gutzon, 151-157, 159, 161-163, 165-169, 189
Bowden, Charles, 184, 195, 225, 227
Bowen, Thomas, 83
Bowen, Mrs. Thomas (Mary Blount), 7, 18, 83
Bowers, Claude, 222-223
Bowman, Isaiah, 185-186, 189-190, 192
Bradford, Gamaliel, 173
Bragg, Braxton, 229
Brooks, Phillips, 80
Brown, Mrs. Duncan, 145
Brown, Mrs. Ed, 108
Brown, John, 116
Brown, Joseph E., 14, 16, 43, 66-68, 71
Brown, Mrs. Joseph E., 66-68
Brown, Orton Bishop, 71
Brown House, 88
Buck, Mrs. Gordon, 230
Bullitt, William C., 179
Bullitt, William Marshall, 179
Bullock, Rufus E., 42, 47
Burge, J. W., 50
Burke, J. W., Gold Medal, 31
Burnett, Mrs. Lewis, 115
Burt, Struthers, 180
Butler, Benjamin ("Beast"), 57, 58, 59, 61
Butler, Billy, 84-85
Butler, Marion, 84
Butler's Historical Record of Macon, 22

Callaway, James, 210
Callaway, Louise, 145
Cameron, Benehan, 156
Campbell, Mrs. A. C., 114
Campbell, Charles, 9, 267
Campbell, Mrs. S. J., 203
Canby, Henry Seidel, 174, 176-177
Cannon, Joseph, 65
Carlisle, John G., 66, 99
Carlisle, Mrs. John G., 66
Carnegie, Andrew, 34
Carpenter, Senator, 57
Caudle, Mrs. Theron Lamar, 172, 185
Central of Georgia Railway, 266

Chamberlin, Eva, 106
Cheatham, B. F., 206
Chennault, Claire, 225
Cherry, George F., 50
Chiang Kai Shek, Madame (Mei-Ling Soong), 265-266
Children of the Confederacy, 136, 145
Churchill, Winston, 140-143
Civil Works Administration, 214-219
Clancy, Duffus, 36
Clarke, George Herbert, 173
Cleveland, Grover, 66, 68, 70-71, 95-98, 179-180
Cleveland, Mrs. Grover, 59, 68-69
Clisby, Editor, 42
Clisby, Warner, 35
Clisby, Mrs. Warner, 34
Clisby family, 22
Cobb, Mrs. Alice Culler, 30-31
Cochran, Bourke, 70
Coleman, Birdie, 26-27
Coleman, Daisy, 26-27
Coleman, Sam, 26
Coleman's Hill, 26, 88, 148
Collins, Appleton, 48
Colquitt, Governor, 66
Colquitt, P. H., 9
Columbia University, 33, 177
Columbus Light Guards, 9
Comer, Mrs. B. B., 185
Comer, Sallie B., 33, 98
Confederate Constitution, 129-130
Confederate Memorial Society, 130
Confederate Veteran Magazine, 138
Conkling, Roscoe, 63
Connor, Grantville, 9
Cook, Mrs. Edwin W., 191
Coolidge, Calvin, 154
Corbin family, 22
Corkle, William, 48
Cotton, Clifford, 22, 26, 30, 242
Cowles Hill, 3, 21-22, 26
Cowles, Jere, 26, 266
Cox, James M., 211-213
Craig, D. D., 50
Craig, Marlin, 127
Curzon, Lady, Vicereine of India, 69
Curzon, Viceroy of India, 69

. 278 .

INDEX

Dabney, Charles W., 183
Davis, Jefferson, 4, 16, 40, 59, 62-63, 66, 88-90, 120-125, 129, 136, 151, 153, 223, 228, 269, 273; Highway, 114-115; Historical Foundation, 121; Memorial, 135
Davis, Mrs. Jefferson, 90
Davis, John A., 178
Davis, Margaret, 88-90; (Mrs. Hayes) 90-91
Davis, Senator, 55
Davis, Winnie, 88
de Graffenreid, Claire, 75
Dennison, L. A., 80
DeRenne, Mrs. G. W. J., 129
DeRenne, W. J., 129
DeRenne, Wymberly, 129, 130
DeRenne Library, 129-130
Derry, Professor, 87
DeWitt, General, 125, 127-128
Dickenson, Jean, 192
Dodd, William E., 178
Dooley, Isma, 108
Douglas, Fred, 60
Dowell, Spright, 186
Doyal, L. T., 9
Dunlap, Capt., 14
Dunmore, Lord, 141
Du Pont, Mrs. Alfred I. (Jessie Ball), 203, 205
Dure, Mrs. Leon, 215
Durell, Judge, 57

Edwards, Harry Stillwell, 269
Ellis, Mrs. Lee, 103
Ellis, Theo W., 50
Ely, Hanson, 128
Emporia Gazette, 179
Encampment Hill, 266
English-Speaking World, 141
Ethridge, Mark, 215
Ethridge, Willie Snow, 169, 215
Ezekiel, Sir Moses, 112

Fargo, L. K., 29
Farrow, Harry, 50
Fellows, John R., 70
Felton, W. H., 82, 221
Fenner, Charles E., 90

Field, Mrs. Alexander, 200
Findlay's Foundry, 12
Finley, John, 139, 178, 180
Finney, Mrs. Tommye, 191
First Baptist Church (Macon), 174
First Presbyterian Church (Macon), 105, 174, 260
Fisher, Dorothy Canfield, 181
Fitten, Flora, 107
Fleming, W. P., 267
Floyd Hotel, 2
Floyd Rifles, 2, 4, 9, 11, 50
Flying Tigers, 225-226
Ford, Mrs. A. C., 202-203
Foster, Stephen, 183
Freeman, Alice, 76, 78
Freeman, Azel, 82
Freeman, Douglas Southall, 122, 125, 177, 189, 196, 206, 223
Frelinghuysen, Secretary, 60
French, John C., 181, 185
French Protestant Huguenot Church, 180
Freud, Sigmund, 124

Gadski, Johanne, 261
Gaines, Mrs. Myra Clark, 56
Gaines, Emma Townes, 8
Gaines, Francis P., 179
Gambrell, James Bruton, 117, 119
Garrett, Mrs. Rufus, 203
Geer, Mrs. A. J., 203
George, Walter F., 129
Georgia Association Opposed to Woman Suffrage, 210
Georgia, University of, 3, 30, 33
Gibson, Gertrude, 185
Gibson, Gertrude Lanier, 185
Glasgow, Ellen, 177, 180
Glass, Carter, Jr., 125
Glass, Carter, Sr., 125
God Is My Co-Pilot, 227
Gone With the Wind, 224
Gonzales, William E., 178, 180
Gordon, Caroline, 70-71
Gordon, Fanny, 70-71
Gordon, John B., 70-71, 99
Gordon, Mrs. John B., 56, 62, 70-71, 100

INDEX

Grace, Mrs. Walter J., 153-155, 157, 159, 161-163, 165
Grady, Henry W., 65
Grant, Ulysses S., 23, 42-43, 47, 51, 54, 57-59, 61, 141
Graves, Charles A., 138-139
Graves, John Temple, Jr., 152-153, 261
Graves, John Temple, Sr., 232
Gray, Gordon, 271
Greeley, Horace, 39-40, 42, 43, 44, 46, 47, 51, 232
Green Bag, 33
Griffith, Mrs. Bowie Dorsey, 29
Gustin, George W., 50

Hale Nui, 30, 83, 92, 101, 259-260
Hancock, C. J., 50
Happ Brothers Factory, 88
Hardeman, Tom, 2, 7, 9, 43, 46
Hardeman, Mrs. Tom, 2
Harding, Warren G., 154
Harper, Eunice, 204
Harper's, 33
Harris, Albert Grady, 174, 197
Harris, Charles Jenkins, 35
Harris, Mrs. Charles Jenkins (Mary Wiley), 19, 35
Harris, Corra, 108, 109
Harris, D. C., 150
Harris, Iverson, 2, 3
Harris, Joel Chandler, 182
Harris, Julia, 230
Harris, Rufus C., 186
Harris, Stella, 76
Harris, Walter A., 144, 147, 196, 198, 226
Harris, William A., 230
Harris, Mrs. William A. (Julia Wheeler), 230
Harrison, Benjamin, 60, 95
Harrison, Mrs. Benjamin, 59
Harrison, Mrs. Fairfax, 201
Harrold, Mrs. C. C., 213
Hawes, Mrs. Harry B., 202
Hayden, John, 230, 231
Hayes, Rutherford B., 99
Hayes, Mrs. Rutherford B., 59
Hayes-Davis, Jefferson Addison, 136

Hazlehurst, William, 24
Henderson, J. J., 150
Heyward, Dubose, 178
Hill, Benjamin H., 45, 46, 61
Hitt, Robert R., 93
Hoadly, Governor, 73
Hoadly, Laura, 73
Hoar, George Frisbie, 62, 63
Hodgewick, Louise M., 78
Hoge, John, 105
Holman, William S., 93, 94
Holmes, J. P., 226
Holt, Asa, 15
Holt, Hamilton, 179
Holt, Thaddeus, 3
Holt, Mrs. William F. (Hennie Dean), 62
Honti, Joseph, 175
Hood, John Bell, 15, 16
Hopkins, Harry, 215, 218, 219
Hopson, Georgia, 87
Hopson, Virginia Connor, 87, 168
Hopson, W. A., 168
Howell, Clark, 160
Huff, W. A., 23, 41, 48, 50, 51
Hume, Alfred, 178
Hyacinth, Père, 90
Hunt, Stella, 74

Ickes, Harold L., 183
Ingalls, Senator, 67
Inge, Dean, 179
Iverson, General, 15

Jackson, Thos. J., 121, 135, 142, 151, 153, 167
Jacobs, Eddie, 218
Jannerone, John Robert, 133
Jefferson, Joseph, 29, 87
Jelks, Mrs. Doris, 150
Jemison, R. W., 46
John Brown's Body, 228
Johns Hopkins University, 181, 184, 185, 189, 192
Johns Hopkins University Press, 176
Johnson, Andrew, 128
Johnston, Ben B., 164
Johnston, Joseph E., 16, 59
Johnston, Marsh, 88-89

INDEX

Johnston, Mary Ellen, 85
Johnston, William B., 3, 86
Johnston, Mrs. William B., 27
Jones, Bruce Carr, 204-205
Jones, Geo. S., 50
Jones, Mrs. Frank F. (Mary Callaway), 172, 191, 196
Jones, Percy, 58-59
Jones, Stuart, 82, 86

Kane, Harnett, 56
Kappa Alpha, 267
Keller, Helen, 179
Kelley, "Pig Iron," 61, 65, 99
Kelly, State Senator, 167
Kilbreath, Miss, 211, 213
King, Campbell, 74
Knox, Helen, 178, 203
Ku Klux Klan, 24-25, 43-44, 50, 56, 70

Ladies' Memorial Association, 25
Ladies' Soldiers' Relief Society, 12, 25
LaGuardia, Fiorella, 176
Lamar, Alberta, 104
Lamar, Fannie, 104, 105
Lamar, Henry, 104
Lamar, Henry J., 61
Lamar, Jack, 104
Lamar, John B., 2
Lamar, L. M., 7
Lamar, L. Q. C., 61-64, 99
Lamar, Valeria (Mrs. Ed McLaren), 103-105
Lamar, Virginia, 4
Lamar, Walter Douglas, 62, 101-108, 169, 187, 204, 215-216, 228, 230, 250, 260, 264
Lamar, Mr. (Walter's father), 104, 106
Lamar, Wileyna, 104
Lang, Alton, 241
Lanier, Charles Day, 166, 171
Lanier, Mrs. Charles Day (May Field), 188, 191, 199-202, 205
Lanier, Clifford, 170, 185
Lanier, Mary Day, 171-172
Lanier, Mary Day (great-granddaughter of poet), 192

Lanier, Sidney, 5, 7, 32, 120, 167-168, 170-183, 185-200, 206, 250, 256, 260, 266-267, 269, 273; Lanier Bridge, 182; Lanier Centennial, 184-187; Lanier High School, 185; Lanier Hotel, 185; Memorial Association, 164; Memorial room, 165; Mount Lanier, 183
Lanier, Sidney (grandson of poet), 191-192
Lanier, Sterling, 169
LeConte, Anna, 4
Lee, Bolling, 127
Lee, G. W. Custis, 138
Lee, Hannah, 206
Lee, Henry, 206
Lee, Mary, 128
Lee, Richard, I, 206
Lee, Robt. E., 38, 115, 121, 125-127, 141-142, 151, 153-154, 161-162, 166-167, 199-200, 206, 223; "Duty" quotation, 137-140; Foundation, Ins., 178, 191, 200-201, 205-206; Memorial Award, 133-134
Lee, Thomas, 200-206
Lee Family Society, 202
Legg, Mrs. Leila, 87
Leiter, Mary, 69
Lester, Laura, 71
Lester, Rufus, 71
Life magazine, 225
Liliuokalani, Queen, 95-98
Lincoln, Abraham, 122-124, 128, 141
Lindsey, Judge Ben, 210
Lipscomb, Mrs. Lamar R., 108
Little, Arthur D., 180
Logan, John A., 99
Long, Mrs. Breckinridge, 203
Long, Jeff, 42, 44-46, 48-50
Long, Pulaski, 49
Longfellow, Henry Wadsworth, 182
Louisville Courier-Journal and Times, 178
Lowe, Tillman, 48
Lowell, Amy, 182
Lowell, James Russell, 182
Lowther Hall, 16
Lukeman, Augustus, 159, 161, 162, 164

.281.

INDEX

McAdoo, William G., 147
McCreary, Representative, 94
McElroy, Robert, 191
McEnery, Gov.-Elect in Louisiana, 57
McKay, Clifford, III, 185
McKay, Mrs. John, 182
McKay, Sally, 185
McKean, Sandra Lanier, 192
McKenzie, Mrs. Oscar, 162, 163
McKinley, William, 33, 229
McKinney, R. L., 146
McLeod, Governor, 155
McPherson, J. H. T., 181, 187

Mabbott, T. C., 181
Macarness, Roger, 141
Mackay, William R., 269
MacKaye, Percy, 270
Macon Community Concert Association, 260
Macon Cotton Factory, 21
Macon Female College, 266
Macon Guards, 7
Macon News, 146, 148
Macon Symphony Orchestra, 260
Macon Telegraph, 162, 164, 169, 210, 215, 219, 221
Macon Telegraph and Messenger, 42-47, 49, 51, 56, 84, 87
Macon Volunteers, 2, 4-5, 9, 11, 50, 82, 146
Maerz, Mrs. Glenn Priest, 150
Malone, Ted, 182, 186
Marsh, John, 224
Mason, Mrs. F. T., 155
Massee Gin Works, 21
Maury, Matthew Fontaine, 135; U. D. C. Award, 133
Maynard, Congressman, 51
Meldrim, Caroline, 185
Mencken, Henry L., 177
Mercer University, 22, 24, 29, 37-38, 117, 186, 221
Millay, Edna St. Vincent, 186
Miller, Vernon, 150
Milwaukee Press, 33
Mims, Edwin, 169, 181, 186, 188
Mississippi, University of, 178-179
Mitchell, Margaret, 123-124, 224

Monroe Railroad, 266
Morgan, Miss A. E. F., 77-78
Morgan, Helen, 81
Morris, Harrison, 181
Morton, Radical Party Whip, 57
Moseley, J. R., 221
Mount de Sales Academy, 22
Mount Holyoke College, 179
Mount Rushmore Memorial, 166
Mount Vernon Ladies Association, 201
Mulberry Street Methodist Church, 37
Murrow, Edward R., 140
Muzzey, *History of the United States*, 122

Nance, Steve, 215, 219
National Association Opposed to Woman Suffrage, 209
Newcomb, Simon, 179
New York American, 156
New York Herald-Tribune, 96, 99
New York Philharmonic Symphony Orchestra, 192
New York Public Library, 192
New York Sun, 137
New York Times, 33, 180, 201
New York University, 137, 172, 191-192, 195
Nicholson, Meredith, 178
Nisbet, Eugenius, 23
Nisbet, John W., 15
Nordica, Lillian, 146
North American Review, 33
North Carolina, University of, 223
Nutting, C. A., 44-46
Nutting, Mattie, 106

O'Bear, Mayor, 23
O'Connor, Herbert, 185
Oglethorpe University, 5
O'Neal, Representative, 94
O'Neal, Mrs. B. P., 26
Ortmann, Otto, 179
Ottley, Mrs. John K., 108

Paine, Tom, 188
Palaver Club, 222
Patterson, Caroline, 210
Peabody Conservatory of Music, 179

INDEX

Peabody Institute, 184
Peel, William Lawson, 261
Peel, Mrs. William Lawson, 114, 261
Pendleton, Colonel, 221
Penn, William, 179
Perrin, Mrs. J. S., 117
Pershing, John J., 119
Peter, H. J., 50
Phelps, William Lyon, 185
Philadelphia Centennial Exhibition, 183
Philadelphia Ledger, 33
Phillips, Wendell, 77
Philomatheans, 74
Phinizy, Mrs. Billups, 111
"Pilgrimage of Poetry," 182
Pinchard, Mrs. S. J., 211
Pio Nono College, 22
Pitts Place, 13, 14, 16
Plane, Mrs. Helen, 152-153, 161, 163
Plant, George, 35
Pleasants, Mrs. W. S., 211, 212
Plummer, Buck, 50
Poe, Clarence, 179
Poe, Edgar Allan, 176, 181, 182
Poe, Washington, 46
Poe, Mrs. Washington, 12
Polhill, Hope, 22, 87
Pope, Edith, 138
Pratt, Daniel, 7, 18, 83
Progressive Farmer, 179

Quay, Senator, 99
Queen's University, 173
Quillian, William F., 264

Rabun Gap-Nacoochee School, 267
Raines, Cadwallader, 3
Raines, Mrs. L. H., 111
Raines, Parthenia, 3
Raley, Loker, 181
Ralston, Hall, 44
Randall, Samuel J., 94, 99
Randolph, Hollins, 154-158, 160-164, 166
Ransom, Ronald, 215, 219
Ransom, Senator, 99
Rayner, Mrs. H. W., 133
Reed, Walter, 188

Reese, Mrs. Anderson, 56
Reid, Thomas B., 65-66
Review of Reviews, 171, 178
Richards, Mrs. Alice H., 201
Richmond Sentinel, 138-139
Ricketts, Mary, 3
Rise and Fall of the Confederate Government, The, 121, 125
Ritchie, Albert, 179
Ritchie, Andrew, 267-268
Ritchie, Mrs. Andrew, 267-268
Rivers, Eretus, 158, 160
Rivoli, 263-265, 269
Roberts, Walter Douglas, 196
Roberts, Warren, 196
Robinson, Joseph T., 179-180
Rogers, Rock, 37
Rollins College, 179
Roosevelt, Franklin D., 214, 216, 219
Roosevelt, Mrs. Franklin D., 215-217
Roosevelt, Theodore, 90-91, 231-232
Root, Elihu, 178, 180
Ross, William H., 50
Ross, Mrs. William Henry, 9
Rouquie, Margaret, 172, 191
Rourke, John, 215
Rush, T. L., 177
Russell, Richard B., Jr., 178
Rutgers University, 173
Rutherford, Mildred, 111-114, 163, 210
Rutledge, Archibald, 178

Saint Cyr, Military Training School, 115
Salisbury, John, 82
Sandhurst, military school, 115
Sanford, Steadman Vincent, 130
Sass, Herbert Ravenel, 179
Saturday Morning Music Club, 171, 262
Saturday Review of Literature, 174
Saussy, Judge Gordon, 185
Saussy, Mrs. Gordon, 185
Savannah and Macon Railroad, 266
Scandrett, Mary, 145, 148
Schofield's Iron Works, 21
Schuler, Hans, 184, 189
Scott, Robert L., Sr., 225
Scott, Mrs. Robert L., Sr., 225

INDEX

Scott, Colonel Robert L., Jr., 225-227
Scott, Mrs. Robert L., Jr. (Catherine), 227
Scott, Winfield, 126
Second Georgia Battalion, 9, 11
Selden, Mrs. Lucile Flanders, 169
Sellers, N. M., 44
Selznick, David, 224
Semmes, Raphael, 115
Seney, George I., 263
Shaw, Albert, 178
Shepherd, Heyward, 116
Shepperson, Gay B., 217-220
Sheridan, Philip Henry, 57
Sherman, William Tecumseh, 14-18, 60, 229
Shorter, Edward, 168
"Sidney Lanier, the Musician," (Lamar), 183
Siebert, L. R., 130
Silver Grays, 14
Simmons, T. J., 44
Simpson, Julia C., 119
Skerrit, Admiral, 98
Smart, Herbert, 258
Smith, Governor James M., 42, 47, 49
Smith, Burton, 71
Smith, Cosby, 87
Smith, E. P., 50
Smith, Marion, 130
Smith, Robert A., 5, 7
Smith, Ruth, 74
Soldiers' Wayside Home, 12-13
Sousa, John Philip, 72
"Southern Cavalcade," 120
Southern Commercial Congress, 231
Southern Literary Messenger, 181
Spalding Grays, 9
Spangler's School, Miss, 4
Sparks, W. B., 82
Sparks, Mrs. W. B., 74
Speer, Representative, 42, 47
Spencer, Lady, 238
Sprague, Kate Chase, 100
Springer, Representative, 94
Stallings, Laurence, 228
Stanton, Edwin McMasters, 21, 128
Starke, Aubrey Harrison, 176
"Stars and Bars," 2, 56

Stein, Gertrude, 125-127
Stephens, Alexander H., 64-65
Stephens, Linton, 45
Stephens, Mrs. T. T., 158
Stevens, Mrs. Daisy McLaurin, 112
Stevens, John L., 96-98
Stevens, Thaddeus, 21
Stewart, Charles E., 200
Stone Mountain, 151-152, 155, 162-164, 166; Memorial Association, 152-165, 168; Memorial coins, 154, 155, 159, 161
Stoneman, General, 15
Stoneman's Raiders, 15
Stover College, 116
Stowe, Harriet Beecher, 129, 190
Stratford, 127, 178, 191, 199-203, 205-206, 267
Sumner, Charles, 21
Sun Yat Sen, Dr., 265
Surratt, Mary Eugenia, 128

Taft, William Howard, 231-232
Tallulah Falls School, 108, 268-269
Talmadge, Eugene, 214-215, 217-218
Tarkington, Booth, 143
Tate, Allen, 223-224
Tatten, Pearl, 116
Tattnall Square, 24, 37, 46, 95, 106
Terrell, William H., 152
Thomas, Bob, 45
Thornton, Matt, 50
Thurmond, Strom, 52
Thurston, Lorrin A., 95
Tilden, Samuel J., 99
Tilley, John Shipley, 185
Tilley, Mrs. John Shipley (Wilsie Lanier), 185
Time magazine, 123
Toombs, Robert, 66
Toomer, Dorothy Lamar Chappell, 17
Toomer, Loretta Lamar, 17
Tracy, Phil, 5, 7
Tragic Era, The, 222
Trimmer, Dr. Maurice, 174
Trimpi, Michael Lanier, 192
Troutman family, 22
Tucker, J. G., 155-156, 166
Tufts, Edith, 77

INDEX

Tulane University, 186
Turnbull, Eleanor, 184
Turpin, W. C., Jr., 196

U. D. C., Chapters: Atlanta, 157; Habersham, 182, 192; Major Charles M. Stedman, 129; Sidney Lanier, 111, 149, 159, 172, 185; William Alexander, 188, 199; Conventions: Baltimore, 110; Charleston, 140, 162; Houston, 189; Memphis, 119; Richmond, 124; San Francisco, 113, 115; Tulsa, 130-131; Washington, 117; Crosses: of Honor, 117, 119, 130-132; of Military Service, 125, 227
U. S. Military Academy, 132-133, 139
U. S. Naval Academy, 132

Valentine, Mrs. Granville, 202
Vanderbilt, Cornelius, 40
Vanderbilt University, 173
Van Deventer, Mrs. Horace, 202
Vandiver, C. E., 215
Van Dyke, Henry, 172
Van Zandt, Hiram, 150
Venable, H. S., 154-155, 158-161, 163
Venable family, 152, 154
"Vigilantes," 143
Vinson, Carl, 218
Virginia Military Institute, 112, 122, 134-135
Virginia, University of, 138
Voorhees, Harold O., 191
Voorhees, John R., 267

Wade, John Donald, 173
Walker, Billington Sanders, 182
Walker, Dawson, 47, 48
Ward, Frederick, 29, 87
Warnoth forces, 57
Washington, Booker T., 188
Washington, George, 206
Washington, Mrs. George, 211-212
Washington, Lawrence, 237
Washington and Lee University, 179
Washington Memorial Library, 165, 200
Waverly Seminary, 74

Weinman, Mrs. John F., 121
Weiss, Rabbi, 221
Wellesley College, 75-78, 80-82, 90, 259
Wesleyan College, 3, 22, 26, 30, 74, 150, 259, 262-267, 269; Dorothy Blount Lamar Scholarship, 264; Wesleyan Conservatory, 171-172, 264, 266, 269
What Price Glory, 228
Wheeler, Annie, 72, 228-230
Wheeler, Birdie, 72, 228, 230
Wheeler, Caroline, 72, 228, 230
Wheeler, Joseph (Little Joe"), 15, 71-72, 228-231
Wheeler, Mrs. Joseph, 72, 228
Wheeler, Julia, 72, 228, 230
Wheeler, Camp, 118, 230, 270-271
White, Mrs. Walter C., 203
White, William Allen, 179
Whitman, Walt, 182
Whitney, W. C., 236
Whittle, Judge L. N., 26
Wilcox, Mrs. John M., 191
Wild, H. Douglas, 173
Wiley, Charlie, 2, 3, 5, 9, 14, 19, 32, 105, 170
Wiley, Colonel, 118
Wiley, Jack, 2, 4, 6, 7
Wiley, Mrs. Jack, 7, 8, 10, 19, 53
Wiley, Judith Gambrell, 117-119
Wiley, Mamie, 105, 118
Wiley, Sidney, 118
Willingham, Calder, 87
Willkie, Wendell, 52
Wilson, Woodrow, 34, 112, 146-147, 212, 231
Winchester, Harriotte, 145
Winn, Cooper, 206
Winship, Blanton, 119, 191
Winship, Mrs. Isaac, 25
Winship Grammar School, 188
Winter, Roger, 160
Wirz, Major Henry, 117
Women's Defense League of Macon, 270-271
Wommack, A. J., 149-150
Wood, Miss Leila, 35
Wood, Miss Minnie, 35

. 285 .

INDEX

Woodbury, Mrs. John L., 115, 182
Woodliffe, Ed, 41
Woodring, Harry, 127
Woolley, Mary E., 179
Wright, General, 45
Wright, Mrs. R. D., 185
Wrigley, Miss Julia, 12

Wummer, John, 192
Wyse, Mrs. W. E. P., 211-212

Yarborough, Mrs. C. A., 185

Zouaves, 50

www.ingramcontent.com/pod-product-compliance
Lightning Source LLC
Chambersburg PA
CBHW030129240426
43672CB00005B/74